EVERYBODY LOVES ICE CREAM

THE WHOLE SCOOP ON AMERICA'S FAVORITE TREAT

By Shannon Jackson Arnold

Emmis Books
1700 Madison Road
Cincinnati, Ohio 45206
www.emmisbooks.com

The recipe for Rich Vanilla Custard-Based Ice Cream is reprinted with permission from the July/August 1993 issue of *Cook's Illustrated* magazine. For a trial issue of *Cook's* call 800-526-8442. Selected articles and recipes, as well as subscription information, are available online at www.cooksillustrated.com

The original recipes for Butter Pecan Ice Cream and Peach Frozen Yogurt appeared in the Instruction and Recipe Booklet for the Cuisinart® Flavor Duo Frozen Yogurt-Ice Cream & Sorbet Maker, ©2002. Cuisinart® is a registered trademark of Cuisinart, Stamford, CT.

Please Note: While the author and publisher made every effort to include accurate information in this book, we recommend that you call ahead to confirm hours, prices and other details before traveling to any of the places listed herein. Further, the author and publisher cannot be held responsible for any loss, injury or inconvenience sustained by any person using information from this book.

For further information, contact the publisher at

 Emmis Books
1700 Madison Road
Cincinnati, Ohio 45206
www.emmisbooks.com

ISBN 1-57860-165-7

Library of Congress Cataloging-in-Publication Data   2004106426

Cover designed by Dana Boll
Interior designed by Heather Leahy
Edited by Jack Heffron

For Michael, who makes my life so much sweeter,
and Grace, the sweetest thing in my life.

Also,
For Ed Marks and all of the passionate Ice Screamers who are
preserving ice cream's rich history for future generations.

In memory of my Grandma Jackson, who gave me her
sweet tooth, and my Grandpa Eisele, who never
turned down a cone of butter pecan.

Acknowledgments

While writing this book, I talked to hundreds of people about ice cream, and I thank each one for sharing their enthusiasm and knowledge. While space does not permit me to thank each person individually, I would like to acknowledge those who were particularly helpful:

For their insights on ice cream, I thank Brian Butko; Walter Vogel at the Historic Washington House; Bruce Weiss at Blue Bell; Lisa Piasecki and Sarah Flood at Good Humor-Breyers; Terry Reeves at Dippin' Dots; John Harrison at Dreyer's; Laura Springer at Häagen-Dazs; Luconda Dager at Velvet Ice Cream; Kim Forbes at Zerroll; Ted Galloway of Galloway Company and Classic Mix; Brue Tharp of Tharp's Food Technologies; Scott Rankin, assistant professor of food science at the University of Wisconsin–Madison; Charlie Beaton of Big Dipper Ice Cream; Bruce Becker of Max & Mina's; Pete Benfaremo of Lemon Ice King of Corona; Craig Bero of the Bespeckled Trout; Jeni Britton of Jeni's Fresh Ice Cream; the folks at Chocolate Shoppe Ice Cream; Matt Lachut at Handel's; Bud Rinehart at Kopp's; and Jon Snyder of Il Laboratorio del Gelato. Special thanks to Steve Sauter at Ice Cream Source for great service and tasty choices and Judi and Sam Sottile at Divino Gelato in Waukesha, Wisconsin, for their help and for providing my local ice cream fix.

For their delicious recipes, I thank Terese Allen; Jeni Britton of Jeni's Fresh; Bea Delpapa; Candace Hartzler; and Kathleen Jones. For help with permissions, I thank Melissa Baldino and Jack Bishop at *Cook's Illustrated*; Amy Stern at Cuisinart; and Yvette Ehler at www.vegweb.com. Special thanks to Elizabeth Brigham for recipes, longtime friendship and culinary expertise.

For generous sharing of photographs and collections, I thank Carl and Sherry Abell at America's Ice Cream and Dairy Museum at Historic Elm Farm; Rob Chambers; Chris Chapman; Allan "Mr. Ice Cream" Mellis; Thomas and Angela Sarro; John and Carol Skurulsky; Tod Swormstedt at the American Sign Museum; Laurie Mapes; Jane Swanson; Dr. Steven C. Wilson; and Good Humor-Breyers.

For research assistance and cheerleading, heartfelt thanks to Mary Christensen; Dennis Cleary and Clare Kilbane Cleary; Jim Ellison; Doris Larson; Kat Lemcke; Tonya Malench; Janet Okoben; Julie Clark Robinson; and Nita Sweeney.

Special thanks to Lisa Blumer for her website expertise and design talent. And extra-special thanks to Ed Marks for his knowledge and generosity.

This book was shepherded by the talented team at Emmis Books. Special thanks to Jack Heffron, pistachio ice cream aficionado, for his encouragement, patience and vision. To Dana Boll, home granita maker, for her inspired designs for this book. To Heather Leahy, lover of coffee ice cream and coffee with ice cream, for her fun and eye-catching page layouts. To Katie Carroll, Ben & Jerry's fan, for her keen eye and great copy-editing. To Katie Parker, frozen custard fan, and Mary Groza Schuetz, fellow Tom's Ice Cream Bowl fan, for sales acumen. To Howard Cohen, charter member of the egg cream fan club, and Meg Cannon, Aglamesis alum, for their publicity savvy. And to Richard Hunt, ace scout of Twistee Treat stands, for his enthusiasm and leadership.

For their profound influence in my life and career, eternal gratitude to Judy Bridges of Redbird Studios; Alison Hazelbaker; Dr. Anne Kuhry; Barbara McRae of Enhanced Life Coaching; Angela Palazzolo; Roger Snell; Joyce Weisshappel; Ty Wenger; and Roy Wolford.

For longtime support, I thank: Dad and Jane; Mom, Kate and Donovan; the Arnold family; Grandma Eisele; Grandpa Jackson; Rita and Dub Moss; Jennifer Arrasmith and Amanda Rabatin; Aunt Mary; Fern Colon; and the women from Writer's Night Out (including Lora Fish, Pat Snyder, Lynn McNish, Nancy Golden and Diane Cartolano). For especially generous friendship, I thank Dhanu Sant for unfailing encouragement and support (and for good humor while taste-testing our way through the Big Apple) and Kris Babe for always listening and for help with everything from proofreading to understanding low-carb diets. I am indebted to my in-laws, Ross and Gloria Arnold, and to Kristen Lance and Liz Millman for providing loving childcare for my daughter; without them, this book could not have been written.

Most importantly, thanks to Grace for making my life richer in every way and ensuring I always have a reason to smile. And to Michael, who contributed so much to the completion of this book he should be listed as coauthor. I thank him for the big and little things he did (from fact-checking to shooting photographs to grocery shopping to cleaning up after recipe testing) that helped make this dream of mine a reality. To him, chocolate milk shakes and coffee ice cream cones always.

Introduction

I don't remember my first taste of ice cream, but I know that, as a child, there wasn't any dessert that made me as happy as ice cream did. My love of ice cream only deepened through the years. During college, it even had vocational benefits. One summer in New York City, I spent five nights a week scooping ice cream at Steve's on the Upper West Side. My biceps got quite a workout, scooping the hard ice cream and hand-mixing toppings into the flavors. After three months of all the free samples of ice cream I wanted, I still loved it. I knew then that my love for ice cream was the real thing.

Wherever I've traveled and landed, from Italy to Illinois, I've made it my mission to sample the local ice cream. In Boston, I discovered Toscanini's, Herrell's, J.P. Lick's and Emack and Bolio's. In Columbus, Ohio, I fell in love with Graeter's, and its huge chocolate chips, Jeni's inventive flavors, and, just an hour away, thick cow milk shakes from Young's Jersey Dairy in Yellow Springs. In the Milwaukee, Wisconsin, area, where I live now, there are frozen custard stands nearly everywhere I go and a great gelateria that I visit more often than I care to admit.

When I got an ice cream maker as a wedding present from my Grandma Jackson, I learned how easy and delicious it is to make at home. I now serve ice cream for ordinary Tuesday dinners, as well as the summertime ice cream social my husband and I host for our friends and neighbors. (Forget what Dale Carnegie said. The way to win friends and influence people is to offer them ice cream.)

I share all this because the roots of my love for ice cream aren't especially grand or pedigreed. I'm not a dairy scientist, a seasoned parlor owner or a chef. I'm just a person who loves ice cream in all its glorious forms. And while I may be more fanatical than most, I know I'm not alone in my love for it. Ice cream is, after all, our nation's favorite dessert.

This book is a celebration of our collective love affair with ice cream and the essential user's guide for ice cream lovers everywhere. *Everybody Loves Ice Cream* offers everything you need to know about enjoying America's favorite dessert, from ice cream's rich history to how to make your own.

We start with a look at ice cream's icy beginnings, the key role Nancy Johnson's hand-crank maker played and why America went on an ice cream binge after World War II. Next, we examine ice cream's role in popular culture, from the invention of the hot fudge sundae to the rise and fall of the soda fountain. Then, there's a look at popular flavors and a glossary of ice cream types, covering everything from Philadelphia ice cream to Mexican paletas. We move on to show you the process of making ice cream, why the industry is nuts over low-carb products and what new items you might see in the freezer case soon. We'll explain why we should thank Howard Johnson's for ice cream chains and offer an up-close look at of the nation's best ice cream parlors. We'll also share everything you need to know about making ice cream at home, including a guide to buying an ice cream freezer and useful tips for a perfect batch every time. Finally, we'll discuss the split over the banana split's invention and what tools you need to create your favorite fountain treats at home.

To further help ice cream fans, there are three appendices, chock-full of information. Appendix 1 lists 550 of the country's best places to enjoy ice cream, with state-by-state listings offering addresses, phone numbers, websites, mail-order information and what's notable about each. Appendix 2 offers 56 easy-to-follow recipes, including several low-carb, diabetic and dairy-free variations. And Appendix 3 has 57 recipes for everything from sauces, sundaes and ice cream sodas to parfaits, pies and pizzelle cones. Nowhere else will you find so much about ice cream in one deliciously convenient place.

It's the perfect time to appreciate the rich role ice cream has played in American culture. This year marks the 100th anniversary of the ice cream cone's wildly popular introduction at the 1904 St. Louis World's Fair. Perhaps no other piece of ice cream history has reached the iconic status of the ice cream cone. (See Chapter 1 for a thorough look at the contenders to the cone's invention.) The marriage of ice cream and cone helped secure ice cream's dominance today, for without the easy portability of the cone, ice cream sales might have declined along with the soda fountain. Instead, sales for ice cream have remained strong through the years.

The innovation that started a century ago hasn't ended. Every year, new ice cream flavors and novelties emerge to delight us. There's always something different to taste and something new to try. It's a sweet deal for ice cream fans, and it's part of the reason ice cream holds such a special place in our hearts.

I

SWEET BEGINNINGS

THE HISTORY OF ICE CREAM

In the beginning, there was light. And then, on the eighth day, there was ice cream. Perhaps not ice cream as we know it, but the promise of ice cream, glistening off the snow-capped peaks of the mountains, icing over with possibility in frozen ponds in the winter.

At least that's how it happened in my mind. But, in truth, we don't know exactly where or how the first ice cream came to be. Legends about ice cream's early history abound: Marco Polo brought back the recipe for ice cream with him from China. Italian Catherine de Medici introduced the treat to France when she married King Henry II. Charles I paid his cook a handsome sum to keep his ice cream techniques a state secret. Most of these grand tales are merely that — tales that have grown taller with time. (As ice cream historian Ed Marks explains, ice cream history is nothing more than "myth, rumor and speculation hardened by media repetition.")

For as long as there's been ice cream, kids of all ages have enjoyed it.

ICE CREAM for You and Me

Although no one has pinpointed the exact date and time of ice cream's birth, we do know a little about its ancestors. Ice cream's lineage is firmly rooted in ice. Without ice or other methods to keep things frozen, there would be no ice cream, merely sweet-tasting milk served at room temperature. Scholars say that the first icehouses were found in Mesopotamia more than 4,000 years ago, and that by 1100 B.C., the Chinese had perfected their icehouse design to the point that they could keep harvested ice through the summer months. As ice became more readily available — although still quite rare and a privilege of the ruling class — people began to develop tasty uses for it. There is evidence that Alexander the Great in 4 B.C. liked snow flavored with nectar and honey, and that Roman Emperor Nero, who reigned from A.D. 54-68, also fancied cold, fruit-flavored drinks and built special rooms for ice storage under his palace. Noted for his cruelty, Nero even sent teams of slaves running into the mountains to retrieve snow and ice; if they didn't get back to the palace before the snow melted, they were executed.

The first documentation of a dish resembling ice cream comes from ancient China, during the Tang Dynasty (A.D. 618–907) It was made from a combination of horse, water buffalo, cow and goat milks that were heated and allowed to ferment and then mixed with flour and camphor. In the Middle East, *charbet*, a drink made with fruit juice and water, was an early precursor of today's sorbets. And slushes made with ice chips and fruit go back to eleventh-century Japan.

1600s: Ice Cream Reaches a Freezing Point

In the late 1600s, ice cream began to have mass appeal. What helped to democratize and popularize ice cream was another milestone in freezing: the discovery of a cool bit of science called the endothermic effect. By using salt to depress the freezing point of ice, the resulting cold can be transferred elsewhere by conduction. In other words, people figured out that if you took some salt and ice, it made other things like, say, a mixture of cream and sugar, cold enough to freeze, too.

The discovery of the endothermic effect led to the creation of the "still pot" method of making ice cream. First, you had to procure ice and chip it into small pieces. They put the cream, milk and sugar in a pewter pot, and next placed the pot in a larger basin surrounded by ice and salt. You had to stir the mixture occasionally and re-incorporate any that had frozen to the sides until it was uniformly frozen. It was time-consuming work, but worth it, given that sweet treats (especially those made with sugar and cream) were a rarity in those days.

What's also significant about the "still pot" method is that for many ice cream historians it marks the point when the history of ice cream becomes solid. The reason the discovery is notable, explains historian Marks, is that it created a standard formula for ice cream making that anyone with access to cream, sugar, salt and ice could follow.

The first written mention of ice cream is found in 1672, when a guest at Windsor on the Feast of St. George writes about the king being treated to "One plate of white strawberries and one plate of Ice Cream." The rest of the guests were left in the cold. Across the channel, though, commoners

1861

Until the late 1800s, there was a distrust of drinking cold drinks. British cookery writer Mrs. Beeton in 1861 warned that the "aged, the delicate and children should abstain from ices and iced beverages, even the strong and healthy should partake of them in moderation." She warned that eating cold treats could result in indisposition or even "produce illness which have ended fatally."

Ice cream serves up sweet memories of favorite childhood haunts, such as the regional Ohio-Pennsylvania chain of Isaly's (left).

had access to ice cream. Paris's Café Procope opened in 1670 as the city's first café and the first to serve water ices to commoners.

As the popularity of places like Café Procope spread, ices became readily available in Europe's cities. By 1718, ice cream was no longer the privilege of only the ruling class; it was firmly in the hands of the masses when the confectioner to Queen Anne published *Mrs. Mary Eales Receipts* and included the first ice cream recipe. It called for first filling two "Tin Ice Pots" with plain or sweetened cream and fruit (if so desired). Then, the bottom of the second pot was lined with straw and the first pot placed inside with 18 to 20 pounds of ice and a "Pound of Bay-Salt" layered around it. Finally, the ice cream was left for four hours to harden in a cellar "where no sun or light comes."

1700s: Ice Cream in the New World

It's believed that ice cream crossed the Atlantic with European settlers in the 1700s. The first written record of ice cream in America dates from 1744 when Maryland Governor Thomas Bladen served the delicacy for his guests. One attendee wrote of a "Dessert no less Curious; Among the Rarities of which it was Compos'd, some fine Ice Cream which, with the Strawberries and Milk, eat most deliciously." By the mid-1770s, confectioners were offering ice cream alongside pastries and jellies. Philip Lenzi advertised that he carried

Did you know?

Some say that credit for being the first successful commercial ice cream manufacture should go to Augustus Jackson, a former White House chef who settled in Philadelphia in the late 1820s. Jackson ran a prosperous and brisk business selling his ice cream in tin cans to area restaurants.

MAD FOR MELLORINE

When rationing was in effect during World War II, ice cream manufacturers began to look for substitutes to satisfy the nation's appetite for ice cream. In Texas, some manufacturers began adding non-dairy fat (such as coconut oil or cottonseed oil) to their ice creams as a replacement for hard-to-get butterfat. First marketed under such names as Frosty Creme, Mello Creme and Great Goodness, the Texas Dairy Institute adopted the term *mellorine* in 1951 to cover all ice cream substitutes.

Mellorine's popularity peaked in the early 1960s when almost 1,800 plants produced the product. By the 1980s, however, it had melted into obscurity. However, mellorine still has a large following in Great Britain, racking up 75 percent of all ice cream sales.

"any sort of ice cream" at his store on Dock Street in New York City in 1774.

It seems that even the likes of George Washington saw the need to have ice cream available on a daily basis. He had two "Cream Machines for Making Ice" at Mount Vernon, and during the summer of 1790 racked up a bill for $200 in ice cream alone at a New York merchant. Thomas Jefferson likewise developed a sweet tooth for ice cream — a taste acquired during his days as ambassador to France in the 1780s. He returned home with two French ice cream machines, a love of adding vanilla for flavor and a fussy, 18-step recipe for French-style ice cream wrapped in a pastry shell. Jefferson could make ice cream year-round, thanks to the 62 wagon-loads of ice kept in his ice house at Monticello.

While Jefferson and Washington made ice cream at home, ice cream was an official state dish by 1813 when it was served at the second inaugural ball for President James Madison. It featured cream from the cows at Madison's farm in Virginia and strawberries from First Lady Dolley's garden. History books give Dolley a lot of credit for helping to popularize ice cream, but some believe the credit more rightfully belongs to a talented, African-American cook from Wilmington, Delaware, Aunt Sallie Shadd, who reportedly gave Dolley the recipe for her delicious ice cream.

Until the invention of hand-crank freezers, such as the White Mountain model shown (above), ice cream was a rare treat enjoyed only by the elite.

1800s: Doing the Hokey Pokey

By the mid-1800s, ice cream was a favorite indulgence of Americans, as restaurants and leisure activities became more popular and commonplace. Grand "pleasure parks" were built, where visitors could promenade and sample some ices or ice cream, and taverns that once catered only to travelers were now serving locals looking for a meal out. Homemade ice cream, too, became something that the average housewife could make. Cookbooks from the 1700s might have offered one or two recipes for frozen desserts, but by

In the late 1800s, the two primary venues for purchasing ice cream were at the local drugstore soda fountain (this page) and from the carts of the hokey pokey men (opposite).

the mid-1800s most cookbooks contained several variations for homemade ice cream. An 1851 Philadelphia cookbook, for example, offered recipes for 34 types of ice cream and 18 varieties of water ices.

Making ice cream at home got much easier after 1846, when Nancy Johnson invented the first hand-cranked freezer. Her design (Patent No. 3254) for an "artificial freezer" had only three main parts: a tall tub, a thinner tub with a tight lid that could fit inside the larger tub and a dasher, or mixing paddle, with a removable crank. It was an easier way to make ice cream, and a faster one, too. Where the still pot method took four or five hours to freeze ice cream, Johnson's invention produced "iced" cream in about 20 minutes.

Johnson's idea caught on quickly, and other inventors started tinkering with her freezer. From 1847 to 1877, more than 70 improvements to ice cream churns were patented as ice cream became a staple of kitchens across the land. Homemade ice cream had become so commonplace that in 1850 an editor for the popular women's magazine *Godey's Lady Book* proclaimed that a party without ice cream "would be like breakfast without bread or a dinner without a roast."

Another factor that helped ice cream spread was the rise of the hokey pokey men. After the Civil War, there was an explosion in street carts selling cheap — both in price and quality — ice cream. They would walk down the streets, singing "Here's the stuff to make you jump; hokey-pokey, penny a lump. Hokey-pokey, sweet and cold; for a penny, new or old." (The term "hokey pokey" is derived from the Italian vendors who shouted *"Ecco un poco,"* meaning "here is a little" or "try a sample.") These small tastes of ice cream, which were served in small glass containers called penny licks, made ice cream a luxury anyone could afford.

As Main Street America's sweet tooth for ice cream grew, businesses scrambled to meet demand. Milk dealer Jacob Fussell, Jr., made ice cream from the extra cream he had during the summer months. His venture was so successful that he converted his dairy plant into an ice cream plant in 1851 and became the first commercial ice cream manufacturer in the United States. Fussell was able to sell his ice cream at a cheaper price (25 cents per quart compared to the going rate of 60 cents), and his brisk sales enabled him to expand rapidly with factories in Boston, New York and Washington D.C.

Besides making ice cream more readily available and setting the template for all future ice cream factories, Fussell also helped the spread of ice cream across America. Fussell took a friend — a down-on-his-luck-banker named Perry Brazelton — under his wing and trained him in ice cream production methods. Brazelton then set out on his own and founded factories in

A Scoop of History

1800s

Oyster and ice cream parlors were popular in the 1800s. Since ice cream was a summertime food, oysters were served the rest of the year — during the "r" months, when they were in season.

Chicago, Cincinnati and St. Louis. In their book *Frozen Desserts,* authors Caroline Liddell and Robin Weir assert that Fussell "more than anyone else, was responsible for starting the Americans' love affair with ice cream."

The spread of soda fountains during the mid–1800s helped, too. In the early 1820s, pharmacists began to offer soda water from spigots in their stores. The popularity of spas like Saratoga Springs, New York, and the purported medicinal benefits of mineral water (which was said to cure everything from depression to indigestion) led to the creation of artificial mineral water. By the 1840s, however, soda water was no longer considered a curative, merely a tasty and enjoyable drink. "Today it is hard to imagine the novelty and excitement surrounding the first soda fountains," writes Anne Cooper Funderburg in her thorough look at ice cream's history, *Chocolate, Strawberry and Vanilla.* "Imagine how a glass of icy water must have tasted on a humid August day to a man laboring outdoors in the blazing sun, a woman wearing a long dress and several layers of petticoats, or a clerk in a stifling office without even an electric fan to stir the air."

It didn't take long for soda fountains to evolve from bare-bones spigots into showy, marble masterpieces and a community gathering place. At first, people simply flavored their bubbly water with syrups, but, by the late 1800s, they began adding ice cream, too.

Between the rise of the soda fountains and increased access to ice cream through home hand-cranks and commercial ice cream operations, inventors began to look at efficient ways to dispense and serve ice cream. In 1878, William Clewell, a confectioner from Reading, Pennsylvania, received a patent for the first ice cream dipper. Made of steel, the dipper was approximately eight inches long and had a deep conical-shaped bowl with a hand-turned key on top that moved a scraper inside to dish the ice cream onto a plate. With ice cream being scooped up more easily, cooks and clever entrepreneurs turned their attention to better ways to serve it. Ice cream was traditionally served in metal, glass or paper cups, but wouldn't it be more efficient, they thought, — and certainly tastier — to serve ice cream in an edible container? The evolution of the ice cream cone had begun.

1900s: A Cornucopia of Cones

Perhaps the first documentation of the ice cream cone is found in Mrs. Agnes Marshall's book *Fancy Ices* (1884), which had a recipe for "cornets with cream." Marshall suggested the cornets, as she called her cones, could be filled with ginger ice water and apple ice cream. In 1896, Italo Marchiony, an ice cream street vendor on Wall Street, was frustrated that all his glass serving cups either got broken or stolen and designed an edible ice cream container. He successfully filed a patent for what some say is the first ice cream cone. But his invention looks more like ice cream teacups, complete with a flat bottom and handles for easy holding. The patent for his device, which operated much like today's waffle irons, was granted December 1903.

It wasn't until 1904 at the St. Louis World's Fair that ice cream cones became the preferred carryout container for ice cream lovers everywhere. The fair, also known as the Louisiana Purchase Exposition, ran for seven months and was an elaborate spectacle covering more than 1,200 acres and housing 1,500 buildings. More than 20 million people came to view the sights. There were some 50 ice cream vendors and dozens of waffle makers in attendance at the fair, making the popularization of edible ice cream cones — then called cornucopias — virtually inevitable.

In the decades following Nancy Johnson's 1846 invention of the hand-crank freezer, other manufacturers such as Gem (above) produced their own models.

EVERYBODY LOVES ICE CREAM

19

Immigrants arriving to Ellis Island in the 1920s were given ice cream as part of a typical American menu. Some new arrivals mistakenly spread this "frozen butter" on their bread.

Mix Masters: Soda jerks memorized hundreds of recipes for everything from a Green River to a sarsaparilla.

Charles Menches of Akron, Ohio, claims to have invented the ice cream cone at the fair on July 23 when he ran out of plates at his concession stand. Necessity being the mother of invention, he figured out how to roll up waffle cookies into cones using a tapered wooden tool called a fid, which was traditionally used to separate ropes. (Menches is also credited with the invention of the hamburger and the recipe for Cracker Jack.) Turkish immigrant David Avayou maintained he introduced the concept of ice cream cones at the fair; he said he had seen paper cones in France and set out to make an edible one. But many historians say the person with the best claim to popularizing ice cream cones in St. Louis that year was Ernest Hamwi, a Syrian immigrant who sold rolled waffle-like pastries coated in sugar called *zalibia*. According to popular legend, Hamwi was selling zalibia when a nearby ice cream vendor ran out of dishes and Hamwi offered his pastries as handy holders.

What bolsters Hamwi's title as King of the Cone is that two other cone claimants, Abe Doumar and Nick Kabbaz, had ties to Hamwi. Nick Kabbaz worked for Hamwi and said he and his brother had developed the idea for edible cones prior to the fair and then shared their discovery with Hamwi. Abe Doumar was at the fair selling paperweight souvenirs filled with Holy Water from the Jordan River. He liked to serve up his merchandise in a rolled paper cone. Doumar reputedly told a fellow ice cream vendor (who may have been Hamwi) that serving ice cream in a waffle cone would be good for business. According to one story, the 16-year-old Abe advised the vendor that his penny waffles could become 10-cent cones by adding ice cream. In another version, Abe himself sold the ice cream cones to fellow concessionaires after the fair closed each evening. Regardless, there's no question that a star was born in the ice cream cone.

1920s: Brewing Up Ice Cream Dominance

The nation's demand for ice cream only got bigger in the decades after the World's Fair. By 1919, American were making 150 millon gallons of ice cream each year — a whopping 750 percent increase over the amount made in 1899. Certainly, technological advances in

FITTING THE MOLD

In Victorian times, proper hostesses wouldn't dream of just serving a scoop of ice cream on a dish. The fashion was to present your ice cream in elaborate shapes made from pewter molds. Molded ice cream, or Fancy Forms, remained popular through the mid–1930s, but they fell out of favor in 1965 when the U.S. government prohibited their use because of fears of lead poisoning.

Thankfully, St. Clair Ice Cream in South Norwalk, Connecticut, keeps the tradition alive by creating edible masterpieces using aluminum reproductions of old pewter molds. St. Clair offers more than 40 shapes, ranging from strawberries to walnuts, day lilies to seashells, yule logs to corn on the cob.

You can order a dozen mini Easter eggs in six colorful flavors, or a golf ball made from coconut ice cream with a chocolate fudge center. They are almost too beautiful to eat, but eat you must as they begin to lose their shape after about 10 minutes. You can order St. Clair's creations by calling 203/853-4774 or online at www.stclairicecream.com. Ray's Ice Cream in Royal Oak, Michigan, also offers molded ice creams. 888/549-5256, www.raysicecream.com

manufacturing and distribution — ranging from steam power, electricity and automobiles to homogenization and the development in 1926 of continuous batch freezers — aided ice cream's popularity. People at home benefited from such innovations as the ice block refrigerator and new ways to fill their new freezers with ice cream, thanks to the introduction of the ice cream cabinet in 1923 at the 1,200 groceries owned by A&P.

But the enforcement of Prohibition in 1920 did the most to raise the spirits of ice cream lovers. Soda fountains had spread since the 1800s when the temperance movement started. By the early 1900s, soda fountains outnumbered bars in places like Atlanta, New York City and Chicago. But Prohibition secured soda fountain dominance. The remaining bars and saloons quickly retooled to offer sundaes and sodas. Major breweries, including Anheuser-Busch and Stroh's, began turning out barrels of ice cream instead of spirits.

The smug ice cream industry trade journals kept a running list of

Food for the family: Early ice cream ads depict ice cream as a wholesome food any mother would be proud to serve.

The Broad Street Pharmacy in Philadelphia had the first soda fountain with a counter you could stand behind installed in 1903. Prior to this, fountains were mounted directly to the wall.

breweries that had been converted into ice cream manufacturing plants. Typical of the giddiness within the industry was a song from the Pacific Ice Cream Manufacturers Convention in 1920:

> *Gone are the days when Father was a souse,*
> *Gone are the days of the weekly family rows,*
> *Gone from this land since prohibition's here—*
> *He brings a brick of ice cream home instead of beer.*

Besides the boost in sales and ice cream consumption, Prohibition also increased competition in the industry, which led to several innovations in ways to enjoy ice cream. The 1920s brought the invention of frozen treats on a stick (the Good Humor bar and the Popsicle); ice cream covered in chocolate (the Eskimo Pie, the Klondike bar) and ice cream in a portable paper cup (the Dixie Cup). The frozen novelty category — as all treats of this nature are called, being "novel" ways to enjoy ice cream — were big business in the 1920s. The Eskimo Pie was introduced in 1921; by 1922, American consumed a million bars a day. The demand for materials to produce the treats was so high that it reportedly caused the price of cocoa beans to rise by 50 percent and single-handedly lifted the economy of Ecuador (a major cocoa exporter) out of a depression.

In many ways, the 1920s were the golden age of ice cream. By 1929, each American consumed nearly nine quarts of ice cream annually, and the United States led the world in ice cream consumption.

1930s: Ice Cream's Great Depression

Unfortunately, things began to sour in the 1930s. By 1933, ice cream production was down 50 percent compared to 1929, the result of several converging factors. First, the Depression made any food choice a weighty one for cash-strapped Americans, and some resorted to buying poor quality black-market ice cream from bootleggers. Secondly, Prohibition was repealed in 1933 with the passage of the Twenty-First Amendment, and soda fountains took a hit as saloons and bars reopened. (The ice cream industry scrambled to respond, going

HOW ISALY'S STRUCK GOLD WITH KLONDIKES

In the 1920s, frozen novelties were an effective way for ice cream manufacturers to entice customers to buy their brand. In Ohio and western Pennsylvania, a popular regional chain of dairy stores, Isaly's, already had a popular novelty in its four-inch-high **Skyscraper cones**, scooped tall and thin with a patented spoon designed expressly for them. But in 1922, it launched another one: 10-cent **Klondike bars** available in six flavors — strawberry, chocolate, vanilla, grape, maple and cherry. (The name is thought to be a nod to the Klondike Gold Rush of the 1890s in the Yukon Territory of Canada.)

Unlike many of the other novelties on the market, though, the Klondike was aimed at an adult consumer. According to Brian Butko, author of the definitive history on the chain, *Klondikes, Chipped Ham & Skyscraper Cones: The Story of Isaly's*, Klondikes were originally sold in glassine bags, but eventually the signature foil wrapper was added. "Klondike bars are still foil wrapped, which makes them kind of special," he explains. "And they were one of the first novelties with a square block." Klondikes were also unique in that one in every 12 had a pink center; if you were lucky enough to get one, your next Klondike was free.

For more than 50 years, Klondike bars were available only through Isaly's large network of stores (in the 1940s there were more than 300). But Isaly's stores began to close in the early 1970s due to increased competition. The company was eventually

ICE CREAM KLONDIKES
The Biggest Bargain in Town!

6 for 1.49

28¢ EACH

America's favorite ice cream bar . . . rich vanilla ice cream with a thick, tasty coating of chocolate. Choose plain or krispy.

sold, and new owners decided to push the Klondike brand. By the early 1980s, the Klondike was sold in 40 states. The Klondike brand is now owned by the **Good Humor-Breyers Ice Cream Co.** Since 1996, they've been the best-selling adult frozen novelty on the market. For more information on Isaly's, check out Brian Butko's website at www.brianbutko.com

The 1920s brought new and novel ways to enjoy ice cream, from Dixie Cups to Brownie ice cream sandwiches to Fudgicles.

so far as to suggest possible ice cream and liquor concoctions and even asserting that ice cream was an effective hangover cure.) A third factor added insult to injury for soda fountains: increasing competition from the roadside stands and eateries that were popping up on the newly expanded highway system.

Lastly, and perhaps most importantly, was the fear over the safety of scoops. Until the late 1930s, much of the nation's milk supply was poorly regulated. Pasteurization was common but not yet universally mandated. There were wide variances from city to city and state to state regarding sanitary procedures and practices, and wide variance in levels of enforcement. (For example, in the 1920s, a vague Massachusetts law granted a dairy license to anyone deemed a "suitable person.") Many diseases — including typhoid fever, diphtheria, scarlet fever, pneumonia and tuberculosis — were spread via the milk supply. Ptomaine poisoning from ice cream was commonplace. Paul Dickson in his seminal 1972 history of ice cream, *The Great American Ice Book,* quotes an *American Journal of Public Health* article from September 1926 stating that tainted ice cream caused 417 cases of diphtheria in Rhode Island and 350 cases of typhoid in Alabama.

To regain the public's trust, ice cream manufacturers sought to allay consumer fears. Images of mothers feeding their children ice cream and words like *clean, pure, quality, healthy* and *nutritious* were frequently employed by ice cream ad copywriters. A circa-1930 advertisement for the Carver Ice Cream Co. promises that "Properly Pasteurized Milk Means Absolute Safety and Purity.... A trial will convince you of Carver Superior Quality."[sic]

It helped, too, that the public's love for ice cream and soda fountain culture did not wane, regardless of risks or marketplace threats. Ice cream and soda fountains were too ingrained a part of American culture. Hollywood helped by perpetuating the nation's love affair with ice cream. Dozens of movies in the 1930s featured ice cream and soda fountains in prominent roles, a symbol of good, wholesome fun on America's Main Streets. Hollywood starlets distributed promotional photos of themselves enjoying a soda or a sundae. Even President Franklin D. Roosevelt, a confirmed fan of chocolate ice cream, helped to keep ice cream in the spotlight. Ice cream was a regular

FUN Facts

First-class passengers on the *Titanic* were treated to French ice cream for dessert, according to the April 14, 1912, menu. Second-class passengers had to settle for plain, egg-free American ice cream.

White House menu item during his tenure, served at everything from children's Christmas parties to state dinners with King George. By the end of the decade, ice cream sales and consumption were exceeding pre-1930 levels.

1940s: Fighting for Truth, Freedom and Ice Cream

When the United States entered World War II, ice cream's symbolic role became even more significant. Fascist countries attempted to curtail American influence abroad by giving a cold reception to ice cream. Mussolini placed an outright ban on the sale of ice cream. In Japan, the emperor instituted new policies that made selling ice cream unprofitable. Ice cream was no longer just our nation's favorite dessert, it became a symbol of democracy and the American way.

Ice cream held perhaps the greatest pull for homesick G.I.s. It was so important to soldiers that the U.S. War Department listed ice cream among the six items essential for troop morale, ranking up there with toiletries, tobacco products and cleaning kits. By 1943, the U.S. military was the world's largest ice cream manufacturer. At stateside bases, overseas USOs and even Red Cross "leave clubs," ice cream was served in heaping quantities. Even G.I.s at sea were ensured of a regular ice cream fix. Both the *Tang* and *Pampanito* submarines were equipped with ice cream freezers. And in 1945, the Navy built its first floating ice cream parlor at a cost of more than $1 million; it produced 10 gallons of ice cream every seven seconds.

At home, rationing limited civilian access to ice cream. There were shortages of milk, sugar, vanilla and cream, and soda fountains responded by using alternate ingredients and promoting their non-ice cream desserts. Some fountains served up half-and-half sundaes, made with one scoop of ice cream and one scoop of sherbet. Others concocted new recipes based on food items still readily available.

When rationing was lifted in 1946, Americans went on an ice cream binge, consuming a then-unprecedented 20 quarts of ice cream per capita that year. But looming on the horizon were cultural shifts that would forever change the ice cream landscape.

PINCH THE TIP

A CHOCOLATE "walk-home" SUNDAE

ERVED IN A TWINK

SYRUP...IDEAL FOR HOME SERVING

By the 1950s, the portability of ice cream became key. From supermarket half-gallons to carry-out containers, ice cream adapted to meet the needs of America's mobile, suburban society.

1950s to Today: Supermarkets and Super-Premiums

The Three Horsemen of the Soda Fountain Apocalypse were the suburbs, supermarkets and the rise of other ice cream outlets, especially roadside stands. During the 1950s, soda fountains were removed from drugstores at the rate of 1,200 a year. It didn't help that most people were buying their piece of the American dream in the suburbs, a place where the drugstore around the corner gave way to driving to the nearest

Did you know?

Ice cream boosterism rose during World War I, after a newspaper quoted a German officer asserting, "We do not fear that nation of ice cream eaters."

store at a strip mall. Ice cream was still enjoyed at roadside stands, diner counters and candy stores, but the soda fountain had gone flat. Increasingly, Americans enjoyed their ice cream in the comfort of their own homes, often in front of the television. By the mid-1950s, supermarkets accounted for 50 percent of all ice cream sales.

While it was certainly convenient to buy ice cream at the local grocery store, ice cream quality on a national scale began to suffer as more stores opted for in-house brands, so-called private labels, that were often made with artificial ingredients and large amounts of air. Economics pushed manufacturers to find more cost-effective ways of making ice cream, and many smaller manufacturers couldn't compete with large ice cream conglomerates. More than 1,600 ice cream plants closed between 1957 and 1969, even though ice cream production remained constant.

By the late 1960s, consumer demand for quality ice cream returned. Hometown parlors and national chains dedicated to serving premium ice cream took hold, and some chains, such as Baskin-Robbins and Bresler's, grew at the rate of a new store each week. In the freezer case, higher quality ice cream grabbed shelf-space again, too, thanks to the creation of a new market segment: super-premium ice cream for adults.

Ice cream as we know and love it today has it roots in 1961 when Reuben Mattus of Brooklyn, New York, decided to buck industry trends by creating a super-premium ice cream using only the finest ingredients. Mattus was one of the small-time ice cream manufacturers whose market dropped out during the early 1960s. Instead of giving up, he gave his product the made-up, foreign-sounding name of Häagen-Dazs, added to its European aura by placing a map of Denmark on the carton and tacking on an import-worthy price. Initially, Mattus offered his ice cream in three flavors — chocolate, coffee and vanilla — and sold it at New York gourmet shops. But word spread on this super-premium treat and by 1973 Häagen-Dazs was available nationwide.

High quality ice cream was back in vogue by the 1970s. Steve Herrell opened his first Steve's store in Boston in 1973, where he made small batches of all-natural, sinfully rich ice cream in unique flavors like malted vanilla and chocolate pudding. As if his flavors weren't inventive enough, he created the concept of mix-ins, wherein customers could choose whatever crushed candy, cookie or fruit they wanted in their ice cream. The ice cream and the mix-ins were placed on a slab and incorporated by hand into one delicious treat. It was so popular that in 1977 he sold his store to a firm that took the concept national.

Just a few years later, grade-school friends Ben Cohen and Jerry Greenfield opened their first store in a converted gas station in Burlington, Vermont. They, too, specialized in super-premium ice cream that used only the finest ingredients (and, to their minds, the chunkier the ingredients, the better). Their first big hit: Heath Bar Crunch.

In the 1980s, frozen yogurt and lower-fat ice creams found a following, but the biggest hit of the decade was the introduction of cookies and cream ice cream in 1983, which became one of the nation's top five flavors within a year of its introduction. (Even chocolate chip cookie dough, which had a smash debut in 1991, didn't make the splash that cookies and cream did.) Ice cream was such a national icon that President Ronald Reagan designated July as National Ice Cream Month in 1984. "Ice cream is a nutritious and wholesome food, enjoyed by over 90 percent of the people of the United States," he wrote in his proclamation. "It enjoys a reputation as the perfect dessert and snack food…[and] I call upon the people of the United States to observe these events with appropriate ceremonies and activities."

Today, sales of frozen yogurt are declining, but full-fat, super-premium ice cream is scooped up at a record pace. Another area seeing phenomenal growth is special diet ice creams, with a flurry of new products aimed at low-carb dieters, diabetics, the lactose intolerant and low-fat followers seeing record sales. Our ice cream horizons are expanding, too, as the consumption of sorbet, frozen custard and gelato rises. Not surprisingly, we lead the world in ice cream production, churning out some 1.6 billion gallons a year, and we each eat more than 23 quarts of it. There's no sign that Americans' screaming for ice cream will quiet anytime soon. ▪

BLACK RASPBERRY
ICE CREAM

Soda fountains dried up and closed as more Americans ate ice cream in the comfort of their own homes.

2

DIPPING INTO AMERICA'S PSYCHE

HOW ICE CREAM HAS SHAPED AMERICA'S CULTURE

America's love affair with ice cream is more than just an infatuation with food. We love ice cream because we love what ice cream means to us. Say "ice cream," and we think not just of the ingredients on the label, but ice cream's de facto ingredients, too: A generous dose of the lazy heat of summer. A dash of childlike innocence and wonder. And several helpings of fond memories — of your favorite hometown ice cream stands, of chasing ice cream trucks for a Nutty Buddy or a Bomb Pop, of special trips into town for a hot fudge sundae. Say "ice cream," and people smile. For Americans, ice cream is not merely foodstuff. It's the stuff of delicious memories and has become every bit as significant to the U.S.A. as Mom, baseball and apple pie.

The sound of the Good Humor truck was music to kids' ears from the 1940s through the 1960s.

THE SATURDAY EVENING POST

SEPT. 16, 1922   5c. THE COPY

Samuel G. Blythe—Edwin Lefèvre—I. F. Marcosson—F. W. Parsons
Nina Wilcox Putnam—Joseph Hergesheimer—Lucy Stone Terrill

A Scoop of History

1950

Billy Wilder's classic film *Sunset Boulevard* immortalized Schwab's Pharmacy by having the landmark serve as the home base for the film's main character, Joe Gillis.

From the earliest days, Americans knew that ice cream is fine to eat alone, but really it's best when shared with others. Not surprisingly, as soon as ice cream hit the streets of America in the mid-1800s, community rituals developed around it. There were ice cream socials during the late nineteenth century, where folks in their Sunday best gathered at the local church or town green to take turns cranking the ice cream freezer, listen to music and play lawn games. But it was the soda fountain — America's answer to Europe's cafe culture — that became Main Street's gathering spot for more than a hundred years.

Fountain Fads

Part of the reason people began to hang out at the local soda fountain was simply because you had to wait to get your order. In the mid-1800s, pharmacists would have to mix your soda by hand, adding whatever flavoring you desired. They'd take a squirt of this and a bit of that to make ginger ale, root beer, sarsaparilla, lemon or strawberry sodas. In the beginning, there was no carryout, so you drank at the counter. In pre-automobile America, it was the perfect chance to chat with neighbors and catch up on local news. At first, the emphasis at the soda fountain was on soda and nothing more. Most soda fountain owners, feeling it easier and more profitable to concentrate on carbonated drinks, left the ice cream trade to restaurants and confectioneries.

After the Civil War, there was increased demand for unique concoctions (many fountains offered upwards of a hundred different drinks) and unusual flavors, from celery to hoarhound to quince. Part of the allure of going to the fountain was ordering the latest "in" drink, be it a new creation or just old formulas gussied up with novel-sounding names. You could have a Pineapple

Smash, an Orange Puff or a Frigid Lemonilla. Drink names often reflected current fads. Anne Cooper Funderberg, in her book *Sundae Best: A History of Soda Fountains,* writes that the bicycle craze of the 1880s launched such drink names as Pedal Pusher, Sprocket Foam and Cycla-Phate.

For ice cream lovers, the marriage of soda and ice cream has its roots in these fad-loving, post–Civil War taste buds, as fountain drinks with raw eggs and milk became popular. You could order egg phosphates, eggnog and egg lemonades. According to author Funderberg, one Chicago confectioner used 360 eggs per day to make drinks and the New York's Astor Hotel used almost 300. Milk fans tried such offerings as the Middle Eastern treat *koumyss,* which was made with fermented milk, fresh milk and sugar. It was only a matter of time before people started putting ice cream in their favorite fountain drinks, too, and by the 1890s ice cream treats were standard fountain fare.

From the mid-1800s to the mid-1900s, America's "counter culture" centered on the local drugstore.

Ice Cream Gets Hot

Perhaps the most significant ice cream creation from the era was the hot fudge sundae. In the 1870s, soda fountains began offering hot sodas to help spur sales in colder climates. Contrary to their name, hot sodas did not contain any carbonated water; offerings were more along the lines of coffee, hot eggnog, beef tea and clam broth. While not as popular as other fountain drinks, hot sodas became a year-round staple. Among the hot soda line, one of the best sellers was hot chocolate,

The flamboyant, fedora-wearing Ed Berner ran an ice cream parlor in Two Rivers, Wisconsin. Locals claim it was the first to serve hot fudge sundaes.

and the syrup was often kept warm on a chafing dish by the fountain. At some point during the 1880s, some bright soda dispenser put this warm chocolate syrup over ice cream.

As with seemingly all ice cream inventions, there are many who claim theirs was the first spoon dipped in this perfect mingling of hot and cold. Almost a dozen towns claim to be the originator, including Buffalo, Cleveland, New Orleans, Norfolk, and Plainfield, Illinois. But the most oft-repeated stories of its invention come from Two Rivers, Wisconsin; Evanston, Illinois; and Ithaca, New York.

The earliest date of the sundae's invention comes from Two Rivers, which claims that Ed Berner first dished up a sundae at his parlor at 1404 Fifth Street in 1881. Customer George Hallauer requested chocolate syrup on top of his ice cream. Berner hesitated at first, as the syrup was only supposed to flavor soda water, but Berner liked the result and added it to his menu, charging the same price as a scoop sans syrup — a nickel. A nearby competitor of Berner's, Charles Giffy, liked this new concoction but knew the price was too low to make any profit. So, Giffy decided to serve the treat only on Sundays, when business was slow, to lure customers. It proved so popular that Giffy began to serve his syrup-and-ice-cream combos every day and changed the name to sundae. (Michael Turback, author of *A Month of Sundaes,* discredits the Two Rivers story as balderdash fabricated by popular newsman H.L. Mencken.)

Perhaps the most oft-repeated sundae legend is from Evanston, Illinois, which had the nickname "Heavenston" because of its strong religious streak. The story goes that local druggists invented the sundae to get around an 1890 Blue Law, which forbade ice cream soda sales on the Sabbath. (Zealous preachers criticized the "Sunday Soda Menace," calling soda "frilly" and admonishing those who liked to "suck soda.") To boost sales on Sunday, one of Evanston's pharmacists put syrup over ice cream instead. Out of respect for the Lord's Day, he changed the spelling to sundae.

Did you know?

In France, sundaes are called *coupes* after the wide-mouthed, stemmed glasses they are served in.

The story with the most solid footing for documentation-loving historians comes from Ithaca, New York. According to author Turback, Ithaca created the sundae in 1892 when a Unitarian minister stopped by Platt & Colt's pharmacy after he finished Sunday services and was served a scoop of ice cream with cherry syrup and a cherry on top. The minister liked his treat so well that he suggested naming it after the day he first tasted it. While Ithaca would seem to be a latecomer to the sundae invention lineup, its assertions are bolstered by an ad that appeared in the local newspaper on May 28, 1892. The ad announces the "Cherry Sunday, a new 10 cent Ice Cream Specialty, / Served only at Platt & Colt's." So, while we may never know who was the first inventor, Ithaca can safely lay claim to the title of earliest sundae documentation.

The Princes of Phosphates

With such delicious choices as sundaes, milk shakes and hot chocolate, Americans had more and more reasons to swing by the local soda fountain. By the turn of the twentieth century, there were 75,000 soda fountains in the United States. Their popularity was bolstered by the Temperance Movement's disdain for saloons and bars. Bars were smoky and dark places, with a reputation for attracting the fringes of society. Soda fountains, on the other hand, had a squeaky-clean image aided by the sanitary standards required of a pharmacy. They were finely appointed with marble counters and backsplashes, brass light fixtures, and china on which to serve

My heart is *SHAKING* only for you

SODA FOUNTAIN SLANG

Apple In: Pineapple ice cream soda

Bucket of Mud: A large scoop of chocolate ice cream

Burn It and Let It Swim: An ice cream float

Dog Soup: Water

Dusty Miller: A chocolate sundae with malted milk

Fix the Pumps: Look at the woman with the large breasts

Fizz: Carbonated water

Go for a Walk: A take-out order

Hold the Hail: No ice

Mud: Chocolate ice cream

No Cow: Without milk

One All the Way: Chocolate soda with chocolate ice cream

One on the Country: Buttermilk

Patch: Strawberry ice cream

Salt Water Man: An ice cream mixer

Spla: Whipped cream

Suds: Root beer

Through Georgia: Chocolate syrup added

Twist It, Choke It and Make It Cackle: A chocolate malted with egg

Virgin Coke: Coke with cherry syrup

White Stick: A vanilla cone

Yum-Yum: Sugar

your order. The atmosphere was more country club than Cotton Club.

By the early 1900s, they were the social epicenter of town life across America and the place to see-and-be-seen in town. If you got a new outfit and wanted to show it off, you went to the parlor for an ice cream soda. Taking a special someone out on a date? Head to the fountain and share a milk shake. As British writer Sir John Fraser observed in a *London Standard* article from the era, "Young people do not go for country walks in America. They chiefly consort in ice cream parlors."

One of the main reasons people kept coming back to the fountain was the soda jerk. At center stage — and key to many a fountain's success — was this prince of the phosphate and master of the milk shake. Part grand showman, part acrobatic linguist, part Mr. Congeniality and part master mixologist, soda jerks were responsible for making the treats, knowing all the recipes by heart and keeping the customers returning for more.

Soda jerking, which got its name from the "jerking" motion needed to get carbonated water from the spigot, was a respected profession in its day, ranking right up there with pharmacists in society's estimation. It was considered a stepping stone for up-and-coming lads with bright futures. The trade took its craftsmanship seriously. Training lasted almost six months, and wanna-be jerks had to bide their time bussing tables and washing dishes until they got their chance in the limelight. Top-notch jerks fetched top-dollar salaries, and some soda jerks, like Ralph Hersch at the Waldorf Astoria in New York, were national celebrities. There were industry magazines that covered the art of soda jerking and detailed dispensing guides (many with diagrams showing the exact ratios) on various formulas for popular drinks. The 1906 *Standard Manual of Soda and Other Beverages* told soda jerks to never display dirty towels or sponges or watch the patrons eat or drink. The manual advised soda jerks to "study each customer's desire and endeavor to remember the particular way in which he likes his drinks mixed and served."

Soda jerks were also encouraged to develop their own schtick in serving drinks, from cracking an egg with one hand to tossing a scoop in the air and catching it in a parfait glass. The *Los Angeles Times* in a July 3, 1907, article described the soda jerk as "a fellow of infinite skill, able to produce a milkshake with a few deft moves with large containers and a mixing machine. His sorcery done, he poured with a flourish, usually at arm's length from a great height."

Soda fountain's heyday in Hollywood was the 1940s, when dozens of films featured fountain scenes. This 1947 promo shot is for the Warner Bros. film "*My Girl Tisa,*" starring Lilli Palmer and Sam Wanamaker.

What added to the soda jerk's cachet was the playful dialect that they invented to describe orders. A "crowd of boats" meant three banana splits. "Adam's ale" was water. "In the Hay" was a strawberry milk shake. Calling out "81" let the workers know that someone needed service, while a shout of "95" meant a customer was leaving without paying. What stopped the jerks in their tracks, though, was a "vanilla" or an "87 1/2" — phrases alerting them that a pretty lady had walked in the door.

A handsome — and available — soda jerk often had a crowd of swooning ladies sitting at the counter and would add extra ice cream or another shot of syrup to the orders of those he fancied. The ultimate soda jerk come-on was setting down a dish with two spoons, an invitation to share ice cream — and perhaps other treats — after work.

In the 1920s and '30s, soda jerks were at the height of their cult status, thanks in large part to one of their biggest fans — Hollywood. Soda fountains

Hitting the Newstands

Ice cream's iconic status sold magazines in the early twentieth century. Mainstream magazines such as *Life* and *The Saturday Evening Post* frequently chose images of ice cream as cover art, while trade magazines, such as *Soda Fountain*, catered to the burgeoning soda fountain sector.

DRINK Coca-Cola

DELICIOUS AND REFRESHING

Ice cream trays, such as this one for Coca-Cola, were standard equipment for soda fountain wait staff from the 1910s through the 1940s.

I SCREAM FOR THE I SCREAMERS

If you're a history buff, passionate collector of ice cream objects or just a fan of a scoop of chocolate chip, you'll find good company among the members of the Ice Screamers. Founded in 1980, the group publishes an informative newsletter that covers everything from collectible straw holders to the debate over the invention of the ice cream cone. They also host an annual convention in Lancaster, Pennsylvania, that includes an auction, memorabilia displays, ice cream tastings and lectures. The group has more than 800 members on its rosters, and you can join, too. Dues are only $20 a year. For more information, call 215-343-2676 or log on to www.icescreamers.com

This ice cream stand in Cleveland, Ohio, is typical of circa-1950 roadside stands: slanted roof, easy walk-up windows and big signage.

A Scoop of History

1819

The first soda fountain patent was granted to Samuel Fahnestock.

and soda jerks sprang up as prominent features of dozens of movies, ranging from star billing in *The Soda Water Cowboy* to the lavish ice cream fantasy at the end of *Kid Millions* (complete with dancers skating on slabs of Neopolitan ice cream). The classic Andy Hardy movies, starring Mickey Rooney, almost always worked in a scene or two featuring a soda fountain.

Part of Hollywood's fascination was art reflecting life: soda fountains were the preferred hangout for dozens of celebrities. The legendary Schwab's Pharmacy, at Hollywood and Crescent boulevards, opened in 1932 and drew the likes of Judy Garland and Orson Welles, and, in later years, James Dean and Marilyn Monroe. Charlie Chaplin could often be found behind the counter making his own milk shake. Lore about the pharmacy claimed that Lana Turner was discovered there (an untrue story, but one that stuck and raised Schwab's profile nonetheless). Such was Schwab's role as a favorite movie setting that Paramount even had the fountain reproduced on its own backlot.

Main Street America was starstruck, too, and the "Hollywood Lunch" of a sandwich and a malted shake became a popular choice as more fountains became full-service restaurants during this period. Dixie Cups took advantage of Hollywood's ice cream love affair and featured picture lids with "Big Name Movie Stars." And even the usually staid ice cream trade journals, whose idea of sexy was to have centerfolds of the latest in soda fountain counter design, featured such pinups as Dorothy Lamour, Bette Davis and Claudette Colbert on their covers — all indulging in ice cream, of course.

By 1946, there were more than 120,000 soda fountains in the United States generating $1.25 billion in sales. But, as noted in the previous chapter, soda fountains and their prominence in America culture had waned by the late 1950s. Today less than 300 hundred remain. (See Appendix 1 on page 129 for a guide to some of them.)

Two Scoops for the Road

The rise of the automobile — and the roadside stands and restaurants that followed in its path — changed the way we enjoyed our scoops of ice cream. Ice cream was a perfect fit for the automobile society. It was a quick stop, and, if needed, you could eat it in the car. Where soda fountains were all about lingering and providing a luxurious setting in which to enjoy your ice cream, the roadside stands offered convenience and speed. They were located along the highways where passersby could easily spot them, and they were set back just far enough from the road to offer plenty of parking. They sported glass fronts so there wasn't any doubt about what goodies were inside. And you could walk up and place your order at a to-go window and eat it casually outside.

Most importantly, these roadside stands knew how to catch a customer's eye. Unlike drugstore soda fountains, which had to fit in with the landscape of Main Street, the signage at roadside stands could be big and bold. Huge signs — often in neon — beckoned travelers, and some buildings were an advertisement in and of themselves, built in the shape of giant ice cream cones, hand-crank ice cream freezers or Lily Cups, a common container from the 1930s.

Adding to the novelty of the roadside stands was what was on the menu. Hard ice cream was standard fare at ice cream parlors. Roadside stands, on the other hand, specialized in soft-serve ice cream and frozen custard. Not only were these new treats tasty, they were more profitable, too. Unlike a traditional parlor, which often relied on suppliers for product, a roadside stand made its own ice cream on-site in small batch freezers, cutting out the middleman and increasing profits.

Greek immigrant Thomas Carvelas didn't set out to become one of the kings of soft-serve, but a fateful trip on a hot day in 1934 made him one. When his ice cream trailer got a flat in Hartsdale, New York, Carvelas, who then went by the more Americanized last name of Carvel, thought fast and started selling his melting ice cream in a parking lot. People loved the now-soft ice cream, and so he opened up a shop in Hartsdale called Carvel's. For the next two years, Carvel worked to find a way to manufacture soft ice cream, and by 1939 he patented the no-air-pump, super-low-temperature ice cream machine.

By 1947, Carvel had sold 71 of his Custard King soft-serve machines to other ice cream shops, but he noticed that some of his buyers were defaulting on their payments. When he analyzed the reason for their financial struggle, he found that many of these shop owners made the same mistakes: they chose a poor location for their shop, they kept unpredictable hours, and they didn't rank cleanliness as a high priority. Carvel decided to oversee these shops directly, sharing his ice cream and business expertise and imposing uniform standards for each store. By 1949, he was allowing others to open their own Carvel stores. Once again, Carvel accidentally happened upon a new concept: the franchise. By the mid-1960s, Carvel's empire grew to 800 stores in 17 states. Key to his success was locating the stores along the burgeoning highway system. The stores — with their distinctive glass fronts and pitched roofs — became an icon along the Eastern seaboard.

The rise of soft-serve roadside stands can also be traced to the pioneering efforts of J. F. McCullough of Illinois and his son, Alex. The McCulloughs, who owned a plant that made ice cream mixes, thought soft ice cream (before it was sent to a freezer to harden) tasted better. To test their concept they set up shop for a day at Sherb Noble's walk-in store in Kankakee, Illinois, on August 4, 1938. They enticed customers with a deal that was hard to refuse: all the ice cream you could eat for 10 cents. In two hours, they dished out

DOUBLE-DIPPING ON MEMORABILIA:
ICE CREAM COLLECTIBLES

For some people, their love of ice cream is only surpassed by their love of collecting stuff about it. There are ice cream collectibles for every taste, from scoops and pewter molds to straw holders and ice-cream-themed Valentines. Chicagoan Allan Mellis, who calls himself "Mr. Ice Cream," has what is widely considered the best private collection of ice cream memorabilia in the country, with more than 10,000 pieces to date. He has penny licks, old signs, a rare Manos heart-shaped scoop and binders full of postcards, pictures and trade cards.

In Fayetteville, Arkansas, Steve "Doc"

Wilson has the world's largest collection of ice cream freezers. There are more than 200 in his collection, including an 1865 butter churn-ice cream freezer combo unit, the world's smallest steam-operated ice cream freezer and an 1878 Benham freezer by the same craftsmen who made the orb and cross on London's St. Paul's Cathedral. Wilson's collection is open to the public for free, and a visit even includes a scoop of free homemade ice cream. (Check out his website at www.users.nwark.com/~piperw/icpage.htm for details.)

If you're interested in doing some collecting of your own, a good starting point is *Ice Cream Collectibles* by Ed Marks (Schiffer Publishing, 2003). It includes a price guide and pictures of everything from penny licks to milkshake machines.

Once Allan "Mr. Ice Cream" Mellis (above) and Steve "Doc" Wilson (above right) got a taste of ice cream collectibles, they were hooked.

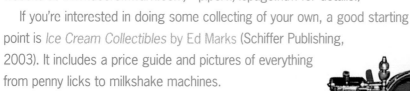

Harry Burt (above) didn't realize he was cooking up a revolution in the ice cream industry when he created the Good Humor bar.

more than 1,600 servings. Their taste test a success, they next needed to figure out how to manufacture their soft-serve ice cream easily and in quantity.

Alex spotted a prototype freezer made by Harry Oltz of Hammond, Indiana, at a trade show in Chicago. Oltz's ice cream machine could produce a continuous flow of soft serve ice cream. Noble was so impressed he called the freezer the Queen — the name stuck and became the inspiration for their chain of soft-serve stands, Dairy Queen. The first store opened on June 22, 1940, in Joliet, Illinois. Today, there are more than 5,000 Dairy Queens worldwide.

Between the spread of national soft-serve chains that catered to America's newly mobile society and local outlets that recognized the advantage of being close to traffic, roadside ice cream stands spread rapidly.

Ice (Cream) Man Cometh

Beginning in the 1940s, ease of purchase became key to many businesses' success, and ice cream was no different. Perhaps the epitome of convenience could be found in the Good Humor man. What could be easier than ice cream available right outside your door? From the 1940s to the 1960s, the Good Humor man patrolled the nation's neighborhoods selling ice cream bars and other treats right from his truck. *Time* magazine said they were "better known than the fire chief, more welcome than the mailman, more respected than the corner cop."

The fleet of Good Humor men got their start in Harry Burt's Youngstown, Ohio, basement. Burt, already a popular local confectioner known for his Good Humor sucker, had been dabbling in creating ice cream products for several years. During the "novelty craze" of the 1920s, Burt learned of the Eskimo Pie and set out to come up with a recipe

The Good Humor men in their signature uniform were as memorable as the treats they served from their trucks.

for chocolate-covered ice cream treats. One night, he found the magical combination in a blend of cocoa butter and coconut oil and rushed upstairs to let his daughter Ruth taste it. Ruth loved the bar, but it made a terrible mess, with chocolate all over her face and hands. Then, a suggestion by one of Burt's other children struck gold: why not use the wooden sticks from lollipops for the ice cream bars? Burt did, inventing the first ice cream bar on a stick.

While Burt's Good Humor bar was certainly an innovative product, what was truly unique was the way Good Humor bars were marketed and sold. Burt painted his candy truck a crisp white and outfitted it with a set of bells from the family's bobsled. He outfitted the driver, too, in all white. The bells would attract the people — children in particular — to see what the fanfare was about, and the pristine truck and professional-looking driver made people feel confident in their purchase. In short order, Burt had a dozen Good Humor trucks on the streets of Youngstown.

FUN *Facts*

FAMOUS SODA JERKS

Lou Costello

Bob Dole

Duke Ellington

Gene Hackman

Bob Hope

Jack Kerouac

Danny Kaye

Gene Kelly

Jerry Lewis

Leonard Nimoy

Tyrone Power

Martin Sheen

Harry Truman

Malcolm X

Source: *A Month of Sundaes* by Michael Turback

EVERYBODY LOVES ICE CREAM

Good Humor men were such a fixture of the American suburban landscape that they spawned a movie and, in 1964, a Golden Book for children.

When Burt died in 1926, the family sold the rights to the patent to a group of Cleveland businessmen. The Good Humor Corporation, as the Clevelanders called their new company, began selling franchises to anyone willing to put down $100 as a down payment.

One of the early franchisees was Tom Brimer, who first opened a Good Humor franchise in Detroit and then, in 1929, a second outlet in Chicago. The ice cream barely had time to harden in the freezer before the mafia showed up at Brimer's door and demanded $5,000 for "protection." Brimer refused. Thankfully Brimer was smart enough to increase the insured value on his trucks because a week later eight Good Humor trucks were blown up. The episode received a lot of publicity, and the resulting increase in sales allowed Brimer to pay his stockholders a 25-percent dividend, an unheard-of amount during the financial collapse of 1929.

The dividend caught the attention of investor Michael Meehan, who paid $500,000 to secure national rights for Good Humor. Under Meehan's direction, the company took on a military discipline, with strict codes of conduct for its drivers and a zeal for spotless trucks. Drivers wore a standard uniform that consisted of white pants and jacket, a blue bow tie, a white hat with a black brim, a shoulder belt and a moneychanger. Drivers were inspected before going on duty to ensure their uniforms, from head to toe, were in tip-top shape. The company even published a detailed manual, called *Making Good with Good Humor,* which covered everything from personal hygiene ("change your socks every day") to being a courteous driver ("always give the fellow the right of way"). According to a *Business Week* article in 1932, any driver who said "Good

Humor ice cream," instead of the regulation "Ice cream Good Humor," could find himself out of a job.

The strict discipline must have worked, though, because Good Humor men had an impeccable reputation for being helpful, polite and courteous. Countless newspaper articles described their Good Samaritan acts, from rescuing kittens out of trees to driving women in labor to the hospital to rescuing children from burning homes. Good Humor men became a vital part of the neighborhoods they served. They knew nearly all of the kids by name (and remembered what flavors they preferred), and they made small talk with isolated housewives, who were often home all day while the typical husband — driving the family's sole car — worked. At its peak, there were more than 1,000 Good Humor trucks in the United States.

Good Humor men were a staple of American culture — even spawning a Golden children's book and a movie — until the company phased out the trucks, and the Good Humor man, in 1976. Some trucks are still in operation with independent operators, and the company continues to make ice cream bars in such flavors as strawberry shortcake and toasted almond. But like the drugstore soda fountain, the distinctive ting-a-ling of the bells and the chipper "May I serve you?" are now only faint memories of the past.

Did you know?

At age 14, onetime soda jerk Duke Ellington wrote his first composition, "Soda Fountain Rag."

PHOSPHATES PRESERVED: GREAT ICE CREAM AND SODA FOUNTAIN MUSEUMS

America's Ice Cream & Dairy Museum at Elm Farm
Medina, Ohio
1050 Lafayette Rd., 330-722-3839, www.elmfarm.com
This collection includes a restored 1900s soda fountain with a 20-foot green-and-white Italian marble counter; old ice cream freezers, scoops and milk bottles; and several restored milk and ice cream delivery trucks.

America's Ice Cream and Dairy Museum at Elm Farm

Biedenharn Candy Company and Coca-Cola Museum
Vicksburg, Mississippi
1107 Washington St.
601-638-6514 www.preservevicksburg.com/1biedenharn.htm
Housed in the building where Coca-Cola was first bottled, the museum has a restored 1900 soda fountain and an 1890s candy counter.

Chippewa Valley Museum
Eau Claire, Wisconsin
Carson Park Drive, 715-834-7871, www.cvmuseum.com
The museum features a working soda fountain that operated in the Eau Claire area from 1895 to 1924.

The Dr Pepper Museum and Free Enterprise Institute
Waco, Texas
300 S. Fifth St., 254-757-1025, www.drpeppermuseum.com
This spot offers a display about old-time drugstores and has a working Dr Pepper–themed soda fountain.

Dublin Dr Pepper Bottling Co.
Dublin, Texas
105 E. Elm St., 888-398-1024, www.drpep.com
The oldest bottler of Dr Pepper soda — and the only plant still making it according to the original formula — has a museum and Old Doc's Soda Shop, where you can sample a Frosty Pepper.

Dundy County Historical Society
Benkelman, Nebraska
522 Arapahoe, 308-423-2750
Its working soda fountain was a local fixture at Reade's Drug Store until it was moved to the museum in 1993.

Durham Western Heritage Museum
Omaha, Nebraska
801 S. Tenth St., 402-444-5071, www.dwhm.org
The museum, housed in the art deco Omaha Union Station, has a 1930s restored soda fountain.

Fort Smith Musuem of History
Fort Smith, Arkansas
320 Rogers Ave., 479-783-7841, www.fortsmithmuseum.com
Housed inside their exhibit for an old-style drugstore is a working soda fountain.

Historic Washington House
Two Rivers, Wisconsin
1622 Jefferson St., 920-793-2490
Visitors can try an ice cream sundae in a replica of Ed Berner's Ice Cream Parlor, named for one of the sundae's purported inventors.

Kansas City Museum
Kansas City, Missouri
3218 Gladstone Blvd., 816-483-8300, www.unionstation.org/kcmuseum.cfm
After dipping into some regional history, grab a float at the museum's 1910 soda fountain.

The Museum of Science and Industry
Chicago, Illinois
57th Street and Lake Shore Drive, 773-684-1414, www.msichicago.org
A 1917 Hyde Park ice cream parlor lives on in the museum as Finnigan's Ice Cream Parlor.

National Museum of American History
Washington, D.C.
14th Street and Constitution Avenue, NW, 202-357-2700, www.american-history.si.edu/
Head to the basement to partake of a banana split at the museum's vintage ice cream parlor, complete with sweetheart chairs and a long bar.

McGill Historical Drugstore Museum
McGill, Nevada
11 Fourth St. (U.S. Route 93), 775-235-7082, www.idsely.com/~wpmuseum/McGill_Drug/mcgill_drug.html

This wonderfully preserved small-town drugstore (thanks to an owner who never threw anything away) features a working 1930s terra cotta soda fountain.

New Orleans Pharmacy Museum
New Orleans, Louisiana
514 Chartres St., 504-565-8027, www.pharmacymuseum.org
This museum features a fascinating collection of 1800s apothecary items, including a rare 1855 Italian black-and-rose marble soda fountain.

Wichita-Sedgwick County Historical Museum
Wichita, Kansas
204 S. Main St., 316-265-9314, www.wichitahistory.org
Museum attractions include The Drug Store, with a refurbished marble soda fountain and cabinetwork from a 1910 Kansas pharmacy.

World of Coca-Cola
Atlanta, Georgia
55 Martin Luther King, Jr., Dr., 404-676-5151, www.woccatlanta.com
At the restored Barnes Soda Fountain, you can learn from a soda jerk how to make an old-fashioned Coca-Cola.

Yakima Valley Museum
Yakima, Washington
2105 Tieton Dr., 509-248-0747, www.yakimavalleymuseum.org
Order a treat from an operating, late-1930s soda fountain that serves as a living history exhibit for the museum.

Ye Olde Mill

Ye Olde Mill
Utica, Ohio
11324 State Route 13, 740-892-3921, www.velveticecream.com
The Velvet Ice Cream Company has an ice cream museum and a nineteenth-century ice cream parlor where you can taste twenty-first-century flavors.

SALTED
CARAMEL

SPECIAL *Flavor*
wildberry

MILK CHOCOLATE

HONEY
VANILLA

3

YOU SAY GLACÉ, I SAY GELATO

FROZEN TREATS DEFINED

Mexican chocolate ice cream. Hazelnut gelato. Pear-champagne sorbet. Toffee Coffee frozen custard. Watermelon ice. Even herring and ketchup ice creams. With so many choices available, it's no wonder Americans consume nearly 185 scoops annually. We need go no further than our nearest ice cream shop, our local grocer's freezer case or a trusty home ice cream maker to have our favorite flavors at our fingertips. It used to be that ice cream came in a limited array of flavors. Not that long ago, Baskin-Robbins' 31 flavors seemed like a mind-boggling range of choices to a vanilla, strawberry and chocolate world. Now, there are gelaterias serving up dense and richly flavored gelato, Mexican *paletas* carts selling mango popsicles and rice-flavored ice cream on a stick, and cookbooks telling you how to make chili and tomato-basil granitas.

Jeni Britton (left) of Jeni's Fresh Ice Creams in Columbus's North Market serves up a myriad of frozen delights: gelato, frozen yogurt, sorbet and, of course, ice cream.

Ice Cream 101

To sort through the myriad of choices, you need to understand a bit about ice cream ingredients and manufacturing. Like fine wine, it's helpful to have a little knowledge of varietals and craftsmanship before sampling. Whether you are talking about *glacé,* Philadelphia ice cream or Argentinian-style gelato, it's still the lovely language of ice cream. But what makes each unique is the ingredients and their ratios and how the ice cream is processed. The addition of egg yolks in frozen custard means a richer, smoother and creamier taste. The absence of dairy in sorbets and ices allows the fresh and vibrant flavors to shine. The crystalline texture of granita comes from not using an ice cream maker at all.

To truly appreciate the various vintages and blends of ice cream, you must first master ice cream itself. At its purest form, ice cream consists of a frozen mixture of cream and usually some other milk product (whether it's fresh milk, dry powder or condensed milk), a sweetener, flavoring and often chunks of nuts, cookies or candies, which are called "solid additions" in the food manufacturing world. Eggs are sometimes added, but not always.

Food scientists talk about essential ice cream ingredients in such unappetizing terms as: stabilizers (like sugars, corn syrup, guar gum or arrowroot), which keep ice crystals from forming; emulsifiers (such as egg yolks or lecithin), which add fat and give ice cream its satisfying taste; dairy products (it is called ice cream, after all); and aeration, which is the amount of air present in the final product. The U.S. Food and Drug Administration requires that all ice cream must have at least 10 percent butterfat and no more than 50 percent air. Super-rich, super-premium ice creams have as much as 25 percent butterfat and less than 15 percent air. Premium ice cream, which accounts for about 50 percent of all ice cream sales in the U.S., averages 30 percent air. Gelato, the densest of all ice creams, can have as little as 4 percent air.

There are so many varieties of ice cream on the market, it can be difficult to keep them all straight. Here's a guide to the range of ice cream available:

ICE CREAM: This is a generic term to cover a frozen mixture of flavored cream and sugar or another sweetener. It can include eggs and other tasty add-ins, such as chocolate chips, almonds or pieces of Key lime pie.

AMERICAN OR COUNTRY-STYLE ICE CREAM: This is ice cream made with the addition of eggs. Before there was concern over the risk of salmonella, this often meant raw eggs were added to the recipe.

FRENCH ICE CREAM: This ice cream is made from a cooked custard base. This makes for a richer ice cream, thanks to all the egg and the use of more cream than milk. The yellow from the egg yolks is what gives French Vanilla its characteristic buttery appearance.

PHILADELPHIA ICE CREAM: This is what put American ice cream on the map back in the day: a simple ice cream traditionally made from an uncooked base with just cream, sugar and flecks of vanilla beans.

ICE MILK: There's no cream in ice milk, just milk, which means ice milk is

No matter what style of ice cream you like or how you like it served, ice cream is something worth shouting about.

lower in fat than traditional ice cream. Ice milk is usually served before hardening, soft-serve style. Most commercial soft-serve ice cream is, in fact, soft-serve ice milk.

SOFT-SERVE ICE CREAM: This term usually refers to soft-serve ice milk (see above), but also covers any ice cream that's served before it's ripened, or hardened, in a freezer.

GELATO [jeh-LAH-toh]; **GELATI** [jeh-LAH-tee], pl.: This is Italian-style ice cream that is dense and full-flavored. Its name is derived from the Italian verb *gelare* meaning "to freeze." Gelato typically uses milk instead of cream, has less air and has only a fraction of the butterfat found in super-premium brands. It's sold in places called "gelaterias," where the brightly colored gelati are displayed under glass in stainless steel tubs. Gelato is served at a slightly warmer temperature than regular ice cream, giving it more of a soft-serve consistency and is scooped into dishes and waffle cones using a paddle instead of a scoop. Popular flavors are *bacio* (chocolate hazelnut), amaretto, *nocciola* (hazelnut) and tiramisu. Gelato is currently one of the fastest-growing sectors of the U.S. ice cream market.

ARGENTINIAN GELATO: Large numbers of Italians fleeing Mussolini

Pete Benfaremo of Lemon Ice King of Corona in Queens, New York, serves up his refreshing ices in easy-to-squeeze paper cups.

emigrated to Argentina in the 1940s, and they brought their love of gelato with them. What evolved was a gelato that's less creamy than Italian-style gelato and relies more on flavors like coffee, chocolate and caramel.

Dulce de leche, made by carmelizing the sugar in milk, is a signature flavor.

GLACÉ [glah-SAY]: This is what the French call their ice cream. *Glacé* is typically made with an egg-custard base and flavoring is intense, vibrant and full, similar to the punch that gelato packs. But *glacé* is creamier than its Italian counterpart because it uses more cream than milk.

GRANITA [grah-nee-TAH]: From the Italian word for *grain,* granita is a frozen ice with fluffy granular crystals. It's made with water, sugar and liquid flavoring, ranging from fruit juice to wine to espresso. Egg whites and gelatin are sometimes added as a stabilizer. Typically, granita recipes call for a ratio of four parts liquid to one part sugar. A bonus to making granita is that it doesn't require any fancy equipment for the home cook: the granita mixture is placed in a metal bowl in the freezer, and then all you have to is stir at regular intervals while it turns to ice.

ITALIAN ICE: An Americanized version of granita, it's sometimes called water ice. Usually served in paper cups and emphasizing sweet fruit flavors, ice is very popular in Philadelphia and in New York City. Typically, the consistency of ices is smoother than snow cones but not as granular as granitas.

KULFI [KOOL-fee]: India's answer to ice cream, it's made from milk boiled down to a thick liquid. Traditional kulfi flavors are cardamom, saffron, pistachio, almond and mango.

PALETAS [pah-LAY-tas]: Mexican fruit popsicles made from pure juice of mangoes or strawberries. *Paletas de crema* are popsicles with cream and swirls of fruit in them. They are sold in parlors called paleterias or from carts.

SEMIFREDDO [say-mee-FRAYD-doh] (Italian); **SEMIFRIO** [say-mee-FREE-oh] (Spanish): Meaning "half cold" in Italian, *semifreddo* refers to any chilled or partially frozen desserts, from cakes and ice creams to custards and whipped cream.

ANYONE FOR A DOUBLE SCOOP OF SHRIMP?

Japanese love ice cream in all its forms, but they are especially crazy for the wild and wacky. Here are some of the more inventive flavors:

Squid

Ox Tongue

Sweet Potato

Fried Eggplant

Wasabi

Shrimp

Eel

Chicken Wing

Cactus

What's Your Flavor Profile?

In his book *What Flavor Is Your Personality?*, Dr. Alan Hirsch, neurological director of the Smell and Taste Treatment and Research Foundation in Chicago, outlines the key personality traits associated with liking a particular type of ice cream. Here's what your favorite scoop says about you:

VANILLA: Ambitious, impulsive and colorful with a busy schedule

CHOCOLATE: Charming, engaging, creative and attention-seeking

BUTTER PECAN: Orderly, fiscally conservative and ethical with a strong competitive drive

BANANA: Laid-back and generous

STRAWBERRY: Shy, detail-oriented and self-critical

CHOCOLATE CHIP: Successful, generous and competitive

ROCKY ROAD: Interesting, charming and professionally goal-driven

MINT CHOCOLATE CHIP: Pessimistic with an argumentative streak

COFFEE: Lively and flirtatious, but often stretched too thin

SHERBET [SHER-biht]: Derived from charbet, a Middle Eastern drink made with sweetened fruit juice and water, sherbets are lighter than ice cream, but creamier and firmer in consistency than ices. Many sherbets contain milk, egg whites or gelatin and often are fruit-flavored.

SORBET [sor-BAY] (French/American); **SORBETTO** [sor-BET-toh] (Italian): This is a dairy-free frozen dessert made from juice or a strained juice puree and usually some form of sweetener. Sorbet has a softer consistency than sherbet and a smoother texture than an ice or granita. Sorbets are served as both a dessert and a palate cleanser between courses and are usually served in a cup, rather than a cone. Sorbetto means "something frozen" in Italian.

FROZEN CUSTARD: Similar to French-style ice cream in its high butterfat and use of egg yolks, frozen custard is served soft, before hardening, and there's no extra air mixed in. Frozen custard is best served soft right out of the machine, and most stands carry three freshly made flavors each day: vanilla, chocolate and a flavor of the day. Frozen custard used to be a regional favorite concentrated along the eastern seaboard and in the Milwaukee area, but in recent years it has become more widely available.

FROZEN YOGURT: Produced when milk is fermented and coagulated by a friendly bacteria and then frozen, frozen yogurt has less butterfat than regular ice cream, but in some cases that lower fat is offset by more sugar than ice cream. (The additional sweetener is often used to offset yogurt's tart, slightly acidic taste.) Since its peak in the 1980s, when frozen yogurt seemed to be on every street corner (even gas stations were carrying it), its popularity has waned.

RICE AND SOY NONDAIRY FROZEN DESSERT: Dairy-free alternatives made with brown rice syrup or soy products, favored by people with milk allergies, vegans and the lactose intolerant.

A Flurry of Flavors

Before there was New York Super Fudge Chunk or bubble gum or rum raisin, there was camphor. During the Tang Dynasty in China, somewhere between 618–807 AD, one emperor employed 94 icemen to produce his favorite gelato-style flavor — camphor — the same tasty stuff that's used in

At Divino Gelato in Waukesha, Wisconsin, mint chocolate chip gelato comes out of the machine still soft and spreadable.

adds to the fun!

PINEAPPLE ICE CREAM

NATURE'S MOST REFRESHING FLAVOR

The Fun Food
The Whole
Family Loves

Ice cream is the perfect backdrop for nearly any flavor, be it pineapple or potato chip.

Did you know?

In Italy, Viagra ice cream is popular.

Vick's Vapo Rub. Sounds strange, but keep in mind that initially ice cream was seen as a medicinal cure for those with weak constitutions. Thankfully, by the mid-1600s, when ice cream started appearing on the menu of Parisian cafes, ice cream was sweetly placed in the dessert category. Early flavors leaned toward the rich and sophisticated — cinnamon and candied pumpkin were found in a 1690 cookbook — because with no refrigeration, ice cream was an expensive and infrequent indulgence of the elite.

While the core of ice cream favorites hasn't changed all that much in 400 years — chocolate, vanilla, strawberry and caramel are still as popular as when Thomas Jefferson was alive — flavors do fall out of vogue. Violet, prune, rose petal and avocado — all popular in the early 1900s — are rarities today. Ice cream recipes using Junket or rennet tablets, made from the digestive enzymes of cows, were a staple of cookbooks until they fell out of fashion in the 1950s. Even rum raisin, a favorite ice cream flavor just 30 years ago, has vanished from top 10 lists.

One constant, though, has been our long-standing love affair with vanilla; it's always been number-one in our hearts. Vanilla outsells its next closest competitor, chocolate, by more than three to one, and 70 percent of all ice cream flavors use vanilla as a base. Of course, vanilla's popularity is helped by the fact that it goes so well with other sweets: milk shakes, pie, cake, brownies. But certainly part of the appeal of vanilla is what aficionados claim: vanilla allows the true character of the ice cream to show through.

Want to know how good an ice cream is? Try the vanilla. A mediocre ice

FUNKY FLAVORS FROM MAX AND MINA'S

At Max and Mina's Homemade Ice Cream and Ices in Flushing, Queens, brothers **Bruce and Mark Becker,** below, turn out some of the most unique ice cream around. Their menu board has featured such flavors as potato chip fudge, beer and nuts, ketchup, horseradish and Nova lox. "We're opening up a whole new world of taste," says Bruce Becker.

The Beckers' flair for experimentation is partly genetic. Their grandfather, **Max Sockloff,** was an organic chemist who created recipes for everything from paints to toothpaste. Sockloff made ice cream, too, and growing up, the Becker brothers were often called to sample their grandfather's latest creation, be it lychee or mango.

When Bruce Becker cleaned out his grandparents' home in the mid-1980s, he found a notebook full of his grandfather's recipes. He put the notebook in a safe deposit box until 1997 when the brothers opened the parlor named in honor of their grandparents.

While their retail store gets a brisk neighborhood business, Max & Mina's

wholesales to restaurants and caterers in the New York area and nationally. They've found a niche making custom flavors for events and restaurants — like tobacco and clove flavors for a *Cigar Aficionado* event or corn ice cream for an all-corn menu. Another selling point for the shop is that the Beckers, both Orthodox Jews, offer only kosher ice cream.

For the Beckers, the flavor research is ongoing. Their standard, first and foremost, is that it must taste good. Some never make it off the drawing board. "Pickle never had a chance," Bruce says. "It was just bad."
Max and Mina's, 71-26 Main St., Flushing, Queens, 718-793-8629.

25 MOST POPULAR ICE CREAM FLAVORS

1) Vanilla
2) Chocolate
3) Neapolitan
4) Butter Pecan/Pecan
5) Chocolate chip
6) Strawberry
7) Candy
8) Cookies and Cream
9) Mint Chocolate Chip
10) Cakes/Cookies/ Brownies
11) Coffee
12) Cherry
13) Cookie Dough
14) Fudge
15) Vanilla/Chocolate
16) Caramel
17) Raspberry
18) Almond
19) Banana
20) Peach
21) Peanut Butter
22) Dulce de Leche
22) Mint
24) Chocolate Fudge
25) Malt

Source: International Ice Cream Association

cream can hide behind gobs of fudge and caramel swirls, gummy bears and chocolate-covered pretzels; but a truly fine ice cream is delicious as plain old vanilla.

Of course, we Americans could never be satisfied with just one flavor; we love choices. And perhaps part of the reason we love ice cream so much is that there's no shortage of choice. In many ways, ice cream is the perfect American dessert because it's so democratic. Regional preferences can be easily accommodated — Grape Nut ice cream for New Englanders or pecan flavors for Texans, for example — and it's still yummy.

At the vanguard of ice cream invention are the chefs at trendy restaurants, who've been pushing gourmet ice cream to new heights and expanding our taste buds in the process. Menus are showcasing such innovative flavors as beet, goat cheese and fig, black truffle, lavender-honey, fenugreek, extra virgin olive oil and charred mango-turmeric. And the ice cream isn't just for dessert anymore. At Victor's in the Ritz-Carlton in New Orleans, a recent menu item featured freshwater prawns with an exotic fruit compote and peanut satay ice cream. Boston celebrity chef Todd English of Olives has paired sweet vidalia ice cream with grilled cheddar cheese fondue or Kentucky lima bean ice cream with honey bacon and quail.

This is all a far cry from the kid stuff served by the hokey pokey man of yore, and it's representative of one of the biggest trends in the industry today: the maturing of ice cream.

Companies certainly market to kids, but adults buy ice cream, too. That's why manufacturers are launching new chocolate and coffee flavors as fast as we can spoon them up, and now there's even a market for such of-age flavors as Guinness Stout and Jack Daniels. A sampling of flavors from Dallas's Out of a Flower reads like the specials at a five-star bistro: tequila and cilantro, rosemary and black peppercorn, and red ginger and red port. New Jersey's Ciao Bella has flavors that span the globe: Moroccan spice, grapefruit vodka, rhubarb crème fraîche and blackberry Cabernet. At Taos Cow in New Mexico, the local harvest of pine nuts is put into such gourmet flavors as piñon caramel and cherry ristra. Even in the heartland, at Jeni's Fresh Ice Creams in Columbus, Ohio, flavors are anything but vanilla: coriander with fresh raspberry sauce; pumpkin five-

Today, our taste for ice cream runs the gamut from gourmet to international to cartoon-inspired.

Mardi Gras Homemade Ice Cream & Cakes in Columbus, Ohio, offers Indian-style kulfi alongside typical American flavors.

spice with pralines; and pepito, made from roasted pumpkin seeds and honey.

In recent years, our tastes for ice cream have gone upscale and over-the-top. Thanks to the influence of Ben & Jerry's, who popularized chunky ice cream, more and more mix-ins are being added to our pints. Turkey Hill Dairy's Creamy Commotions Chocolate Pretzel includes chocolate-covered Snyder's of Hanover pretzels and fudge swirled through vanilla ice cream. Dreyer's offers a Peanut Butter Bones ice cream that has vanilla and chocolate ice creams with bone-shaped bits of peanut butter cookie dough and chocolate-coated pieces of peanut butter cookies.

The Dreyer's Bones flavor showcases another growing trend in ice cream: marketing tie-ins and co-branding with movies, television shows and other established products such as candy bars and cookies. Dreyer's has deals with the Cartoon Network and Warner Brothers Pictures to make flavors inspired

BRAIN FREEZE FACTS

• Ice cream headaches are caused when something cold hits the nerve center at the roof of your mouth, causing the blood vessels in your head to dilate. The extra pressure on the blood in your head is what causes the pain.

• The scientific name for the condition is *sphenopalatine ganglioneuralgia.*

• Most ice cream headaches only last 15 to 30 seconds, but some can linger up to five minutes.

• The *British Medical Journal* published a study by an Ontario, Canada, middle-schooler which found that kids who ate ice cream too fast were more likely to get brain freeze.

• Want to avoid an ice cream headache? Keep the ice cream to the sides of your mouth, away from the roof your mouth.

by the Powerpuff Girls and Scooby-Doo (hence, the creation of the bones flavor). In 2002, NBC signed a deal giving Baskin-Robbins license to market flavors tied to its shows *Ed, American Dream,* and the popular daredevil reality show *Fear Factor.* (The Fear Factor sundae was topped with broken Oreos and gummy spiders to make it look like you were eating dirt crawling with insects.) These clever concoctions are aimed at kids and help explain why candy-infused ice cream is the fastest-growing ice cream flavor at the moment.

According to the International Ice Cream Association (IICA), other flavors on the rise include mint chocolate chip, banana, peanut butter and what trend watchers call the "brown flavors" — chocolate, caramel and coffee. *Dulce de leche,* a caramel-flavored ice cream that means "dessert of milk" in Spanish, is very big right now, and signifies the trend towards more Hispanic-influenced flavors. (*Trés leche* — a rich, yellow cake with creamy syrup and meringue whose name means "three milks" — is touted as the next hot flavor.) Other trends the IICA says to watch: more global flavors (ginger, lemongrass); unusual combinations (chocolate-curry); and flavors with chunks of popular desserts (tiramisu, Key lime pie). Perry's Ice Cream in Akron, New York, cites marula fruit, blood orange, prickly pear, mascarpone cheese and phyllo dough as up-and-comers. The low-carb craze is influencing flavors, too: nut and berry flavors are on the rise, as are inclusions made from sugar-free chocolates and candies.

And what about cookies and cream, the flavor that made the biggest debut in ice cream history when it hit the market in 1983? It's on the wane, along with chocolate fudge, malt and almond. Perhaps it will stage a comeback. Perhaps a cookies and cream ice cream, with chocolate fudge, malt, caramel and almond pieces is on its way to a freezer near you.

FUN *Facts*

According to the *Guinness Book of World Records,* the Heladeria Coromoto ice cream parlor in Merida, Venezuela, offers the most flavors in the world with more than 700 on the menu. Some of the exotic choices include brandied shrimp, steak and radish. The top-seller: sweet corn.

4

FROM COW TO CONE

HOW ICE CREAM IS MADE

Ice cream is more than just a sweet treat.
It's big business in the United States. With combined sales of $20.7 billion and 1.6 billion gallons being churned out annually, we lead the world in ice cream production. In truth, the cow is the true dairy queen of the ice cream business. Almost 9 percent of U.S. milk production — some 15 billion pounds annually — goes to the manufacture of ice cream. A high volume of milk is crucial for the manufacture of ice cream as it takes gallons of milk to make one gallon of ice cream.

Most ice cream in this country originates with the black-and-white Holstein cows, a breed popular because they produce the highest volume of

Without the cow, there would be no ice cream.

In the early days, ice cream was delivered by a horse-pulled wagon and kept cold by ice blocks and hay.

milk. Other breeds such as Brown Swiss, Ayrshire, Jersey and Guernsey are also used. Jersey and Guernsey cows don't produce as much milk as Holsteins, but their milk has more protein and more fat.

Cows are milked two to three times a day, and the average cow produces about eight gallons of milk. Cows used to be kept in small herds and milked by hand, but today the process is mechanized and it takes less than six minutes to milk each cow. As a result, herd sizes have grown, as have milk yields. At Braum's in Tuttle, Oklahoma, which operates 280 dairy stores in the region and makes its own brand of ice cream, there are 25,000 heads of dairy cattle 10,000 of which are in the milking herd. Thanks to milking machines, Braum's can milk 800 cows in 32 minutes and produce about 30,000 pounds of milk an hour.

From Milk to Mix-ins: The Making of Ice Cream

Early ice cream dairies and ice cream factories weren't fastidious about cleanliness. Before health and food safety laws went into effect, it wasn't uncommon to find extra "goodies," ranging from teeth to tobacco, in your ice cream. There were no labels that listed ingredients, either, so you couldn't be sure that only milk, cream and sugar were added. Thankfully, ice cream manufacturers now have squeaky-clean environments where workers wear lab coats and hair nets, and most of ice cream manufacture takes place within the confines of gleaming stainless steel machines. At the larger plants, nearly everything is done by machine, from filling pint containers and cutting ice cream for ice cream sandwiches to dipping ice cream into chocolate for bars and pouring ice pops into molds for freezing. Smaller plants may do some steps by hand. (For example, Matterhorn Cones, a popular West Coast

ICE CREAM UNIVERSITY

You can get your degree in the science of ice cream making at Penn State University's esteemed Ice Cream Short Course. Penn State was the first to offer college-level instruction in ice cream, beginning in 1892. The course was offered in the slower winter months, when "the boys could best be spared," and the only cost to students was $5 to cover lab fees and incidentals. Today, the weeklong course is still held in January, but it now costs more than $1,000. The well-regarded program graduates a "who's-who" list of ice cream industry names; even Ben Cohen and Jerry Greenfield are alums.

frozen novelty made in Caldwell, Idaho, hand-dips four million of their huge vanilla-topped cones into chocolate and nuts each year.) But typically ice cream today is carried, churned, shot, squirted, mixed, swirled, coated and packaged with little human contact.

Step 1: The Mix

The first step in making ice cream is creating the mix. Milk travels via an insulated tanker truck from the farm to the processing plant or ice cream factory. While each company's formula varies in levels of fat, sweetness and ingredients, all mixes include cream and other milk ingredients, plus sweeteners and any stabilizers or emulsifiers that are added. The ingredients are then poured into a huge blending tank and mixed with a large beater.

There are two kinds of mixes made: vanilla or chocolate. All the hundreds of varieties of flavors are made from these two base mixes. The largest production goes to making the vanilla mix because it's so widely used as the starting point for ice cream flavors; strawberry, cookies and cream, rum raisin and bubble gum, for example, all start out with a vanilla base.

Whether the ice cream maker creates its own mix is largely a matter of company size and processing capabilities Nearly all the big manufacturers make their own mix, as do many micro-creameries and some retail shops with specific standards for their recipes. Smaller manufacturers and ice cream retail shops tend to buy their mix from a dairy processor. Pasteurized and homogenized mixes are delivered to the store or plant in large plastic bags, but the addition of flavorings and ingredients and the freezing of ice cream are done on-site. Whether the mix is made in-house or out, the steps to making ice cream are the same.

BEST-SELLING ICE CREAM BRANDS

1. Private Label (includes in-house store brands)
2. Breyers
3. Dreyer's/ Edy's Grand
4. Blue Bell
5. Häagen-Dazs
6. Ben & Jerry's
7. Dreyer's/Edy's
8. Well's Blue Bunny
9. Healthy Choice
10. Turkey Hill

Source: Information Resources Inc. (2002)

Step 2: The Pasteurizer

After the mix is blended, it is pumped into the pasteurizer. In the 1860s, Louis Pasteur found that quick heating of foods destroyed harmful bacteria without ruining the basic composition of the food. Today's pasteurizer quickly heats the mix to 175 degrees Fahrenheit for 15 to 25 seconds to kill any bacteria and give the mix a longer life. One downside to pasteurization is that it denatures healthy enzymes and protein naturally present in the milk, too.

Step 3: The Homogenizer

After a quick trip to the pasteurizer, the hot mix is sent directly to the homogenizer to streamline the milk's fat globules into a uniform size so they don't separate. (If you've seen non-homogenized milk, you'll notice the thick layer of cream on top. The cream, full of large, buoyant fat globules, rises, whereas the skim milk below is fat-free.) The homogenizer "mashes" the milk by applying pressure of 2,000 pounds per square inch to break down the fat globules into small, uniform particles. The mix is quickly cooled to 30 or 40 degrees Fahrenheit and then set aside to "age" in a refrigerated tank anywhere from several hours to overnight. Flavorings and colorings are added, and the mixture heads to a freezer to become ice cream.

Step 4: The Freezer

Most large manufacturers use a continuous freezer, which can churn out as many as 2,000 gallons an hour. With continuous freezers, a steady stream of ice cream mix and air (the amount of air varies depending on desired overrun) runs through the freezing chamber. While in the freezer chamber, dashers, or mixing paddles, incorporate the air; this prevents the ice cream from

A COOL JOB: ICE CREAM TASTE-TESTER

John Harrison is the official taster for Edy's Grand Ice Cream. It sounds like a cake job, but taste-testers play a crucial role in a company's success by developing new flavors and ensuring quality standards.

Edy's takes Harrison's job so seriously that his taste buds are insured for $1 million. Harrison tastes up to to 120 spoonfuls of ice cream a day. (He doesn't swallow, though; he spits it out after tasting it.) For his job, Harrison babies his taste buds, eschewing spicy foods, coffee, alcohol and smoking. He even uses a gold-plated spoon because there's no aftertaste associated with it. For at-home tasters, Harrison suggests consuming whatever you buy within a week and sampling the ice cream with the spoon turned upside down — that way, all you taste is the ice cream.

At the Chocolate Shoppe, in Madison, Wisconsin, ice cream first goes through a freezer (above) before being stored in a room that's -15 below zero (right).

being a rock-solid mass and keeps the ice crystals small, which is critical if you want a smoothly textured product. It takes only a few seconds to freeze the mix, and then, like magic, the ice cream comes out, looking much like very soft, soft-serve. Next, a "flavor feeder" injects everything from cookie pieces to peanut butter cups to fudge swirls. Finally, the ice cream is squirted into containers or novelty molds.

Small manufacturers use a similar process, but they use batch freezers, instead, which make only 60 gallons an hour. With a batch freezer, the mixture is poured into the top of the machine by hand. The proper freezing time and temperature is programmed into the machine, and in less than 10 minutes, the freezer pours the soft ice cream through a "mouth" in the front

PAMPERING YOUR PINTS

You'd think all you'd need to know about eating ice cream would involve a scoop, a spoon and a dish, but in fact there are several things you can do to ensure your ice cream is fresh and tasty and that it stays that way. Try these tips, culled from the International Ice Cream Association and other experts:

■ Make the ice cream freezer your last stop in the store and place it separate from other groceries in your cart.
■ Pack your ice cream in a freezer bag or double brown paper bags to insulate it for the trip home.
■ Head immediately home from the grocery store, so your ice cream doesn't have the chance to melt.
■ Store ice cream as far back in the freezer as possible; even better, store it in your deep freezer, if you have one. Never store it in the freezer door.
■ Do not set a carton of ice cream on your counter and subject it to multiple thawings and refreezings, which

deteriorates the consistency of the ice cream. Portion only the ice cream you need and return the carton back to the freezer.
■ Do not store ice cream alongside foods with pungent odors, like coffee or fish. Wrap carton in a plastic freezer bag or a brown paper bag to prevent the ice cream from absorbing smells.
■ When scooping ice cream, scoop gently and evenly. Pushing down too hard on the ice cream can break down the ice crystals and ruin its texture. And scooping only from the middle ruins the ice cream on the side of the container.

of the machine. Then, any inclusions or swirls for the flavor are stirred in by hand. Filling pints or other containers is done by hand, too; some shops use a machine to dispense the accurate amount of ice cream into each pint, but a person still needs to work the machine and place lids on each container.

Step 5: Hardening

The final stage of the production process is the hardening room, a big walk-in freezer where the ice cream is completely frozen to temperatures ranging from 20 to 40 degrees. To keep the ice cream as fresh and smooth as possible, fans often blow air around the freshly made ice cream to speed the hardening process. Larger manufacturers have warehouse-size hardening areas, in which workers, who look like they're dressed for an Arctic expedition, stack and sort the ice cream. (Workers spend 45 minutes in the hardening room and 15 minutes out, to give them a chance to warm up.) Once the ice cream has hardened for six to eight hours, it is moved to a storage room that is cold, usually around 20 degrees, but not nearly as frigid as the hardening room. From there, the ice cream is ready to be eaten and enjoyed by consumers.

At Handel's in Youngstown, Ohio, ice cream is made in small quantities using a batch freezer.

The Art of Making Ice Cream

It's not that hard to make ice cream. But making great ice cream is as much art as science. As Bruce Tharp, a professor emeritus from the distinguished

While you might not see the word *seaweed* listed among the ingredients on your carton, you may see sodium alginate or carrageenan, both seaweed derivatives that are used as stabilizers to keep ice cream smooth and tasty. Sodium alginate is made from extract of brown kelp, while carrageenan is derived from red algae, which was once harvested from the coast of Ireland, near the village of Carragheen.

Pennsylvania State University dairy program and an international dairy consultant, puts it, "Ice cream is a complex material. It's one of the most complex foods we eat."

Part of what makes ice cream so complex is that it is the only food that's designed to be eaten frozen. It needs to stay frozen throughout its distribution cycle from factory to your doorstep to be fully enjoyed. Too much fluctuation in temperature, called "heat shock," is a disaster. Ice cream manufacturers take great care to ensure their ice cream stays ice cold; some even handle distribution to the grocery store to ensure that the ice cream never thaws even the slightest bit.

"Physiologically, ice cream is a fragile product," explains Ted Galloway of Galloway Company and Classic Mix in Neenah, Wisconsin. His company supplies frozen dessert mixes to retail shops throughout the Midwest. "It's very delicate."

Ice cream's fragile nature comes primarily from the fact that it isn't completely frozen, even at zero degrees. Even at this seemingly frigid temperature, 5 to 10 percent of the ice cream's water content is still liquid. Water crystals in the ice cream keep thawing and re-freezing, and over time the smoothness and creaminess disintegrate. "Once ice cream starts to destabilize," Galloway says, "it's progressive." This means that once ice cream's texture starts to deteriorate, there's no turning back to the Land of Smooth Creaminess.

To be completely frozen, ice cream needs to be kept at -20 degrees, the temperature of choice for ice cream warehouses and grocers' freezer cabinets. Anytime the temperature fluctuates above that in the ice cream's journey from plant to freezer cabinet to home refrigerator (where inevitably the temperature rises as most home freezers are kept at five below to zero degrees

Fahrenheit) there is the potential for damage to the product.

To limit the effects of heat shock, manufacturers add stabilizers (such as carrageenan and guar gum) that reduce the amount of ice crystals that form in the product. They even make on-site visits to grocery and convenience stores to ensure their product is kept at the right temperature. A well-frozen ice cream is good ice cream, and the efforts by manufacturers to make it so are something we can all appreciate.

The safe transport of ice cream from plant to your local freezer case is a top priority.

Churn, Baby, Churn

Today, some 500 companies feed our nation's appetite for ice cream. Ice cream manufacturers usually fall within four categories: the big companies with a national presence; regional companies with name recognition in their area; small, specialty makers with limited distribution; and wholesalers who don't deal with the public but supply ice cream to restaurants, coffeehouses and the like.

Increasingly, ice cream manufacturing is done by a handful of companies. Recent years have brought a spate of mergers: Dreyer's merged with Nestlé

Looking for the latest flavors? Check your local freezer case in January or February when new ice cream flavors are typically introduced. New ice cream novelties come out in March.

Ice Cream Company in 2003, and now its holdings include the Häagen-Dazs brand and Nestlé's line of Drumsticks, Fruit 'N Juice bars and other novelties. In 2001, Suiza merged with Dean's Foods in a $10-billion deal that placed 14 different regional ice cream brands within one organization. British-Danish conglomerate Unilever owns both Ben & Jerry's and the Good Humor-Breyers Company. Even the holdings of Good Humor-Breyers, which include the Popsicle and Klondike frozen novelty lines, is the result of several mergers over the last 50 years.

But no matter how large the companies are today, nearly everyone in the ice cream business started out small. The founding stories all follow the same arc: the company's founder(s) started making a few gallons in the back of the store, the kitchen or wherever, and over time, their great ice cream gained a following. Most of the major national and regional ice cream manufacturers started producing ice cream in the 1920s and '30s as family-owned operations.

Two of the top seven best-selling ice cream brands are still family-owned: Wells Dairy in Le Mars, Iowa, makers of the Blue Bunny line of ice cream and the largest family-owned dairy in the country, and the Texas-based Blue Bell ice cream, which is the number three ice cream manufacturer in the country, despite only selling in 14 states.

Even though the top 10 ice cream brands generate about half of the take-home sales in the country, there's still a big piece of the ice cream pie left for smaller manufacturers. Regional dairies, such as Turkey Hill in Pennsylvania, Pierre's and Velvet in Ohio, Perry's and Ronnybrook Farm in New York and Mayfield, and Purity in Tennessee, hold their own in their respective markets.

ICE CREAM UP-CLOSE: GREAT FACTORY TOURS

What better way is there to appreciate your next scoop of ice cream than to understand how it's made? At these factory tours, you can witness how milk becomes ice cream, learn some company history and, most importantly, sample their wares when you're done. Always call ahead to confirm tour times and availability.

If you can't make it to an on-site factory tour, log on to one of these websites for a virtual tour instead.:
Ben & Jerry's (www.benjerry.com), **Purity Dairy** (www.puritydairies.com), **House of Flavors** (www.houseofflavors.com) **or Boulder Ice Cream** (www.bouldericecream.com)

Ben & Jerry's Homemade
Waterbury, Vermont
Tours are offered on a first-come, first-served basis. No ice cream production on weekends. $3; seniors, $2; children under age 12, free. 866-BJ-TOURS, www.benjerry.com

Blue Bell
Brenham, Texas
The plant is closed for tours on weekends, but the Country Store and Ice Cream Parlor are open most Saturdays. Tours are also offered at their Broken Arrow, Oklahoma, and Sylacauga, Alabama, plants. $3; seniors and children, $2; under age 6, free. 800-327-8135, 979-830-2197, www.bluebell.com

Braum's Ice Cream and Dairy Stores

Tuttle, Oklahoma
Tours offered by appointment only. 405-478-1656, www.braums.com

Ice Cream Capital of the World Visitors Center
Le Mars, Iowa
Open year round, but hours are limited from September to April. $3; children, ages 5–12, $1. 712-546-4090, www.bluebunny.com

Mayfield Dairy Farms
Athens, Tennessee
Tours are offered every day except Wednesday and Sunday. Ice-cream diehards might want to avoid Saturday's tour since no ice cream is made that day. There are tours at their Braselton, Georgia, plant, too. Free. 800-872-5444, ext. 2253, www.mayfielddairy.com

Oberweis Dairy
North Aurora, Illinois
Tours are offered Mondays and Wednesdays at 10 a.m.; reservations required. $3; children over age 7, $2 (no children under age 7 admitted on tours). 630-801-6100, www.oberweisdairy.com

Perry's Ice Cream
Akron, New York
Tours are offered Monday through Friday by appointment only. $1. 800-8PERRYS, ext. 230, 716-542-5492, www.perrysicecream.com

Velvet Ice Cream
Utica, Ohio
Tours are offered May through October. Free. 740-892-3921, www.velveticecream.com

THE SKINNY ON ICE CREAM LABELS

Labels on the ice cream carton will tell you a lot about how much fat is in the ice cream. If the carton just says ice cream, it has at least 10 percent butterfat. (Premium and super-premium will have even more fat.) But if you're looking for something lighter, here are your choices:

■ **REDUCED FAT:** 25 percent less fat than the referenced product (either an average of leading brands or the company's own brand.)

■ **LIGHT:** 50 percent less fat or 33 percent fewer calories than the referenced product.

■ **LOWFAT:** no more than three grams of total fat per serving.

■ **NONFAT:** less than 0.5 grams per serving.

Other companies, like Palazzolo's Gelato and Sorbetto in Douglas, Michigan, and Olympic Mountain Ice Cream near Puget Sound, Washington, maintain a low-profile and a discerning client base by selling wholesale to restaurants and other businesses. These wholesalers manufacture a stable of popular flavors, but they also must become masters at custom flavors, working with chefs and caterers to design creative fare to match a menu or fill a company's request for a flavor in keeping with a particular theme. (Olympic, for example, has developed a Douglas fir champagne sorbet and asparagus ice cream for clients.)

Still other artisanal manufacturers find their niche in gourmet markets and via online ordering by working in small batches with top-notch ingredients. Out of a Flower's exotic herb and flower-infused sorbets, Straus Creamery's farm-fresh organic flavors, and Ciao Bella's intensely flavored gelati and sorbets probably will never be found in every grocer's freezer, but that's not the point. Their ice creams are made with same care as a fine wine or a four-star meal.

The beauty of the ice cream business is that there's market demand for the range of manufacturers. Perhaps Luconda Dager, a third-generation ice cream maker and vice president of sales for Velvet Ice Cream, gets to the heart of why so many ice cream companies do well and why consumers love them: "We're not selling ice cream," she says. "We're selling fun."

AT YOUR SERVICE

The Flavor's There

HOOD'S
old fashioned
ICE CREAM

Massachusetts-based Hood's has been in business since 1846.

SERVING Smith ICE CREAM

Most ice cream companies got their start as small-time, family outfits.

Future of Ice Cream

One thing that remains constant in the ice cream business is the changing marketplace. Between shifts in consumer preferences, demand for a constant stream of new and improved products, and technological advances, ice cream manufacturers are always doing research and development. New flavors and new products are rolled out each year to meet demand. The current emphasis on ice cream for special diets is playing a big role. In the last two years, there's been a glut of lactose-free, low-carb and no-sugar-added products introduced to meet consumer demand. (No-carb ice cream could be on the horizon; researchers at the University of Wisconsin are working on one.) Low-fat ice

FLAVORS WORTH FINDING

Here are some artisanal ice cream manufacturers worth seeking out. Note that some do not have distribution outside of their area, but many will ship direct to your doorstep. The website www.icecreamsource.com is an excellent one-stop resource for many of these micro-creamery brands.

Blue Moon Sorbet
Quechee, Vermont
802/295-1165

Dandy Don's HomeMade
Ice Cream
Van Nuys, California
818/994-0111
www.dandydonsicecream.com

Gelati-Da
Edina, Minnesota
952/926-8744
www.gelatida.com

Out of a Flower
Dallas, Texas
214/630-3136

Reed's Ginger Ice Cream
Los Angeles, California
800/997-3337
www.reedsgingerbrew.com/
icecream.asp

Seattle Sorbets
Seattle, Washington
800/747-4518
www.morethanicecream.com

Sibby's
Westby, Wisconsin
608/634-3828
www.sibbysfarm.com

Strafford Organic Creamery
Strafford, Vermont
802/765-4180

Straus Family Creamery
Marin County, California
www.strausmilk.com

Note: many artisanal manufacturers have a retail store in addition to grocery store distributions. See Appendix 1 on page 129 for information on the following brands: Boulder Ice Cream, Ciao Bella, Crema Café/Sonny's Ice Cream, Créme Crémaillére, Dave's Hawaiian Ice Cream, Double Rainbow, Dr. Bob's Ice Creams and Ronnybrook Farms.

EVERYBODY LOVES ICE CREAM

78

cream, thought to be a category whose time was done, is gaining attention once again. Low-fat ice cream bars and sandwiches are seeing brisk sales, and Dreyer's recently unveiled light ice cream made with its new "slow churn" technology; the process, according to the company, makes low-fat cream taste like the full-fat version. Sales for non-dairy frozen desserts made from rice and soy are on the rise, too. (From 1999 to 2000, sales in this category rose by more than 36 percent.) And there's even an oat-based frozen dessert on the market— OatsCreme from Minneapolis-based American Oats.

There are other innovations, too. According to an October 2002 *Food Technology* article entitled "31 Ingredient Developments for Frozen Desserts," everything from fiber to flavored raisins to flaxseed could show up on ice cream ingredient labels someday. Even winter-wheat protein might become a staple for manufacturers, as food scientists at the University of Guelph in Ontario, Canada, investigate how to isolate the proteins from cold-thriving plant and animal sources to keep ice cream stable when frozen.

Another big trend is the increased complexity of inclusions — as the additions of everything from cookies to cake batter to candy are called. Ice cream, like many American products in recent years, has gone extreme. Expect to see more shaped candies, more swirls and more add-ins in general. Two decades ago, ice cream with one inclusion (cookies and cream or chocolate chip cookie dough, for example) was considered indulgent. Now, three inclusions are commonplace.

The market segment that is perhaps garnering the most attention today is frozen novelties, a category that covers everything from frozen ice pops to ice cream sandwiches to sundae cups. Sales are up — 7.6 percent from 2002 to 2003 — and it looks like the trend will continue.

FUN

10 BEST-SELLING MARKETS FOR ICE CREAM

Des Moines, Iowa

Roanoke, Virginia

Spokane, Washington

Jacksonville, Florida

Tampa/St. Petersburg, Florida

Hartford, CT/ Springfield, MA

Green Bay, Wisconsin

Salt Lake City, Utah

Richmond/ Norfolk, Virginia

Portland, Oregon

Source: International Ice Cream Association (2001)

A 2003 "Frozen Novelties Planning Guide" from Columbus, Ohio-based Norse Dairy Systems stated that the frozen novelties category "presents the greatest growth opportunity in the overall frozen dessert market." Ice cream sandwiches, cones, push tubes and cakes, pies and rolls have all seen double-digit growth in recent years. For adults, there's increased interest in low-fat, low-carb and no-sugar-added novelties. For kids, product developers are looking at ways to make novelties even more appealing; everything from three-dimensional frozen ice pops, which is already popular in Europe, to novelties that change color as you eat them are on the drawing board.

Even the now century-old cone is getting an update. Norse Dairy

Systems, which manufactures cones, cups and wafers for the ice cream industry, has developed coffee-flavored cones, red-and-blue-striped cones, and cone cups, an innovation that would make the inventor of edible cups, Italo Marchiony, proud. ■

VANILLA: ANYTHING BUT PLAIN

Vanilla is often a synonym for bland, plain and ordinary. But vanilla is far from ordinary: It comes from the pod of the orchid *Vanilla planifolia*, the only one of more than 20,000 orchid varieties that produces an edible fruit, and has a complex bouquet with more than 250 flavor components.

Vanilla is the world's most labor-intensive crop, taking several years to reach the market. It takes three years for the plant to flower, which it does only once a year. Workers then quickly hand-pollinate all the plants to produce the bean and wait nine months for the bean to mature on the plant.

Once the green, cigar-shaped pods are harvested, they go through an elaborate curing process to achieve their characteristic color and flavor. First they are plunged in water, and then for several months they are alternately baked in the sun by daylight and sweated in closed containers by night.

Because the flower is so rare and the labor so involved, vanilla has always been a precious commodity. In the last few years, vanilla has become even more of a luxury item as prices have skyrocketed due to a devastating cyclone in 2000 that ruined 30 percent of the crop in Madagascar. (Seventy-percent of the world's vanilla comes from Madagascar, but Indonesia, Tahiti, Mexico, Costa Rica and other areas grow it, too.) A gallon of vanilla extract was $47 a gallon in 2000; in 2003, the price was nearing $300.

For the next few years, cost for vanilla beans and pure vanilla extract will remain high. But many cooks won't settle for anything else and will continue to buy it.

You can purchase quality vanilla beans and extract from these companies: Nielsen-Massey, 800/525-PURE, www.nielsenmassey.com; Penzey's Spices, 800/741-7787, www.penzeys.com; and the Vanilla Company, 800/757-7511, www.vanilla.com.

5

ICE CREAM NIRVANA

WHERE TO FIND AMAZING ICE CREAM

Perhaps one reason ice cream is America's favorite treat is that it embodies much of what makes this country so great: a sense of democracy and pluralism, equal opportunity and a steadfast belief in the inalienable right to the pursuit of happiness. The beauty of ice cream is that it's as unique, varied and ethnically rich as we are as a society. Ditto for the range of places that sell ice cream. There are mom-and-pop stands, country dairy bars, sleek gelaterias, five-and-dime soda fountains, and trendy micro-creameries. There are national chains that got big because they knew a thing or two about good ice cream, and the shop in your neighborhood that makes the very best ice cream on earth (and no one can tell you otherwise). Each type of ice cream retailer serves its own distinct twist on ice cream, and I say it's all good.

A couple vows to be eternally faithful to Ted Drewes in St. Louis.

Selling the Scoops

Our love of going out for ice cream is reflected in the numbers: almost 65 percent — $13 billion — of total ice cream sales is spent at scoop shops, parlors and other retail outlets. In all, there are some 17,000 ice cream shops in the United States. According to the National Ice Cream Retailers Association (NICRA), the number of shops has been steady since the mid-1990s, with new shops opening to replace those that have shuttered their doors.

What NICRA is seeing, however, is a change in the kinds of shops that are popular today. The sit-down parlor with glass tulip cups and a menu of soda treats is giving way to the fast-service scoop shop. At a scoop shop, you might stay a few minutes to eat your ice cream, but you're just as likely to grab and go.

Competition among the scoop shops is intense. Ice cream is largely a seasonal business with most ice cream sales occurring in the summer. A successful business depends on selling a lot of scoops, and there are a lot of stands vying for our business. In some highly desirable locales, there are as many as six ice cream stands within a mile of each other.

The last five years have seen aggressive expansion by upstart ice cream franchises. There's been tremendous growth among what one newspaper writer called "the slabberies," including Cold Stone Creamery, Marble Slab Creamery and Maggie Moo's, all shops that feature ice cream hand-mixed on a frozen marble or granite slab. Cold Stone Creamery, in particular, has been growing fast. Its first franchise opened in 1995, and by 2003 there were 560 stores open nationwide and another 750 in development. Another growth area is frozen custard. Two of the largest frozen custard

The many faces of ice cream shops: Jim Aglamesis and old-time charm at Aglamesis Brothers in Cincinnati (above); Judi Sottile and gelato at Divino Gelato in Waukesha, Wisconsin (lower right); and neon custard at Kitt's in Milwaukee, Wisconsin (next page).

A Scoop of History

1919

Frozen custard first appeared at Coney Island as a carnival treat and became a staple of the East Coast resort communities before spreading westward.

chains, Culver's and Ritter's, have opened new locations throughout the Midwest and, in the case of Ritter's, in Florida. Texas, in particular, is a frozen custard hotspot, with as many as 40 frozen custard shops slated to open in the next two years.

Even existing franchises have added stores: Carvel, the longtime East Coast institution and the fourth-largest ice cream chain, grew by 220 percent in 2003, signing more than 114 new franchise agreements. Even the frozen yogurt franchises, which have had a tougher go of it since the 1980s when frozen yogurt was the craze, are growing. Nearly all of them have added traditional ice cream to their offerings.

Ice cream chains got started in 1935 when Howard Johnson, who already operated two profitable grill and ice cream shops in Quincy, Massachusetts, arranged a deal to sell his products at a Cape Cod stand operated by an old schoolmate. Before Howard Johnson's was known as a motel, it was known

IT'S SO MUCH FUN TO CHOOSE

HOWARD JOHNSON'S ICE CREAM
28 FLAVORS

FROM 28 WONDERFUL FLAVORS!

HOWARD JOHNSON'S
RESTAURANTS   MOTOR LODGES
"Host of the Highways"
Howard Johnson's, Inc., 45 Rockefeller Plaza, New York 20, New York

for its 28 famous flavors of rich, 20-percent butterfat ice cream and good, valued-priced food. Over the next several decades, Howard Johnson's became a fixture of the nation's expanding highway system, with its easy-to-spot orange roof. There were more than 400 restaurants in the chain before it embarked into the lodging business in 1954. In the mid–1960s, sales at Howard Johnson's restaurants exceeded the sales of McDonald's, Burger King and Kentucky Fried Chicken combined. In fact, the only organization that fed more people than Howard Johnson's was the U.S. Army. By the late 1970's, HoJo's empire consisted of more than 1,000 restaurants. In the mid–1980s, the restaurant and lodging sides of the company split, and today, there are just 17 Howard Johnson's restaurants, all serving ice cream based on the original 1925 recipe.

Following Johnson's lead, other ice cream chains soon followed in post–World War II America. Dairy Queen, Carvel and Tastee Freeze catered to the increasingly vehicle-dependent public, while chains such as Sonic Drive-in and A&W catered to the teen crowd looking for a place to park their cars after an evening of cruising. Chains such as Baskin-Robbins appealed to Americans who wanted to enjoy their ice cream, but not linger for too long. (At first, the only seats at Baskin-Robbins were a row of school desk chairs.) And since the super-premium renaissance in the late 1960s, scoop shops with gourmet offerings have been popular.

Ice Cream Castles: 10 Shops Worth a Pilgrimage

Some ice cream shops produce such a great product — and usually have done so for a long time — that they go beyond being a local stand and become an institution. In the course of researching this book, a select group of ice cream shops were mentioned again and again — in media reports and in the personal recommendations of folks saying "they have the best ice cream in the world" and truly meaning it.

Here are profiles of some shops where the ice cream is at the peak of perfection. These are must-taste ice creams, served up by places where the fine art of ice cream has been taken to the level of mastery. There are easily 50 more that could be on this list. (Bauder's Pharmacy, Brown's, Double Rainbow, Dr. Bob's, Dr. Mike's, Jake's, Jeni's Fresh, Oberweis, Ronnybrook Farm, Rick's, Ted Drewes, Tom's Ice Cream Bowl and Toscanini's, to name just a few, are worthy of inclusion, too). But in the interest of space, we offer a tasting tour of 10 of the country's best ice cream shops.

AMY'S ICE CREAMS • AUSTIN, TEXAS

Amy's has been an Austin institution for 20 years, and with six stores in the greater Austin area, one in San Antonio and one in Houston, Amy's is a Texas institution, too. Part of its popularity comes from super-premium ice cream offered in such creative flavors as snickerdoodle, peanut butter honey sandwich and Shiner Bock beer. But what keeps the crowds coming back to

At Graeter's (next page, center), the French pot method results in amazing ice cream. The original location of Handel's (next page, lower right) doubled as a gas station.

Amy's is the fun and zany atmosphere. The decor is funky (think disco balls and cow-print vinyl booths), and the servers put on quite a show. Scoops are tossed overhead and caught in the dish, the banter is lively, and often the staff is dressed up like pirates or circus performers, according to a range of themes.

CARL'S • FREDERICKSBURG, VIRGINIA

If you're traveling along U.S. Route 1 in Fredericksburg, it's hard to miss Carl's. There's a bright neon sign with a cone, for one. And there's always a line of people waiting to try the legendary frozen custard. Carl's serves ice cream much as they did when they opened in 1947. It's still a seasonal walk-up stand. There are still only three flavors to choose from. And it's still freshly made before your eyes on the same (now-rare) Electro-Freeze machines. If you want to go, go in the early afternoon: Only a 120 gallons are made each day, and serving 700 customers on busy nights they sometimes run out.

FOUR SEAS ICE CREAM • CENTERVILLE, MASSACHUSETTS

Four Seas is the oldest ice cream shop on Cape Cod and one of the oldest in New England. Since 1934, it has served up 16-percent-butterfat ice cream in such flavors as chip chocolate, cantaloupe and penuche pecan. Most summer

SPOTTING GREAT SHOPS AND STANDS

Where to find good ice cream? Well, there's no one common denominator for all great ice cream. (Each has its own unique strengths and gifts.) But here are some traits to look for when scouting out your next scoop:

1. The ice cream is homemade.
2. They use milk from their own herd.
3. There's a line out the door.
4. They've been in business awhile.
5. They've got multiple locations.

6. They have an extensive fountain menu.
7. There are unusual flavors on the menu.
8. The waffle cones are made fresh.
9. There are awards and newspaper clips all over the walls.
10. People are smiling.

nights, the tiny shop's counter is packed three- and four-deep; but the shop's staff of cheerful students (who are required to be on the honor roll to get a job) scoop up the menu's 24 flavors quickly. While the ice cream is delicious on its own, order a sundae with one of Four Seas' homemade toppings. Hot fudge, butterscotch, blackberry brandy and *crème de menthe* are all made on-site.

GRAETER'S •
CINCINNATI, OHIO

Founded in 1870, Graeter's is now so popular that it has 35 stores in Ohio and Kentucky. Part of Graeter's appeal is how the ice cream is manufactured. They use a labor-intensive French pot process, where custom-made freezers featuring large, deep pots spin to freeze the ice cream. To keep the mixture smooth and evenly frozen, a worker must manually scrape down the sides with a paddle. The result is velvety and super-dense. Their signature chocolate chip flavors are made when liquid chocolate is poured into the pots during the final stage of the freezing process; the chocolate freezes upon contact and shatters into giant, irregularly shaped chunks. You haven't had chocolate chip until you've tried Graeter's version; their black raspberry, mint or mocha chocolate chip flavors are to-die-for.

HANDEL'S HOMEMADE ICE CREAM & YOGURT • YOUNGSTOWN, OHIO

Alice Handel started making ice cream out of her husband's gas station in 1945, using fruits from her backyard and old-fashioned recipes. Today, there

There are longtime favorites (like Handel's in Youngstown, above) and new treats, such as Dippin' Dots (far right).

A Scoop of History

1985

Dairy Queen introduced Blizzards, which are soft-serve ice cream mixed with chunks of candy, cookies or fruit. An instant hit, the chain sold more than 175 million of them in its first year.

are more than 20 Handel's locations in Indiana, Ohio and Pennsylvania. Even in the dead of winter, Handel's walk-up-only stands draw crowds for their smooth and freshly made ice cream. There are 40-some flavors available at any time, and anything that's added to them (from the cherries in the cherry vanilla to the marshmallow swirl in the pumpkin ripple) is done by hand. The signature flavor is chocolate pecan, and it's served soft — a tradition that started when demand was so high there wasn't time to let the ice cream harden before serving.

HERRELL'S ICE CREAM • NORTHAMPTON, MASSACHUSSETS

Long before Cold Stone Creamery, Maggie Moo's and the like were mixing in bits of candy, fruit or cookies into their ice cream, there was Steve Herrell, who invented the concept. He first launched Steve's Ice Cream in 1973 before selling it to a company that took the chain national. By 1980, Herrell was back making ice cream again, this time using his last name on the storefront. Herrell's, which also has two stores in Boston, continues to make rich super-premium ice cream in such flavors as chocolate pudding, malted vanilla and maple cream. There are, of course, "smoosh-ins" to add to your ice cream, along with chocolate whipped cream, great shakes and homemade hot fudge sauce.

IL LABORATORIO DEL GELATO • NEW YORK CITY

So serious is the art and science of fine ice cream at this tiny Lower East Side shop that all the workers wear white lab coats. This isn't just any ice cream, after all, but frozen perfection made by Jon Snyder. At the age of 19, he founded the well-regarded Ciao Bella, but he burnt out and sold it six years later. In 2002, Snyder returned to ice cream and opened this shop. He creates

DEEP FREEZE DIPS

Dippin' Dots founder Curt Jones was working in cryogenics at a biotech firm in Lexington, Kentucky, when he began tinkering with how his knowledge of deep freezing could work with ice cream. What he discovered became Dippin' Dots, an innovative ice cream product that the Paducah, Kentucky-based company bills as the "ice cream of the future" and "the coldest ice cream you'll ever eat." Jones's flash-freezing technique uses liquid nitrogen to create small, round pebbles of ice cream. To keep its characteristic shape, Dippin' Dots must be stored at much lower temperatures (-42 degrees Fahrenheit) than normal ice cream, which is why you can't buy Dippin' Dots in your grocery store for your home freezer (neither is cold enough for it). Instead, Dippin' Dots is sold through special freezers at more than 2,250 stores, fairs and festivals, and theme parks worldwide and through vending machines that dispense foil pouches of Dippin' Dots. Kids, in particular, love the novelty of Dippin' Dots, which comes in 16 flavors and a bright rainbow of colors. 270-443-0994, www.dippindots.com

Nitro Ice Cream also uses liquid nitrogen to make its product but with a different result. Thomas (T.J.) Paskach and William Schroeder were two Ph.D. students in chemical engineering from Iowa State when they invented the Nitro Freeze Process to create homemade ice cream in a fraction of the time (a gallon a minute). Paskach and Schroeder say their ice cream is especially good because the extreme cold keeps the mixture from forming ice crystals. Adding to the cachet is watching the machine in action, with clouds of condensed vapor rising out and giving the whole process a witch's cauldron feel. Nitro Ice Cream is offered at several state fairs in the Midwest, and at the company's retail store, Blue Sky Creamery, in Ankeny, Iowa. 515-268-4336, www.nitroicecream.com.

Service with a smile from Jon Snyder at New York's Il Laboratorio Del Gelato (top right) and at Kopp's Frozen Custard in Milwaukee.

custom flavors for the city's top restaurants, and whatever is left over from his wholesale business is sold from the modest ice cream cabinet. On any given day, you might find rosemary, pistachio, prune/armagnac, walnut nocello, mascarpone or green grape sorbet. All of it is exquisite: not too creamy or too icy and the flavors shine through.

KOPP'S FROZEN CUSTARD • MILWAUKEE, WISCONSIN

Did you know?

In Newark, New Jersey, it is illegal to eat ice cream after 6 P.M. without a doctor's note. And it is illegal to carry an ice cream cone in your back pocket in Lexington, Kentucky.

Milwaukee is the Frozen Custard Capital of the United States, with more frozen custard outlets than anywhere else. To stand out among the competition in this market is saying something about how good Kopp's is. Started by Elsa Kopp in 1950, there are now three Kopp's outlets in the area. There's always vanilla and chocolate on the menu, but where Kopp's wows is with its flavor of the day (a concept Kopp invented). Following the adage that you can never get too much of a good thing, Kopp's loads up it daily offering with everything from whole macadamia nuts to pieces of pineapple-upside down cake. Yes, it's rich and thick, but oh-so-good, too.

MITCHELL'S ICE CREAM • SAN FRANCISCO, CALIFORNIA

Mitchell's Ice Cream has a reputation as a friendly family-run shop that offers some of the most exotic flavors around. They didn't start out with unusual flavors, but in the mid-1960s, a friend suggested adding mango ice cream to their menu. They did, and more tropical fruit flavors followed, including avocado, *buko* (baby coconut), guava and *langka* (jackfruit). Mitchell's has more traditional offerings, too (rum raisin, Chicago cheesecake, strawberries 'n cream), and the diverse mix of both gives a wonderful flavor to this 51-year-old institution in San Francisco's Mission District. Order a scoop of something you've never tried and an old favorite, too; then, grab a bench outside and savor this cultural melting pot on a cone.

UNIVERSITY CREAMERY • UNIVERSITY PARK, PENNSYLVANIA

There are many universities around the country that offer ice cream as a byproduct of their dairy science program, but perhaps none is better known than the 108-year-old University Creamery at Penn State. The creamery uses its own cows to make the ice cream, which means it's extra-fresh and extra-good; on average, the ice cream was still milk in the cow just four days ago. Expect a wait on football weekends, when visitors and returning alums flock to the creamery for a scoop of Peachy Paterno, butter pecan or the blue-and-white Alumni Swirl. You might find a line other times, too; more than 750,000 cones are scooped up each year.

As good as these 10 ice cream shops are, what ultimately matters is finding what you like — and then finding the closest place that serves it. With some 17,000 ice cream parlors, stands and shops to choose from, chances are you aren't too far from satisfying your ice cream craving.

FOR LISTINGS OF GREAT ICE CREAM PARLORS NATIONWIDE, SEE APPENDIX 1 ON PAGE 129.

ICE CREAM EVERY DAY

Looking for a good excuse to eat ice cream? You can celebrate all-month long during National Ice Cream Month in July, or throw a big bash on the National Ice Cream Day, held annually on the third Sunday in July. You can also raise a scoop in honor of our nation's favorite dessert on these days:

May 11
Eat What You Want Day

June 2
National Rocky Road Day

June 7
National Chocolate Ice Cream Day

July 1
Creative Ice Cream Flavor Day

July 7
National Strawberry Sundae Day

July 17
National Peach Ice Cream Day

July 23
National Vanilla Ice Cream Day

AUGUST 2
National Ice Cream Soda Day
National Ice Cream Sandwich Day

August 14
National Creamsicle Day

September 21
Birth of the Ice Cream Cone

October 7
National Frappe Day

November 25
National Parfait Day

REGIONAL FAVORITES

While our nation's love for ice cream spans state lines, our preferences for frozen treats has some definite boundaries. Here's a look at favorite flavors in different parts of the country:

Upper Midwest: Green River is a popular flavor for fountain sodas; it has a sweet lemon-lime taste.

Wisconsin: Frozen custard is king in America's Dairyland, especially the Milwaukee area, which has the largest concentration of custard stands in the country.

California's Coachelle Valley: Date shakes are very popular. It is believed that the shakes were introduced in 1947 at the inaugural National Date Festival.

Texas: The Lonestar State loves Dairy Queen; there are more than 600 DQs in the state, more than any other state. Dairy Queen even has a separate head-quarters there. Texans also love anything with pecans.

Hawaii: Shave ice, with its finely ground ice that resembles snow, is a popular treat. Similar to a snowball (see Baltimore) but with a more tropical flavor (sometimes even sweet beans like azuki are used) and often often topped with milk.

Baltimore, New Orleans and southern Texas: A favorite treat is a snowball, which is made from finely pulverized ice and a sugary syrup, all topped with a dollop of ice cream or marshmallows.

New England: Grape Nut, frozen pudding and maple are popular with Yankees.

Michigan: Blue Moon is a popular flavor (it's pineapple-flavored ice cream with blue coloring).

New York: You can still find egg creams on the menu; it's a refreshing concoction of seltzer water, milk and chocolate syrup.

Boston: If you want ice cream in your milk shake, order a frappe. Milk shakes in Beantown contain only milk, ice and syrup.

Chicago: The Moose Tracks flavor — vanilla ice cream with peanut butter cups swirled with fudge — is usually one of the top two best-selling flavors in the Windy City.

Pennsylvania: Black raspberry ice cream is a popular flavor.

Rhode Island: The state drink of Rhode Island is coffee milk, and the cabinet (as Rhode Islanders call their milk shakes) of choice is, not surprisingly, coffee.

Philadelphia/East Coast: The seemingly redundant water ice, sometimes called Italian ice, is a popular treat, especially in hot weather.

Nashville: Folks are nutty for the Purity Dairy's Nutty Buddy, the number-one selling frozen novelty in this market. Purity is one of the last places that makes these vanilla ice cream cones topped with a coating of chocolate and peanuts.

East of Mississippi: Cherry ice cream is made with black cherries; west of the Mississippi it's made with maraschino cherries.

The South: Homemade ice cream is a longstanding tradition; some purists insist that the only way to enjoy ice cream is to make it yourself. Black walnut, butter pecan and peach are popular flavors.

Florida: In the southern part of the state, gelato is the hottest trend.

6

SCOOPS DU JOUR

HOW TO MAKE GREAT ICE CREAM

The beauty of ice cream is that anyone can make it. The ingredients are blissfully simple — milk, cream, sugar and maybe some eggs and flavorings — and it's equally simple to make. Most of the time your results will be quite good. So good, in fact, that as great as ice cream is at your favorite ice cream parlor or brought home from the store, there's nothing quite like making it yourself. For one, ice cream that you make at home is fresh. When properly made, it's especially creamy and smooth, and the flavors are bright and oh-so-yummy. Many ice cream lovers (myself among them) maintain that ice cream is at its peak of perfection right out of the machine — even better if it's licked directly off the dasher.

Plus, when you make ice cream yourself, you have control over the flavors and the quality of ingredients. You can use organic milk, strawberries just

The best — and tastiest — part of making your own ice cream is licking the dasher.

picked at the local patch, or your cousin's signature almond bark. Love peanut butter, banana, cookie dough and chocolate chips? Want to make a low-carb blueberry ginger ice cream for your friend on the Atkins diet? Or a rice milk "ice cream" for your lactose-intolerant daughter? No problem. All you need to make great ice cream are a few base recipes to get you started and one essential tool — an ice cream maker.

Maker Magic

Ice cream makers run the gamut from $40 one-quart electric machines that make ice cream in about 25 minutes to $125 four-quart, hand-cranked throwbacks to $300-plus units that contain their own refrigeration system. No matter the price, all ice cream makers today operate on the same principle: the mixture is poured into a canister that is chilled, and then it's aerated and mixed by a dasher, a paddle-like device, that is inserted vertically into the canister and turned by hand or by motor. What varies from maker to maker is whether they are electric or hand-cranked and what method they use to chill the canister (either by being surrounded by rock salt and ice, by frozen coolant housed within its walls, or by a self-contained refrigerator unit).

Modern ice cream makers are indebted to the inspired design of Nancy Johnson's 1846 hand-crank freezer. Her basic principles — a dasher that sits upright in the center of the canister and the regular turning of the canister within the cooling agent — are still in use today. However, two key components of her invention —

Hand-crank freezers (below right) and Junket tablets (above and next page) are still available, although they aren't as popular as they once were.

ON AN ICE CREAM JUNKET

Junket ice cream may sound strange to modern cooks, but from the early part of the 1900s through the 1960s, most cookbooks contained the requisite recipe using rennet-based Junket tablets. The resulting ice cream was smoother and fluffier because rennet, which is made from the rennin enzyme found in the fourth stomach of cows, breaks down the milk proteins and acts as a coagulant.

Junket tablets got their start when Danish immigrant Christian Hansen arrived in Hanson Falls, New York, in 1878 to supply rennet extract to the area's burgeoning cheese industry. By 1886, Hansen had founded Chr. Hansen's Laboratories and began offering Junket tablets as a quick and easy way to make cheese, milk drinks, custards and ice cream at home.

You can still make Junket ice cream, either from tablets or from a mix. The products are still manufactured in Hanson Falls, about 20 minutes east of Utica. (The company has changed hands several times and is now owned by Redco Foods.) You can find Junket products in some grocery stores, or order them direct from the company via phone (800-556-6674) or its website (www.junketdesserts.com). With advance notice, the Junket folks will even give you a tour of plant operations.

HAVE SOME JUNKET!

DAINTY
DELICIOUS
HEALTHFUL
NUTRITIOUS

the use of rock salt and ice to chill the mixture and the hand-crank that mixes the cream into ice cream — now represent only a small fraction of the ice-cream-making marketplace.

Currently, only one company, White Mountain, still makes a Johnson-inspired, hand-cranked model, and only White Mountain, and its parent company, Rival, offer four- and six-quart models that use rock salt and ice. (White Mountain makes both hand-crank and electric models, while Rival makes only electric.) Critics of these models claim the use of rock salt and ice is cumbersome and messy, but old-school purists maintain that hand-cranked ice cream, nestled inside a tub of rock salt and ice, is best. Ultimately, which maker you choose will depend on several factors.

Here's a guide to the kinds of makers on the market today.

Meeting Your Maker: Choosing the Best Model for You

HAND-CRANKED MODELS

Cost (on average): $100-$180

Brands to Check Out: White Mountain

Reasons to Buy: You get old-fashioned appeal along with great-tasting ice cream in crowd-pleasing proportions.

Details: White Mountain's hand-cranked models make four or six quarts of ice cream, and they use the same patented triple-motion dasher system the company has used since it started in 1853. They are perfect for family reunions, ice cream socials and backyard barbecues. They

While Auto Vacuum Freezers (which attached to your car's engine) are obsolete (next page), the White Mountain brand endures.

There is Money in the White Mountain Freezer.

MONEY TO THE DEALER.

require a good amount of elbow grease, but that's part of the fun. (You feel like you've earned that ice cream cone.) Children, in particular, seem to love taking turns at the crank and sitting on top of the machine to hold it steady as churning gets harder during the final stages of the freezing process. White Mountain's models are heirloom-quality; they've got a reputation for lasting forever. In many families, they are passed down with the same affection as Grandma's bone china. Fans of the hand-crank maintain that these models make the best ice cream. Hand-cranking, they say, gives you intimate control of the speed and duration of the freezing process. They also maintain that rock salt and ice does a better job freezing the mixture and gives it better texture and creaminess.

LARGE-CAPACITY ELECTRIC MODELS

Cost (on average): $30–$200

Brands to Check Out: White Mountain, Rival

Reasons to Buy: Feed a crowd of ice cream lovers without the hard work of cranking it yourself.

Details: These four- to six-quart ice cream makers are much like their hand-cranked kin, except the work of churning is done courtesy of an electric motor instead of your biceps. Rival's models feature plastic tubs and dashers and, as a result, are lower priced, while the more expensive White Mountain models feature pine tubs and metal dashers. Both require rock salt and ice to freeze your mixture, but for your effort, you'll have enough to feed more than 30 people a scoop of ice cream. Of course, you can make smaller quantities, but they are best-suited for parties and large gatherings. If you love ice cream and love to entertain, a large-capacity machine — be it electric or hand-cranked — is a good investment, even if you only use it a handful of times each year. You'll be thankful you can make so many people so happy so easily.

If you don't feel like making ice cream from scratch but still want to make it at home, consider buying a mix. Rival, Parmalat and Junket all make mixes that require little time or effort. And in the case of Parmalat's Sweet Gelato Mix, you don't even have to add milk. Just pour into your maker and freeze.

NON-ELECTRIC GEL CANISTER ICE CREAM MAKERS

Cost (on average): $30–$60

Brands to Check Out: Donvier, William Bound's Chilly

Reasons to Buy: Quietly and quickly make about a quart of ice cream without using rock salt and ice and without electricity.

Details: When Donvier introduced the concept of gel-canister ice cream makers in 1985, it revolutionized the industry. These canisters have refrigerator coolant inside its walls, eliminating the need for layering rock salt and ice. All you have to do is put the canister in the freezer at least 24 hours before you want to make ice cream, pour the cream mixture into the canister, turn it a few times and, *voilà*, 20 minutes later you have ice cream. The other advantage to these motorless models is that they are quiet (most of the motor-driven machines are rather loud) and require a minimum of effort. Unlike traditional hand-cranks, you only need to churn them every so often, not continuously. (William Bound's Chilly model doesn't even require you to turn it; just set it on the counter and wait.) Another benefit to these makers is the smaller yield: making a quart of ice cream is a better size for most families and for every-day use. Their smaller size makes storing them easier, too.

ELECTRIC GEL CANISTER ICE CREAM MAKERS

Cost (on average): $50–$100

Brands to Check Out: Cuisinart, DeLonghi, Krups, Rival

Reason to Buy: With a frozen gel canister ready, you are about 20 minutes away from a fresh quart of ice cream. Plus, its smaller size stores easily and doesn't take up much countertop space.

Details: The electric gel canister models make homemade ice cream a quick and affordable option. These quart- to quart-and-half makers produce family-friendly quantities and they're so effortless you'll find yourself making ice cream on Tuesday night just for the heck of it. There's no rock salt and ice to clean up afterward, and the electric motor means you can pour it in and ignore it for 20 minutes or so until it's ready.

Self-Contained Ice Cream Makers

Cost (on average): $200-$1,000

Brands to Check Out: Musso, Simac, DeLonghi

Reason to Buy: If you're a serious ice cream connoisseur, gourmet gadget fanatic or want to make multiple batches in an evening, these high-end Italian machines are for you.

Details: Often called the Rolls Royce of ice cream makers, these are top-of-line machines imported from Italy. They are sleek and professional-looking machines that give you a quart of ice cream at the touch of a button. They have self-contained refrigerator units so the makers are ready to go without pre-freezing a canister or cooling your mixtures to room temperature. Best of all, they are capable of turning out batch after batch of ice cream with no waiting in between. In little over an hour, you could make three flavors of ice cream. (How about coffee, hazelnut and peppermint for your next dinner party?) Another neat feature is that they automatically stop when the ice cream is ready, which prevents your ice cream from becoming butter when you're not looking. The self-contained units are worth the investment, if you plan to use them regularly. Besides a gourmet-level price tag, these machines are heavy (averaging about 35 pounds), don't like to be moved often and are countertop hogs. You'll want to keep them out and indulge frequently to get your money's worth.

All of these machines will make good ice cream — and some of them make phenomenal ice cream. Try out different recipes to find what works

A CRASH COURSE IN CREAMS

Here's the percentage of fat in the various creams and milks on the market:

Heavy Cream:
36 to 40%

Whipping Cream:
30 to 36%

Light Cream/ Coffee Cream/ Table Cream:
18 to 30%
(20% on average)

Half-and-Half:
10 to 12%

Whole Milk:
2%, 1%, and Skim Nonfat Milk
(self-explanatory)

best in your machine. If you are just starting out making ice cream, I'd recommend buying a one-quart maker for under $100. You can then graduate to a high-end self-contained model or a larger-capacity maker. Once you see how easy it is to make your own ice cream, sorbets, frozen yogurts and slushy drinks, you'll be hooked.

The 10 Commandments of Excellent Ice Cream Making

While ice cream making isn't hard, there are a few things that you should do to ensure excellent ice cream every time.

1. THOU SHALT USE YOUR ICE CREAM MAKER.

Okay, this seems obvious, but there's no value in an ice cream maker that sits in the basement gathering dust. All makers come with a few recipes to get you started, and Appendix 2 on page 158 lists more than 50; try them out, build your confidence, and — trust me on this — you'll soon be making ice cream all the time.

2. THOU SHALT PUT ONLY THOROUGHLY CHILLED INGREDIENTS INTO THE ICE CREAM MAKER.

Never put hot, warm or even lukewarm mixtures into your ice cream maker. The mixture won't freeze properly, and you could end up with an icy batch. Makers need cold to work properly, so be sure all liquid that goes into your machine is thoroughly chilled. For no-cook recipes, milk and cream right out

of the refrigerator is ready for freezing, but for cooked recipes, put them in an airtight container in the refrigerator to cool for at least four hours before pouring into maker. It's even better if you can chill the mixture overnight. The reason: the flavors steep longer, which gives you a better and bolder taste, and the mix becomes more viscous, or thick, resulting in a creamier and smoother ice cream.

3. THOU SHALT KEEP THE RIGHT TOOLS ON HAND

Making ice cream doesn't require a cabinet full of gadgets, but a few tools can be helpful. Besides the requisite ice cream maker and kitchen standards like measuring spoons and cups and mixing bowls, here are some other essentials:

A candy thermometer: A foolproof way to ensure perfectly cooked custard every time. Heat milk until the thermometer reads 175 degrees. Pour part of the mixture into your beaten eggs to temper them, and then combine the eggs and milk and heat until the mixture reaches 180 degrees. Remove from heat immediately. Until I started using a candy thermometer, I had a tough time getting a smooth custard. I'd either overcook or undercook it. Now, my custard-base ice creams are smooth and velvety every time.

A fine-mesh strainer: Handy to strain out vanilla bean pods, steeped mint leaves and fruit seeds, or to ensure a silky-smooth custard.

A whisk or an electric beater: It's essential to make sure that sugar is

Making your own ice cream means you can make whatever flavor you like.

ROCK SOLID FREEZING

Rock salt and ice is an effective refrigerant for ice cream makers because the "brine solution," as the mixture is called, enables the ice cream to freeze at a temperature of 8 to 12 degrees. Thanks to the physics of heat transfer, the salt absorbs the heat from the melting water and lowers the water's freezing point. (The ice on its own would freeze at about 32 degrees, 7 degrees too warm to even begin to freeze the ice cream.) White Mountain recommends that the ideal brine contain a ratio of five cups ice to one cup rock salt. Too little salt and the ice cream won't freeze properly; too much salt and the ice cream gets too hard, too fast.

Source: White Mountain Ice Cream Freezer Instruction Booklet.

completely dissolved, that eggs are properly beaten (they should fall off the whisk or beaters in ribbons when ready) and that all ingredients are fully incorporated. A whisk or an electric beater will ensure your ingredients are properly mixed.

A heavy, medium-size saucepan: For melting chocolate, heating milk and cooking custards. If you're going to cook your ice cream bases, you'll need one of these.

One- and two-quart plastic or glass storage containers: Having some extra storage containers on hand will make cooling and ripening your ice cream easier. When you ripen your ice cream in the freezer, you'll want storage containers with about the same volume as the ice cream you've produced, as too much extra air space in the container will deteriorate the texture and quality of the ice cream.

4. THOU SHALT NOT MAKE ICE CREAM WITH RAW EGGS

Older cookbooks, country-style ice creams and very likely your great aunt Thelma's prize-winning recipe usually call for making ice cream with raw eggs. However, raw eggs can contain salmonella and cause food poisoning. A better bet is to heat milk and eggs to at least 160 degrees Fahrenheit to kill any bacteria presence. You can also use pasteurized eggs (which are increasingly available at grocery stores) or egg substitute (use 1/4 cup to replace an egg in a recipe).

5. THOU SHALT NOT BOIL COOKED-CUSTARD BASES

Many people avoid cooked custard bases because the recipes seem daunting. While cooked-custard bases do take a little more time and require a watchful eye, they result in a lusciously rich ice cream that's worth the effort. The cardinal rule for making custard bases is to heat until thickened, but never boil. There are two ways to ensure the right consistency. The first is simpler, but less exact: Stir the custard mixture constantly with a wooden spoon until it coats the back of the spoon without running and leaves a clear line on the back of the spoon when you run your finger through it. The other way is more exact, and my preferred method, for cooking custards: Using a candy thermometer to monitor temperature, stir constantly until the egg and milk mixture reaches 180 degrees. Promptly remove from heat.

6. THOU SHALT ALLOW ICE CREAM TIME TO RIPEN

Ice cream directly out of the maker has a consistency similar to soft serve. It tastes wonderful, but it's not very firm. If you want your ice cream to hold its shape, it needs to harden, or ripen, for several hours in a freezer before serving. Keep ripening time in mind if you plan on serving ice cream for an event. The ideal timeline for serving ice cream at a dinner party, for example, is to make the base the night or morning before you plan on serving, freeze in a maker in early afternoon and then let ripen in freezer for a few hours before serving.

7. THOU SHALT EAT YOUR ICE CREAM IN A TIMELY FASHION

Unlike store-bought ice cream that usually has stabilizers to keep them

NO MAKER? NO PROBLEM

If you don't own an ice cream maker, you can still make your own ice cream with the help of your kitchen freezer. Place the mixture in a shallow glass baking dish or rectangular plastic container. Cover and put it in the coldest part of your freezer (near the bottom and towards the back); wait about two hours. Remove ice cream from container with a fork and whip up with an electric mixer on low speed. Return to freezer, wait two more hours and then repeat. Allow to freeze for two hours more. Then, about 20 minutes before you plan on serving the ice cream, place the ice cream in your refrigerator to soften. The result will be icier than ice cream from a maker, but still quite good. You can also make granita or ice cream using plastic bags; see Appendix 2 for recipes.

1929

The 1929 edition of the classic *Boston Cooking-School Cook Book* by Fannie Merrit Farmer includes recipes for maraschino ice, pomegranate ice, quince ice cream, brown bread ice cream, orange pekoe ice cream and a clam frappé that calls for 20 clams and ½ cup of cold water.

creamy and smooth months after it's been made, homemade ice cream deteriorates rather quickly. To maximize taste and freshness, eat ice cream the day it's made. Most ice creams are still pretty good the next day, but they become icy and coarse within a few days. The shortest shelf-life comes from the no-cook bases that include only milk, cream, sugar and flavorings as ingredients; these last only a day or two in the freezer. Recipes with eggs or other stabilizers such as gelatin will hold up for at least three days. So, make only the amount of ice cream you will consume in a day or two. When it's gone, you can always make another batch.

8. THOU SHALT EXPERIMENT WITH NEW FLAVORS

Part of the fun of making ice cream at home is that you can customize your ice cream for your individual preferences and cravings. Start off with a good base recipe for chocolate or vanilla and then tinker with whatever flavors strike your fancy. Whether you have a bumper crop of lemon mint this year, a health-conscious spouse who wants fat-free, sugar-free sorbets, or a kid whose favorite foods are blueberries, white chocolate chips and caramel, the great thing about making it yourself is that you can be your own Ben or Jerry. Sure, you may have to tweak the recipe a bit, but it probably won't be a complete flop either. Think about a food you love, think about it with ice cream, and then go for it.

9. THOU SHALT SHARE THY ICE CREAM BOUNTY

This isn't necessarily a commandment, so much as it's a surefire way to make new friends and endear old ones. Unless you have a giant-sized appetite, there will always be extra ice cream to share. Pack up a pint to give to your neighbor, invite some of your child's playmates or your in-laws for dessert. You're sure to impress people, and you'll probably make their day. After all, who wouldn't be happy to receive some freshly made ice cream?

10. THOU SHALT LICK THE DASHER

As any veteran of ice cream making can tell you, the best part of making it yourself is getting to clean off the dasher. The ice cream is at its tastiest, and there's something wonderfully indulgent and childlike about leaning over the sink (you don't want to drip all over the floor) and licking the dasher clean. The golden rule of ice cream making is that he or she who makes the ice cream has first dibs on the dasher. It's a sweet rule to follow, and one that quickly becomes a treasured part of making ice cream at home.

Recipes for Success: More Tips for Making Ice Cream

Now that you've mastered the homemade ice cream commandments, here are some tips to making great ice cream:

Taste the mixture before freezing to check for balance of flavors.
You can add more sugar or more flavoring as needed. Keep in mind that the base will taste less sweet once it's frozen.

Make sure the sugar is fully dissolved.
This is an especially important point for no-cook recipes. Be sure to whisk ingredients together thoroughly until completely smooth. Otherwise, the resulting ice cream will be grainy.

FUN **Facts**

When making gelato, allow your serving to soften to about 10 to 15 degrees Fahrenheit. It will maximize the flavor and texture. Actually, all ice cream benefits from sitting out for 5 to 10 minutes before serving; that is, if you can wait that long.

Lost the instruction booklet for your ice cream maker? Log onto www. makeicecream.com. The site has uploaded instructions for most major brands.

■ **Use vanilla beans whenever possible.**

Yes, it's more expensive, but the flavor leaves a fuller bouquet on the tongue. For any recipe calling for vanilla extract, you can add the beans and pod from half of a vanilla bean. Heat milk, vanilla bean and pod over medium heat until bubbles form. Remove from heat and steep for 30 minutes. Resume recipe, and remove pod prior to freezing.

■ **Speed up the cooling process with an ice bath.**

If you'd like to get your cooked custard base to room temperature quickly, place the mixture in a bowl and then set that bowl in a larger bowl filled three-quarters with ice and water. Stir occasionally until cool.

■ **Add vanilla extract to mixture right before freezing.**

Do as they do at many ice cream shops, and add the vanilla just before you pour it in the freezer. The taste of vanilla will be brighter and more pronounced.

■ **When buying heavy or whipping cream for recipes, look for pasteurized, rather than ultra-pasteurized, varieties.**

Ultra-pasteurized cream has been pasteurized at a higher temperature to kill more bacteria, and, as a result, has a longer shelf life than pasteurized cream. But ultra-pasteurized cream doesn't whip as well as pasteurized, and ice cream made with pasteurized cream is creamier when frozen.

■ **Do not overfill your ice cream maker.**

Ice cream expands when freezing so only add your base up to your canister's fill line, if it has one, or no more than 75 percent full.

■ **When using a machine that uses rock salt and ice, consider making it outside.**

Makers that use rock salt and ice can be messy, so it's often easier to just use

them outside. Remember, too, that when you're finished, dispose of brine solution outside, away from grass and anything else you don't want to turn brown. (Do not pour it down the kitchen drain.) You should also avoid using a metal scoop to dish out the rock salt, since the salt can pit the metal.

■ **Place wax paper or plastic wrap over top of ice cream before sealing container for freezing.**

This will give your ice cream added protection from ice crystals that can form along the surface of the ice cream.

■ **Consider buying a back-up gel canister.**

If you own an ice cream maker that uses a gel canister, you might want to purchase an extra canister. That way you can make a second batch after the first without waiting 24 hours for the canister to refreeze.

If you've never made ice cream before, start with some vanilla and chocolate no-cook recipes first. They are easy and offer quick results. Once you've got those down, try custard-base recipes. The first time making custard may feel awkward, but after one or two batches, you'll have mastered the technique. (And because custard recipes are so rich and creamy, it's worth any learning curve.) Soon, making ice cream at home becomes second nature, and you'll wonder why you ever made anything else for dessert. ■

For Recipes, see Appendix 2 on page 158.

HOW DO YOU RANK?

Think your home-made ice cream is the best? See how it ranks at the annual "Crankfest" in McKinney, Texas. The event, held the third Saturday in August, attracts some 50 participants and more than 1,000 hungry spectators. Several awards are given, from best vanilla to best unusual flavor in the "you made what?!" category. For information, call the McKinney Chamber of Commerce at 972-562-6880.

7

LICKETY SPLIT
OUR FAVORITE FOUNTAIN TREATS

How do you take a nearly perfect food and make it even better? Add more good stuff to it. At least that seems to be the philosophy behind ice cream treats. Ice cream is great on its own, but it's positively heavenly when topped with hot fudge, placed in a cone or mixed up in a shake. It's the perfect accompaniment to most everything sweet, and you can flavor it to suit any need or taste.

In the early days of ice cream, the fact that you had ice cream — or any sort of cold beverage — was novelty enough. By the mid–1800s, Americans were frequent visitors to their local soda fountains, and sampling the latest ice cream creations was all the rage. To keep track of the recipes, soda fountain dispensing manuals listed the myriad of menu options. What is believed to be the first fountain recipe book — *The American Dispenser's Book...Containing*

Sure-fire way to get a smile? Ice cream with hot fudge, of course.

Choice Formulas for Making Soda Water Syrups and Fancy Drinks, or: How to Make a Soda Fountain Pay — was published in 1863. By the turn of the century, many formularies contained more than a thousand recipes. The 1919 edition of *The Spatula Soda Water Guide* included 154 types of syrups, 25 kinds of banana splits and 50 nut sundaes; the names were as imaginative as the ingredients: The Chatauqua Flip, the Yale Shake, the North Pole Sundae.

A Split Decision

What's less documented is where these soda fountain classics were invented. With most of our soda fountain favorites, their exact origins are hazy and often widely disputed. Was it Detroit's Fred Sanders, Philadelphia's Robert Green or Philip Mohr of Elizabeth, New Jersey who invented the ice cream soda? No one is certain. There's even debate over the origin of the banana split. Historians generally credit Latrobe, Pennsylvania, optometrist David "Doc" Strickler with serving the first split in 1904 for 10 cents. The lore is

"A new taste sensation" Banana Split ICE CREAM

At the Bespeckled Trout in New York City, a vintage Hamilton Beach spindle milkshake machine (left) makes old-fashioned milkshakes. The beauty of ice cream is that it tastes even better when put on a cone, made into a float or served up as a banana split.

Did you know?

Steven J. Poplawski invented the first blender in 1922, but it was the 1937 "Miracle Mixer" from Fred Osius and Fred Waring that made blenders a household name.

that Strickler started playing with new recipes, having been inspired by a recent trip to Atlantic City where the soda jerks were offering all sorts of creative fruit sundaes. He was looking for a way to drum up business in his pharmacy by appealing to nearby coeds at Saint Vincent College. Strickler placed three scoops of ice cream on top of a banana sliced lengthwise, added strawberries, raspberries and crushed pineapple, and piled marshmallow sauce and chopped nuts on top.

But other towns lay claim to the invention, too. Davenport, Iowa, says native son Gus Napoulos of Elite Confectionery invented the split in 1906 while looking for something to do with ripe bananas. Columbus, Ohio, claims Letty Lally at Foeller's Drug Store whipped one up in 1904 when a customer asked for "something different." Bostonians maintain that Stinson Thomas, the head soda jerk at the Butler Department Store, was the first, when in 1905 he served a banana split topped with peaches, pistachios and crushed walnuts.

Wilmington, Ohio, also makes a claim. Locals say Ernest "Doc" Hazard invented the ultimate soda fountain treat at his drugstore during the hard winter of 1907. Business was slow, so Hazard held a contest among his employees to devise a new sundae to bring in students from nearby Wilmington College. As it turns out, Hazard won his own contest with a sundae that had split bananas as the base, three scoops of ice cream, three kinds of toppings (chocolate, strawberry and pineapple), whipped cream, nuts and maraschino cherries. Wilmington claims that they are the true inventors since Hazard's creation is so similar to what's now considered the standard banana split formula. The town even holds a Banana Split Festival each year in June to honor Hazard's dish.

TAKE A PACKAGE HOME
Banana Ice Cream

A Nation of Coneheads

Our favorite ice cream concoction may be the ice cream cone. Nearly a third of all the ice cream we eat is consumed this way, popular for both its taste and convenience. As a U.S. Department of Health, Education and Welfare official told *60 Minutes* in 1969, "The ice cream cone is the only ecologically sound package known. It is the perfect package."

After cones made a big splash at the 1904 World's Fair, manufacturers slowly spread across the country. It was a cheap business to enter, and profits were all but guaranteed. At first, cones were made on a modified waffle-maker and rolled by hand. But in 1912, Frederick Bruckman, an inventor from Portland, Oregon, patented a machine to do the job. Molded cones made from specially designed pans or inserted cores soon followed. Clevelander Carl Rutherford Taylor's 1924 invention of a cone-rolling machine made mass-produced cones possible.

By 1924, more than 245 million cones were produced. In part, sales were fueled by the cone's portability. Most ice cream was eaten outside of the home as freezer units weren't commonplace until the 1930s, but even more importantly, cones were the cheapest ice cream treats around, costing only a nickel. In those days, it was far more expensive to buy ice cream in bulk,

Fountain treats were touted as a perfect snack or lunch food during the 1940s.

as automated technology for filling half-gallons and pints hadn't been developed yet.

Cone manufacturers, seeking ways to increase sales in an increasingly competitive field, began introducing new "models" of cones each year. There were dripless cones, cones shaped liked rocket ships, cones shaped like an ice cream sandwich for IcyPi novelties, and Jack and Jill cones with side-by-side cups for two different flavors. Most cones were simply embellished versions of the classic sugar cone, but that didn't stop consumers from checking out the latest fad.

Until the 1940s, most cones were, well, cone-shaped. But in the 1940s Joseph Shapiro invented the first flat-bottomed cone for Dairy Queen, so servers could stand cones on the counter while filling orders. The design caught on, and soon cake cones joined sugar cones and waffle cones, as the dominant styles on the market. By the late 1950s, following the trend of ice cream manufacturers, the number of cone manufacturers had streamlined, too, with less than three dozen factories in business. Today, most cones are made by five companies — Bake-Line, Interbake, Keebler, Nabisco and Joy Cone. The largest of these is the Joy Cone Company, which was founded by the George family in an Ohio grocery store in 1918. The company is the largest manufacturer of cones in the world, churning out more than 1.5 billion cones each year.

While consumers have settled into their cone preferences (like Pepsi versus Coke, you're either a cake or a sugar cone fan), there is still innovation in the industry. In 1999, Richard Hartman of Issaquah, Washington, patented a motorized cone that spins a cup of ice cream around so you can effortlessly lick the cone. The patented Buddy System cone holder is manufactured in

GET SAUCED

For those of us who insist that ice cream is best when drowning in sauce, there are plenty of delicious choices out there. Here are some premium ice cream toppings worth a taste:

Black Hound
212-979-9505
www.blackhound.com
Hip New York store offers three kinds of chocolate truffle sauces, each flavored with liqueur.

Brent's
707-252-4228
www.anettes.com
Six chocolate sauces flavored with wines and liqueurs.

C.C. Brown's
818-878-0032
www.ccbrowns.com
Sauces using original recipes from the now-closed Hollywood landmark.

Fudge Fatale
888-923-8343
www.fudgefatale.com
Handmade sauces by fudgemaker and Hollywood cinematographer Alexander Black.

Herrell's
866-YUM-FUDGE
www.herrells.com
Hot fudge sauce from the legendary Massachusetts ice cream maker Steve Herrell.

King's Cupboard
800-962-6555
www.kingscupboard.com
Eleven flavors of sauces, ranging from Key lime white chocolate to pear cinnamon caramel to orange chocolate.

Lehmann Farms
800-446-5276
www.lehmannfarms.com
Nutty chocolate sauces with either pecans, toasted almonds or walnuts.

Ron's
888-669-7425
www.mothermyricks.com
A sauce that *Yankee* magazine's "Travel Guide to New England" called "sinfully good."

Sander's
800-651-7263
www.sanderscandy.com
Four topping flavors from a favorite Detroit institution.

Scharffen Berger Chocolate Maker
510-981-4050
www.scharffenberger.com
Chocolate sauce from the esteemed artisan chocolate maker.

Timeless Traditions
802-483-6024
ww.ice-cream-toppings.com
Fourteen flavors, including Maple Caramel, Peanut Butter Mud Fudge, and Vermont Apple and Cider.

Top Hat
847-256-6565
www.chocolatebutter-scotchhotfudgedessert sauces.com
Standard flavors and gourmet ones, too, like raspberry fudge and Mayan Legacy (mocha sauce flavored with cinnamon and orange).

Tulocay's Made in Napa Valley
888-627-2859, ext. 32
www.madeinnappa valley.com
Wine-inspired dessert sauces in such flavors as chocolate with figs and Zinfandel, and vanilla caramel with Chardonnay.

GIFTS FOR ICE CREAM LOVERS

Ice cream — and ice cream–related items — make a wonderful present. You can give an ice cream maker, some fountain glasses, a trio of sauces, a T-shirt from a local stand or an express-mailed shipment of a favorite ice cream. Here are some unique ways to please the ice cream lover in your life. (Note: prices do not include shipping and handling.)

■ The web-based **Ice Cream Source** allows you to send an assortment of pints from some of the country's best makers. There are more than 16 "micro-dairies" to choose from; you can even give a membership to the ice cream-of-the-month club. Price varies, depending on order. 920-495-1668; www.icecreamsource.com

■ Illinois-based **Prairie Moon** offers beverage syrup concentrates to concoct whatever flavor of soda you desire. Its Basic Soda Fountain Fun Set ($81.50) includes most everything you need to make authentic ice cream sodas at home — flavored syrups, fountain glasses, even a soda siphon. All you need to add is ice cream. 866-331-0767; www.prairiemoon.biz

■ Online department store **New York First** includes a confectionery with a wealth of ice-cream related items, from a Hot Fudge Sundae Kit ($26) to the Complete Brooklyn Egg Cream Kit ($59) to a Zerroll scoop and spade gift pack ($29). 607-277-0152; www.NewYorkFirst.com

■ Kids will love **freeze-dried astronaut ice cream** ($2 to $3). Developed originally for the Apollo missions, the ice cream is frozen to -40 degrees Celsius, then vacuum-dried (which removes all the liquid) and sealed in a foil packet. Widely available online and at select retailers.

■ **Everything Ice Cream** claims to have the largest selection of ice cream-related gifts on the Net. Among the offerings are scented strawberry milk shake candles ($15.99), ice cream-themed ornaments and plastic ice cream-shaped banks ($6.99). 607-535-7354; www.everythingicecream.com.

■ A **talking ice cream scoop** ($14) really does scream for ice cream. Fashioned in the shape of a Good Humor man or an ice cream truck, you can press a button to hear the call of "Ice Cream" and the ringing of truck bells. Available online at several websites; one to try is 877-665-GIFT; www.funideas.com.

Rochester, New York; it's a polystyrene sleeve that fits over cones to prevent drips and helps keep cones germ-free. Cones have even gone upscale with the offerings from Philadelphia's Cone Guys, a company that wholesales gourmet cones to parlors in such flavors as chocolate chip cookie and pretzel.

The Scoop on Dippers

But where would the cone be without the trusty scoop? Before 1878, ice cream was spooned for serving because there was no such thing as an ice cream scoop or dipper. It made for slow going when a line of customers waited. No wonder soda fountain owners rued all the new-fangled ice cream treats. Fountains needed fewer employees, had higher customer turnover, and made more profit when plain sodas dominated their business. But by the late 1800s, America's love affair with ice cream treats was well past the infatuation stage.

With the invention of the ice cream dipper, getting ice cream out of the tub became much easier, if not completely efficient (Clewell's conical-shaped dipper required two hands to use). Scoops and dippers became the soda jerk's essential tool, and companies actively sought new designs and innovations to keep their brand in heavy rotation at the local fountain.

In all, there were 241 patents for ice cream dippers and scoops issued between 1878 and 1940. (For many years, dipper was the term of choice; scoop didn't catch on until the 1920s.) The first one-handed scoop, which rotated a scraper inside the bowl when the handle was squeezed, was patented by Edson Clement Baughman of Topeka, Kansas, and marketed as Kingery's Rapid Ice Cream Disher. Round scoops in a range of sizes, manufactured by companies like Gilchrist, become popular after 1900. Scoops were numbered, from the petite no. 30 scoop to the sundae-sized, 2-3/4–inch diameter no. 12. The scoop's number correlated to how many servings you'd get from a quart of ice cream with that size scoop.

Early ice cream dippers were often tricky to use and usually required two hands and lots of muscle power to operate.

A Scoop of History

1920s

Malted milkshakes were quite a fad in the 1920s. Sales of malted milk powder jumped from less than one million pounds in 1910 to more than 35 million pounds by 1926.

Nesbitt's, a popular soda
pop and fountain syrup
manufacturer from the
1930s through the 1970s,
was best-known for
its orange flavors.

When the novelty craze hit in the 1920s, inventors responded by creating a slew of scoops specially designed for soda fountain treats. There were oblong scoops for dispensing ice cream on a banana split, triangular scoops for pie à la mode, square and rectangular scoops for ice cream sandwiches, and cylindrical scoops for inserting ice cream into tube-shaped cookies. Perhaps the most fanciful was the 1925 heart-shaped scoop designed by John Manos of Toronto, Ohio. (Today, they are a highly prized and rarely found collectible — only about 1,000 were made.)

One of the best-loved and best-selling scoops of all time was developed in the 1930s by Sherman Kelly of Toledo, Ohio. While on vacation in Palm Beach, Kelly noticed the hands of a worker were blistered from trying to scoop the hard ice cream. Kelly figured he could design something better and set out to create the world's best ice cream scoop. His design, the Zeroll, became an instant classic and the industry standard. Its seamless, one-piece design meant there were no mechanical parts that could break, and ice cream could be scooped easily and neatly with one hand, thanks to the ingenuity of adding a defrosting fluid to the inside of the handle. (The fluid responds to heat from the user's hand and warms up the aluminum scoop so ice cream is more easily scooped.) It also helped that Kelly designed a sleek and elegant scoop. Even New York's Museum of Modern Art has put it on display.

Whether you like your ice cream scooped into a cone or dished into a bowl, you can get as intricate or as bare-bones with your ice cream as you like. It's up to you, your preference and your mood. What's certain is that you'll have no shortage of ways to enjoy it — in a waffle cone, topped with sauce, mixed into a malt. That's the beauty of ice cream, and a major reason it is so popular. Ice cream is one of the most versatile foods around, and it can be adapted to anyone's tastes, be they traditional, gourmet, low-carb or low-fat. And however you like it served up, it's still delicious. No wonder everyone loves ice cream as much as they do.

BRINGING THE FOUNTAIN HOME

WITH THE RIGHT SCOOP — AND PERHAPS A FEW OTHER TOOLS — YOU CAN MAKE ALL OF YOUR FOUNTAIN FAVORITES, FROM ICE CREAM SODAS TO WAFFLE CONES, IN THE COMFORT OF YOUR OWN KITCHEN. FROM TOPPINGS AND SAUCES TO SODAS AND SUNDAES, ICE CREAM TREATS ARE QUICK TO MAKE. (EVEN HOT FUDGE SAUCE FROM SCRATCH WON'T TAKE YOU MORE THAN 15 MINUTES.) YOUR JOB CAN BE EVEN EASIER WITH A FEW WELL-CHOSEN TOOLS, SUCH AS THESE:

Scoops

There are three primary types of scoops on the market today: spades, models with self-releasing handles, and seamless, one-piece scoops. Spades, which look like wide, metal spatulas, are good for getting large amounts of ice cream out of the container or spreading ice cream into a pie or onto a cake. They're also adept at incorporating mix-ins into ice cream (you'll need two spades to do this, though). A spade, while helpful, is optional. A scoop, however, is essential.

It's personal preference whether you get a trigger-release model or one with just a scoop. I like to keep several sizes on hand: A small melon-baller is great for putting a trio of dainty scoops in a dish. An oval-shaped scoop makes the ice cream look elegant. There are even scoops in the shape of a heart or a cube. (You can find Stöckel's shaped scoops at Sur La Table, 800-243-0852, www.surlatable.com.) Good Cook has recently introduced one more variation to the scoop lineup, the Smart Scoop (800-421-6290, www.goodcook.com). It has a Teflon coating and an innovative two-piece scoop that splits apart to drop the ice cream neatly onto the cone.

Fountain Glasses

For maximum effect and ease of serving, it's helpful to have some fountain-style serving dishes on hand. A good starter set would include four each of the following: generous 12- to 20-ounce soda glasses; tall, narrow parfait glasses; footed, tulip-shaped sundae cups; and shallow, oblong banana split bowls. You can also create makeshift fountainware from items already on hand. Champagne glasses can double as parfait glasses. Martini glasses fill in fine for sundaes (so do cereal or soup bowls). Pint glasses make great milk shake containers. The bottom line: be creative. It really doesn't matter what you use, so long as it's made of glass or stainless steel — plastic doesn't keep the ice cream cold enough.

Blender/ Drink Mixer

Fans of milkshakes, freezes and smoothies should get a good blender or drink mixer. Hamilton Beach and Waring are classic choices; their brands have been fountain fixtures for more than 70 years. Drink mixers with a spindle that drops down into a glass or a stainless steel tumbler are the choice of most parlors; an at-home model from Hamilton Beach, Waring or Farberware will cost between $40 and $149, depending on features. There's a wide selection of blenders on the market, too, and in a range of prices (from $30 to $200), but any brand with a record of reliability and decent mixing power will do. (You can even use a hand-held immersion blender to whip up a quick milk shake.) With blenders, however, be sure and invest in one with a glass pitcher; the plastic ones don't keep the drinks as cold.

Straws/Soda Fountain Spoons

If you plan on making fountain drinks, you'll need straws and long-stemmed spoons (either soda-fountain-style or iced tea spoons). And take a tip from soda jerks in the know: keep your glasses and spoons at the ready in the freezer. The colder all the elements are for your fountain drinks (from the milk to the container), the better the taste and the results.

Waffle Cone/Pizzelle Maker

There's nothing better than ice cream on a freshly made cone, and it's not hard to make them. Unfortunately, a regular waffle maker won't work; the grooves are too deep. You'll need a waffle cone or a pizzelle maker. Both produce a thin round waffle that can be rolled into a cone shape. Chef's Choice and Rival sell special waffle cone makers (about $50) that come with a cone mold. A pizzelle maker is intended to produce thin Italian cookies (usually flavored with anise) but can also produce cones, too. (Note: don't use a pizzelle recipe to make a cone; use a specially formulated cone recipe instead). Villaware, Cusinart and Chef's Choice all produce pizzelle makers. If using a pizzelle maker, you'll need to purchase a cone form separately; it's difficult to roll them without one.

Whipped Cream Charger

Nearly all ice cream treats look better — and taste better — when topped off with whipped cream. A whipped cream charger produces light and airy whipped cream in a flash.

All you do is pour whipped cream into dispenser, outfit with a NO_2 cartridge and squirt away. You don't even need to add any sugar. As a bonus, you can easily create flavored and colored whipped creams. Chargers run from $20 to $70; 24 replacement NO^2 cartridges cost about $12.

FOR RECIPES FOR ICE CREAM TOPPINGS, SUNDAES, DRINKS AND PIES, SEE APPENDIX 3 ON PAGE 167.

Soda Siphon

If you love ice cream sodas and egg creams, consider investing in a soda siphon, which makes fresh seltzer water with the help of a CO_2 cartridge. In authentic soda fountain fashion, you can even mix your root beer or cola from scratch by adding flavored syrup. Costs for siphons range from $30 to more than $100; chargers run about $5 for a pack of 10.

CREAM OF THE CROP

550 GREAT AMERICAN ICE CREAM PARLORS

Here are some of the country's best places to enjoy ice cream. All of the parlors and shops mentioned here received favorable reports from at least two of the following sources: on-site visits, media coverage, recommendations from other ice cream fans and phone interviews with the shops. Still, the final criterion for including these places was broad and highly subjective. Some places are included because they've perfected the art of making ice cream; others are listed because they offer a superb atmosphere in which to enjoy it. Many make their own ice cream, but some serve up an out-of-house brand with flair or a fabulous setting. I made a particular effort to list noteworthy surviving soda fountains, too, because they are the living museums of our nation's ice cream past.

That said, this list doesn't even begin to scratch the surface on all the best ice cream parlors in America. Consider it a starting point for expanding your ice cream horizons or a trusty resource to locate ice cream when traveling.

Big Dipper Ice Cream, Missoula, Montana

Note: Before visiting, please call to confirm store hours, available flavors and location particulars.

National and Regional Ice Cream Brands, Chains and Franchises

Note: Ice cream stores with more than 20 outlets are listed in this section.

Ashby Sterling
888-4-ASHBYS
www.ashbyssterling.com
Headquarters: Oak Park, Michigan
Supplies innovative flavors, including banana pudding and English cinnamon crumb cake, to shops using the Ashby name or their own names.

Baskin-Robbins
800-859-5339
www.baskinrobbins.com
Headquarters: Randolph, Massachusetts
Known for 31 flavors, including Pralines 'n Cream and seasonal flavors.

Ben & Jerry's
802-846-1500
www.benjerry.com
Headquarters: Montpelier, Vermont
Mail-Order: Yes
Super-rich ice cream with super-chunky ingredients, such as Cherry Garcia, Phish Food and Core Sundaes.

Braum's Ice Cream and Dairy Stores
405-478-1656
www.braums.com
Headquarters: Oklahoma City, Oklahoma
Some 280 dairy stores featuring an extensive menu of treats. Also, they're the only major ice cream maker that still milks its own cows.

Bresler's
631-737-9700
www.coolbrandsinternational.com
Headquarters: Markham, Ontario
Started in Chicago after the Depression, the chain specializes in premium hard ice cream in flavors geared to kids and teens.

Bridgeman's
763-971-2947
www.bridgemans.com
Headquarters: Brooklyn Center, Minnesota
Most of their shops are located within an existing business (called co-branding). Menu offers cones and some 24 treats.

Bruster's
724-774-4250
www.brustersicecream.com
Headquarters: Bridgewater, Pennsylvania
Walk-up stands known for its velvety ice cream in inventive flavors such as Purple Dinosaur.

Carvel
860-257-4448
www.carvel.com
Headquarters: Rocky Hill, Connecticut
An East Coast institution for soft-serve ice cream and ice cream cakes in shapes like Fudgie the Whale.

Ciao Bella
800-343-5286
www.ciaobellagelato.com
Headquarters: Irving, New Jersey
Mail-Order: Yes, via phone
They offer boutique gelati and sorbetti, such as chocolate jalapeño, blackberry Cabernet and five kinds of vanilla.

Cold Stone Creamery
480-348-1704
www.coldstonecreamery.com
Headquarters: Scottsdale, Arizona
A wide array of mix-ins and toppings can be hand-folded into ice cream on top of a chilled granite stone.

CremaLita
212-645-2000
www.cremalita.com
Headquarters: New York City
Low- to no-fat soft-serve shops with a sleek design.

Culver's
608-643-7980
www.culvers.com
Headquarters: Prairie du Sac, Wisconsin
Casual fast food chain with freshly made frozen custard and ButterBurgers.

Dairy Queen
952-830-0200
www.dairyqueen.com
Headquarters: Edina, Minnesota
With more than 5,000 locations in the U.S., DQ is the nation's largest ice cream franchise, known for soft-serve ice cream cones with the signature curl on top and Blizzards.

Dippin' Dots
270-575-6990
www.dippindots.com
Headquarters: Paducah, Kentucky
Flash-frozen ice cream that forms into small "dots" is available in franchised stores, vending machines and at theme parks and fairs.

Double Rainbow
415-861-5858
www.doublerainbow.com
Headquarters: San Francisco
The super-premium ice cream called the "official ice cream of San Francisco," is available nationally at 19 shops bearing the Double Rainbow name and more than 300 other locations.

Emack & Bolio's
617-739-7995
www.emackandbolios.com
Headquarters: Brookline, Massachusetts
Since 1975, Emack & Bolio's has been known for over-the-top flavors, healthy smoothies and vibrant, funky shops.

Friendly's
413-543-2400
www.friendlys.com
Headquarters: Wilbraham, Massachusetts
Restaurant and ice cream parlor featuring light fare and lots of soda fountain treats.

Goodrich's
866-228-6258
www.goodrichicecream.com
Headquarters: Omaha, Nebraska
Parlors offering old-fashioned fountains treats, such as Orange Cassanovas, and flavors like Goo Goo Cluster and butter brickle.

Graeter's
800-727-7425
www.graeters.com
Headquarters: Cincinnati, Ohio
Mail-Order: Yes
Made using the French pot method, Graeter's ice cream is rich, creamy and especially good in the form of one of its signature "chip" flavors.

Häagen-Dazs
800-767-0120
www.haagen-dazs.com
Headquarters: Oakland, California
Shops featuring their smooth and
rich super-premium ice cream and
treats like Mint Chip Dazzlers.

**Handel's Homemade
Ice Cream & Yogurt**
330-702-8270
www.handelsicecream.com
Headquarters: Canfield, Ohio
Mail-Order: Yes, via telephone
Founded in 1945, Handel's has
made a name for itself with super-
smooth ice cream and indulgent flavors. Their chocolate pecan, which
is served soft, is their best-seller.

Hershey's Creamery
888-240-1905
www.hersheyicecream.com
Headquarters: Harrisburg,
Pennsylvania
Supplies retails outlets with their
premium ice cream (some shops
are called Hershey's, some just
carry the brand).

Howard Johnson's
781-837-2296
www.franchiscassociates.com
Headquarters: Duxbury,
Massachusetts
Ice cream shops and cafes
that still serve Howard Johnson's
original 1925 recipe.

I Can't Believe It's Yogurt
631-737-9700
www.coolbrandsinternational.com
Headquarters: Markham, Ontario
Soft serve frozen yogurt with a
range of toppings.

Ice Cream Club
800-535-7711
www.icecreamclub.com
Headquarters: Boynton Beach,
Florida

More than 100 flavors of hard ice
cream, 22 flavors of hard frozen
yogurt and some 40 flavors of
soft-serve in rotation.

Johnny Rockets
888-8-JOHNNY
www.johnnyrockets.com
Headquarters: Aliso Viejo,
California
Sleek retro diners featuring table-
top jukeboxes, servers in white
paper caps and thick milk shakes.

Kaleidoscoops
630-752-1750
www.kaleidoscoops.com
Headquarters: Wheaton, Illinois
Kaleidoscoops is a co-op of ice
cream stores that markets bold
flavors — Bear Foot Brownie and
Nuthin' But Truffle — in boldly
colored stores.

**Kilwin's Chocolates
& Ice Cream**
231-347-3800
www.kilwins.com
Headquarters: Petoskey, Michigan
Known for their quaint shops
offering chocolates and ice cream.

Kohr Bros.
434-975-1500
www.kohrbros.com
Headquarters: Charlottesville,
Virginia
It was Archie Kohr who first introduced frozen custard to the Coney
Island boardwalk — and the world
— in 1919. Today, Kohr Bros. is
found in 10 states, but they are
perhaps best enjoyed at one their
New Jersey boardwalk sites.

**Lappert's Hawaiian Ice
Cream**
510-231-2340
www.lapperts.com
Headquarters: Richmond, California
Mail-Order: Yes

Started by late Hawaiian icon
Walter Lappert, the chain is known
for such flavors as coconut
macadamia nut fudge, guava
and Kona coffee.

Maggie Moo's
800-949-8114
www.maggiemoos.com
Headquarters: Columbia, Maryland
Known as the most kid-oriented of
the cold-slab creameries and for
its award-winning chocolate and
dark chocolate flavors.

Marble Slab Creamery
713-780-3601
www.marbleslab.com
Headquarters: Houston, Texas
Customer-created ice cream
concoctions that are hand-mixed
on a marble slab.

Oberweis Dairy
630-897-6600
www.oberweisdairy.com
Headquarters: Aurora, Illinois
Oberweis makes extremely rich ice
cream with milk from its own herd.
It also still delivers milk to
customers' doorsteps.

Ralph's Famous Italian Ices
718-448-0853
www.ralphsices.com
Headquarters: Staten Island,
New York
Ralph's offers water ices and
sherbets in more than 50 flavors.

Rita's Water Ice
800-677-RITA
www.ritasice.com
Headquarters: Bensalem,
Pennsylvania
Seasonal walk-up stand featuring
31 flavors of Italian ices.

Ritter's Frozen Custard
317-819-0700
www.ritters.com

Headquarters: Carmel, Indiana
Seasonal walk-up stands featuring
chocolate, vanilla and lite vanilla
frozen custard, plus a nut, fruit
and special flavor each day.

Shake's Frozen Custard
866-742-5648
www.shakesfrozencustard.com
Headquarters: Fayetteville,
Arkansas
Fresh frozen custard served up
in everything from a Pink Poodle
sundae to thick "concrete" shakes.

Sheridan's Frozen Custard
913-341-5339
www.sheridansfrozencustard.com
Headquarters: Overland Park,
Kansas
Frozen custard made fresh daily
and thick "concretes" in such
flavors as Mount Rush S'more
and caramel pretzel crunch.

Sonic Drive-In
405-225-5000
www.sonicdrivein.com
Headquarters: Oklahoma City,
Oklahoma
Sonic started in 1953 and now
it's the nation's largest chain of
drive-ins, known for its cream
pie shakes.

Steak 'n Shake
317-633-4100
www.steaknshake.com
Headquarters: Indianapolis, Indiana
Founded in 1934 in Normal,
Illinois, they have milk shakes,
floats and sundaes, all made with
ice cream from their own recipe.

Swensen's
631-737-9700
www.coolbrandsinternational.com
Headquarters: Markham, Ontario
Parlors with an old-fashioned feel
and a menu of soda fountain
treats.

Tastee-Freez
949-752-5800
www.tastee-freez.com
Headquarters: Newport Beach,
California
Soft-serve chain from the 1950s,
cofounded by former Dairy Queen
executive Harry Axene.

Tasti D-Lite
800-228-2784
www.tastidlite.com
Headquarters: New York City
Longtime Big Apple fixture known
for its low-fat soft-serve in 100
flavors.

TCBY
800-348-6311
www.tcby.com
Headquarters: Salt Lake City, Utah

Serves hard premium ice cream,
soft-serve frozen yogurt and
smoothies.

Thrifty Ice Cream
800-RITE-AID
www.riteaid.com
Headquarters: Harrisburg,
Pennsylvania
When Rite-Aid bought the west
coast chain of Thrifty drugstores,
they kept 400-some, in-store
scoop shops that had become
local favorites.

Twistee Treat
Eye-catching roadside soft-
serve stands in the shape of a
22-foot-high Twistee Treat cone.
Once a franchised chain, all outlets
are now individually owned.

United Dairy Farmers
800-833-9911
www.udfinc.com
Headquarters: Norwood, Ohio
Chain of 200 dairy and
convenience stores featuring
its Homemade brand of ice
cream and scoop shops with
fountain treats.

Yogen Früz
631-737-9700
www.coolbrandsinternational.com
Headquarters: Markham, Ontario
Purveyors of frozen yogurt mixed
with fresh toppings, granita
slushes and smoothies.

Whippy Dip
A 1970s soft-serve chain is now
individually owned and operated.
Some of the remaining stores
can be found in Decorah, Iowa;
Vesterheim, Minnesota; Sandusky,
Ohio; Silver Lake, Michigan; and
Fairlee, Vermont.

Zesto Drive-In
A popular chain of drive-ins
in the 1950s that still exists in
some locations under independent
owner-operators. Known for their
Chubby Decker sandwiches
and a good selection of shakes
and other ice cream treats.
The remaining drive-ins are
concentrated in South Dakota,
Nebraska and the Atlanta area.

State-by-State Listings
Note: Ice cream stores with more than 20 outlets are listed above in the National and Regional Ice Cream listings.

ALABAMA
Loxley
Burris Farm Market
Intersection of highways 59 & 64
251-964-6464
Open: Seasonally
Type: Farm stand
Gulf Shores Highway landmark
serves up produce, fresh pie and
homemade ice cream. Try the
peach or butter pecan.

Tuscumbia
Palace Soda Fountain
100 S. Main St., 256-386-8210
Type: Old-fashioned soda fountain
This refurbished 1833 soda
fountain sells more than 30,000
Harvey Milkshakes each year.

ALASKA
Fairbanks
Hot Licks Homemade
Ice Cream

3453 College Rd., 907-479-7813
www.hotlicks.net
Open: April–September
Type: Walk-up stand
Handmade batches with locally
inspired flavors such as Alaska
Wild Blueberry and Aurora Borealis.

Homer Spit
Frosty Bear
4025 Thompson Boardwalk # 16
907-235-7300 (plus one other
location)
www.willieandme.com
Open: Seasonally
Type: Scoop shop
Homemade waffle cones, hard
and soft ice cream, and a view
of the local sea otters.

ARIZONA
Chandler
Angel Sweet
1900 W. Chandler Blvd.

480-722-2541
www.angelsweetgelato.com
Type: Gelateria
Award-winning local favorite serves
up 24 flavors of gelato each day.

Gilbert
Streamers Ice Cream
Parlor and Grill
1166 S. Gilbert Rd.
480-635-9222
Type: Retro parlor
Try one of the 11 parfaits on the
menu or a Gatsby's summer soda.

Phoenix
Mary Coyle Ice Cream Parlor
5521 N. Seventh Ave.
602-265-6266.
Type: Old-time parlor
In business since 1958. Try a $49
Mountain sundae with seven pounds
of ice cream and four toppings.

Scottsdale
Auntie Em's Frozen Custard
2910 N. Hayden Rd.
480-994-5988.
Type: Scoop shop
Three flavors of frozen custard
daily: chocolate, vanilla and a flavor of the day from German chocolate cake to spiced cranberry nut.

The Sugar Bowl
4005 North Scottsdale Rd.
480-946-0051
Type: Old-time parlor
The city's first parlor hasn't
changed much since 1958; take
a date and have a banana split.

Tuscon
Austin's Old Fashion Ice Cream
2920 E. Broadway Blvd.
520-327-3892
Type: Old-time parlor
Since 1959, they've been serving

up homemade ice cream (try the peach or the ginger) and sundaes like the Wildcat Special.

Eric's Fine Foods & Ice Cream
1702 E. Speedway Blvd.
520-795-2366
Open: Lunch only
Type: Diner/Scoop shop
Homemade ice cream in such flavors as Gentle Persuasion, made with oatmeal and prunes, and Viagra Chip with blue M&M'S candies.

ARKANSAS
Benton
Jerry Van Dyke's Soda Shoppe
107 S. Market St., 501-860-5500
www.jerryvandyke.org
Type: Old-fashioned soda fountain
Enjoy a Jerry's Black & White sundae amidst memorabilia from the career of sitcom comedian Jerry Van Dyke.

Little Rock
The Purple Cow
8026 Cantrell Rd., 501-221-3555
(plus locations in Arkansas and Texas)
Type: Retro parlor-Diner
Renowned for their milk shakes, in such flavors as peanut butter, double chocolate and even Purple.

Mountain View
Woods Pharmacy & Old-Fashioned Fountain
301 W. Main St., 870-269-8304
www.arkansascommunities.com/MtnView/woods.htm
Open: Lunch only
Type: Old-fashioned soda fountain
Have a phosphate or a strawberry daiquiri sundae at the early 1900s soda fountain.

CALIFORNIA
Alhambra
Fosselman's
1824 W. Main St., 626-282-6533
www.fosselmans.com

Type: Old-time parlor
Award-winning maker of more than 40 flavors, from burgundy cherry to green apple sorbet.

Bakersfield
Dewar's Candy Shop
1120 Eye St., 661-322-0933
www.dewarscandy.com
Type: Candy store/Old-fashioned soda fountain
Serving double banana splits, malts and other treats since 1928.

Hollywood
Mashti Malone
1525 N. La Brea Ave.
323-874-6168
www.mashti.com
Mail-Order: Yes
Type: Scoop shop
Try their version of an ice cream sandwich — a Mashti — filled with one of their exotic, Iranian-inspired flavors, like rosewater saffron with pistachios or orange blossom.

Indio
Shield's Date Gardens
80225 U.S. Highway 111,
760-347-0996
www.shieldsdates.com
Type: Roadside stand
Sample a California favorite — date shakes and date ice cream – and also catch a 1940s slide show on "The Romance and Sex Life of the Date."

Julian
Julian Drugstore & Miner's Diner
2134 Main St., 760-765-3753
Type: Old-fashioned soda fountain
Sip a sarsaparilla soda at a 1928 soda fountain housed in a historic 1886 building.

Los Angeles
Al Gelato
806 S. Robertson Blvd.
310-659-8069

Type: Gelateria
In 2000, *Los Angeles* magazine called this gelato the best in town, thanks to an authentic family recipe from Palermo.

Oakland
Fentons Creamery & Restaurant
4226 Piedmont Ave.
510-658-7000
www.fentonscreamery.com
Type: Old-time parlor
Order a gigantic banana special or a Berry Go Round sundae made with Fentons's homemade sauces and ice cream.

Orange
Watson's Drugs & Soda Fountain
116 E. Chapman, 714-633-1050
www.menusunlimited.com/watsondrug/index.htm
Type: Old-fashioned soda fountain
The locals line the stools to trade gossip and indulge in one of the fountain treats at this 1940s-era spot.

Palo Alto
Rick's Ice Cream
3946 Middlefield Rd.
650-493-6553
www.ricksicecream.com
Type: Scoop shop
Inventive flavors such as rose, Computer Chip (orange with chocolate chips), and Hawaiian Rocky Road.

Pasedena
Tutti Gelati
62 W. Union St., 626-440-9800
(plus a Las Vegas location)
www.tuttigelati.com
Type: Gelateria
Flavors such as malaga (rum raisin), sour cherry and cassata, all made with ingredients imported from Milan.

Sacramento
Gunther's Quality Ice Cream
2801 Franklin Blvd.
916-457-6646
Type: Old-time parlor
There are often long lines at this town favorite; locals rave about the creamy ice cream and gigantic sundaes.

Leatherby's Family Creamery
2333 Arden Way, 916-920-8382
(plus a Las Vegas location)
www.deadlinecreative.com/dining/profile/leatherby.htm
Type: Parlor
Homemade ice cream and homemade sauces make the sundaes here a special treat.

Vic's Ice Cream
3199 Riverside Blvd.
916-448-0892
Type: Old-time parlor
Slip into a booth at this shop that dates back to 1947 and order a scoop of homemade ice cream or an authentic fountain drink.

San Francisco
Gelato Classico
576 Union St., 415-391-6667
(plus other area locations)
Type: Gelateria
For more than 30 years, Gelato Classico has been offering its dense and flavorful Italian-style ice cream.

Ghirardelli Chocolate Manufactory & Soda Fountain
900 N. Point St., 415-474-1414
(plus 10 other locations in four states)
www.ghirardelli.com
Type: Retro parlor
At the site of the original Ghirardelli chocolate factory, you can order a decadent hot fudge sundae.

Joe's Ice Cream
5351 Geary Blvd., 415-751-1950
joesicecream.citysearch.com
Type: Old-time parlor
Owner Mutsuhiko Murashige still uses Joe's original recipes, but he's added an Asian twist with such flavors as Rocky Road Ginger and azuki bean.

Mitchell's Ice Cream
688 San Jose Ave., 415-648-2300
www.mitchellsicecream.com
Type: Scoop shop
A Mission District institution for more than 50 years known for its exceptional flavors, including such exotics as *ube* (purple yam) and *macapuno* (sweet coconut).

Swensen's Ice Cream
1999 Hyde St., 415-775-6818
(plus other locations worldwide)
Type: Old-time parlor
Visit the original store in this now-worldwide chain. It's where Earle Swensen first offered ice cream in 1948.

Tango Gelato
2015 Fillmore St., 415-346-3692
www.tangogelato.com
Type: Gelateria
Sample Argentinian-style gelato in such flavors as *dulce de leche* and *giandiusa* (chocolate hazelnut). On select Sundays, you can get a tango lesson with your scoop.

Santa Barbara
McConnell's
201 W. Mission St., 805-963-8813
www.mcconnells.com
Type: Parlor
In business since 1949, this much-praised, super-premium maker offers flavors like Elberta peach and Oregon blackberry.

Santa Cruz
Marianne's Ice Cream

1020 Ocean St., 831-458-1447
Type: Old-time parlor
More than 40 years of experience and some 70 flavors in rotation including cinnamon and *macapuno*.

South Pasadena
Fair Oaks Pharmacy and Soda Fountain
1526 Mission St., 626-799-1414
www.fairoakspharmacy.net
Type: Old-fashioned soda fountain
Have a hot fudge sundae at the place *Sunset* magazine called the "Best Old-Fashioned Ice Cream Parlor in the West."

Upland
Dr. Bob's HandCrafted IceCreams
155 C St., 909-920-1966
www.drbobsicecream.com
Mail-Order: Yes
Type: Scoop shop
Sixty handcrafted flavors including sour cream and brown sugar, and a black raspberry chip using Scharffen Berger chocolate.

Venice
Massimo's Delectables
1029 Abbot Kinney Blvd.
310-581-2485
Type: Pastry shop/Gelateria
Try ginger gelato, pear sorbetto, or one of the pastry-gelato combinations, such as the Livornese or the Capri.

COLORADO
Boulder
Boulder Ice Cream Shoppe
637 G. South Broadway,
303-494-2002
www.bouldericecream.com/shoppe
Type: Scoop shop
Mail-Order: Yes, via www.icecreamsource.com
Flavors such as Island Coconut and Famous Sweet Cream, plus $1 scoops when it's snowing.

Colorado Springs
Michelle's
122 North Tejon St.,
719-633-5089 (plus two other locations)
www.michellecandies.com
Mail-Order: Yes, for ice cream toppings
Type: Restaurant/Confectionery
There's a three-page ice cream menu, including a "Believe It or Not" ice cream sundae that weighs 42 pounds.

Denver
Bonnie Brae Ice Cream
799 S. University Blvd.,
303-777-0808
Type: Scoop shop
Since 1986, Bonnie Brae has been a Denver favorite for flavors such as Triple Death by Chocolate and Grand Marnier chocolate chip.

Gelato d'Italia
250 Detroit St., 303-316-9154
www.gelatousa.com
Type: Gelateria
Flavorful gelato in such flavors as rum truffle, pistachio and blueberry.

Lik's
2039 E. 13th Ave., 303-321-2370
Type: Scoop shop
Choose from flavors such as Jack Daniels dark chocolate chip or peanut butter swirl; if they're out of your favorite flavor, they'll call when it's made again.

Fort Collins
Walrus Ice Cream Company
125 W. Mountain Ave.,
970-482-5919 (plus a location in Greeley)
www.walrusicecream.com
Type: Scoop shop
Saturdaes (their version of sundaes) and flavors such as root beer chip and peach amaretto.

CONNECTICUT
Bethel
Dr. Mike's
158 Greenwood Ave., 203-792-4388 (plus a location in Monroe)
Type: Parlor
Owned by a dentist-turned-ice cream maker, Dr. Mike's turns out well-regarded flavors for sweet tooths. Don't miss the rich chocolate.

Guilford
Ashley's Ice Cream Cafe
942 Boston Post Rd., 203-458-3040 (plus four other locations)
www.guilfordct.com/ashleys/
Type: Parlor
Named for the owner's beloved whippet, the ice cream is (pardon the pun) doggone good. Try the peanut butter or mint.

Hamden
Wentworth's Ice Cream
3697 Whitney Ave., 203-281-7429
Type: Old-time parlor
Set in 100-year-old house, Wentworth's serves up decadent sundaes and rich flavors, such as Kahlúa Heath.

Manchester
Shady Glen Dairy Stores
840 Middle Turnpike East,
860-649-4245
Type: Dairy bar/Restaurant
Known for its fresh ice cream and inspired flavors like Grape Nut, Frozen Pudding and chocolate Almond Joy.

Middletown
Praline's of Middletown
170 Main St., 860-347-2663
www.pralinesct.com
Type: Parlor
More than 50 flavors of homemade ice cream are on the menu, including Graham Cracker Smacker and, of course, Pralines and Cream.

Mystic

Mystic Drawbridge Ice Cream
2 W. Main St., 860-572-7978
Type: Parlor
Homemade ice cream in a pristine setting overlooking the 1922 bascule drawbridge in this historic port.

Old Saybrook

James Gallery and Soda Fountain
325 Main St., 860-395-1229
www.pratthouse.net/
jamesgallery.htm
Open: May–December
Type: Old-fashioned soda fountain
Try a Miss James' Dusty Rhodes sundae, in honor of this circa-1896 fountain's longtime pharmacist.

Oxford

Rich Farm
691 Oxford Rd. (Route 67)
203-881-1040
Open: Seasonally
Type: Farm stand
Century-farm and well-known stand uses the cream from its own herd to make ice cream.

Ridgefield

Mr. Shane's Homemade Parlour
409 Main St., 203-431-8020
Open: April–October
Type: Scoop shop
A small step-down parlor known for its toasted coconut, chocolate malt and Mud Pie.

Ridgefield Ice Cream Shop
680 Danbury Rd. (Route 7)
203-438-3094
Type: Roadside stand
Not your ordinary soft-serve, but delicious frozen custard made from vintage machines.

West Simsbury

Tulmeadow Dairy Farm
255 Farms Village Rd. (Route 309), 860-658-1430
Open: April–October
Type: Farm stand
Time-tested ice cream expertise from a place that's been a working dairy farm since 1786.

DELAWARE

Newark

Caffe Gelato
90 E. Main St., 302-738-5811
www.caffegelato.net
Type: Restaurant/Gelateria
Owner Ryan German traveled to Italy to find the right machines and the right recipe for his gelato.

Hockessin

Woodside Farm Creamery
Corner Little Baltimore and North Star roads, 302-239-9847
www.woodsidefarmcreamery.com
Open: Seasonally
Type: Farm stand
Sample its farm-fresh flavors, made with cream from their Jersey cows.

Lewes

Kings Homemade Ice Cream
201 Second St., 302-645-9425
(plus a location in Milton)
Open: April–October
Type: Old-time parlor
Since 1972, this quaint Lewes parlor has been a favorite spot for locals and tourists on their way to the beach.

Rehoboth Beach

Royal Treat
4 Wilmington Ave., 302-227-6277
Open: April–October
Type: Parlor/Restaurant
In the morning Royal Treat is all breakfast, but in the afternoon people line up for the soda fountain goodies.

FLORIDA

Bonita Springs

Royal Scoop Ice Cream Parlor
15 8th St., 239-992-2000
Type: Scoop shop
Its creamy ice cream was voted Best Ice Cream by its local paper four years running.

Dania Beach

Jaxson's Ice Cream Parlor
128 S. Federal Hwy.,
954-923-4445
Type: Old-time parlor
Pick your favorite choice off the chalkboard menu at this landmark, 1950s-era parlor.

Key Largo

Mr. C's Gourmet Ice Cream
Mile-Marker 98.900
305-453-4256
Type: Scoop shop
Ice creams, gelati and sorbets in such flavors as cantaloupe, German chocolate and black cherry.

Homestead

Knauss Berry Farm
15980 SW 248th St.
305-247-0668
Type: Farm stand
Known for its luscious milkshakes in such flavors as strawberry, mango and raspberry.

Miami

Bacio Gelato
3462 Main Hwy., 305-442-4233
(plus other locations)
www.gelatobacio.com
Type: Gelateria
American franchise of a popular Italian chain offers authentic gelato in a sleek atmosphere.

Walls Old-Fashioned Ice Cream
8075 SW 67th Ave.
305-740-9830
Type: Scoop shop
Thirty flavors to choose from (there's even a beer-flavored stout ice cream), and six different types of cones.

Miami Beach

Frieze Ice Cream Factory
1626 Michigan Ave.
305-538-2028
Type: Scoop shop
Known for fresh flavors like macadamia caramel or tamarind sorbet.

Gelateria Parmalat
670 Lincoln Rd., 786-276-9475
(plus one location in Miami and several shops worldwide)
www.gelateriaparmalat.com/
en/b.html
Type: Gelateria
Creamy gelato in such authentic Italian flavors as *zabajone* and *gianduia*.

Palm Beach

Sprinkles Ice Cream & Sandwich Shop
279 Royal Poinciana Way
561-659-1140
Type: Scoop shop/Cafe
Top vote-getter in a 2003 *People* magazine national ranking of ice cream for its Triple Chocolate Supreme.

Palm Harbor

Strachan's Homemade Ice Cream
100 Palm Harbor Blvd. (Alt. 19 N.)
727-781-0997
www.strachansdesserts.com
Type: Parlor
Ice cream made with an eye for quality and a rotating menu of 18 flavors of homemade hot fudge.

West Palm Beach
La Michoacana
636 Belvedere Rd., 561-514-3030
Type: Paleteria
Mexican-style ice cream parlor featuring fruit popsicles — *paletas* — in fruity flavors.

Sloan's
112 Clematis St., 561-833-3335
(plus one other location)
Type: Scoop shop
Known for inventive flavors and for having what the Travel Channel considers one of the 10 best bathrooms in the world.

Tampa
Matt & Tanya's Ice Cream
1715 N. West Shore Blvd.
(inside the mall's food court)
813-287-1959
Type: Scoop shop
Try Kahlúa Cream Crunch, Mississippi Mud or a massive Lollapalooza sundae.

South Miami
Whip 'N Dip Ice Cream
1407 Sunset Dr., 305-665-2565
Type: Scoop shop
They say it would take 10 lifetimes to try all their possible flavor/topping combinations.

GEORGIA
Athens
Hodgson's Pharmacy
1220 S. Milledge Ave.
706-543-7386
Type: Old-fashioned soda fountain
An Athen's favorite, known for its generous scoops and good value.

Atlanta
Jake's Ice Cream and Sorbets
655 Highland Ave., 404-586-9972
(plus three other locations)
www.jakesicecream.com
Type: Scoop shop/Cafe
An Atlantan favorite featuring such creative flavors Nut Nanner Elvis, Diesel Fuel, and Coffee and Doughnuts.

Lexington Chocolatier
931 Monroe Dr. NE
404-875-0111
Type: Confectionery/Scoop shop
Ten flavors of ice cream are offered, all with made with an eye towards — what else — chocolate.

Paolo's Gelato
1025 Virginia Ave., N.E.
404-607-0055 (plus one South Carolina location)
www.paolosgelato.com
Type: Gelateria
Creamy gelato in such flavors as banana flambé, fig, jasmine, and hazelnut.

Roswell
The Calico Cow Creamery and Café
4401 Shallowford Rd.
678-205-3647
www.calicocow.com
Mail-Order: Yes
Type: Scoop shop/Cafe
Homemade ice cream in such flavors as Lemon Velvet, toasted coconut and Brownie Trifle.

Savannah
Chilly Vanilly Ice Cream Factory
7400 Abercorn St., Ste. 805
912-691-2088
Type: Scoop shop
Hand-crafted ice cream with a Southern twist, in such flavors as Savannah Lemon and Pralines and Cream.

Cafe Gelatohhh!
202 W. Saint Julian St.
(City Market), 912-234-2344

Type: Gelateria
There's always 24 flavors of freshly made gelato to choose from here.

HAWAII
Haleiwa
Matsumoto's Shave Ice
66-087 Kamehameha Hwy.
808-637-4827
www.matsumotoshaveice.com
Type: Shave ice shop/General store
Landmark shave ice stand. Have yours filled with ice cream and azuki beans and topped with shave ice and your choice of flavor.

Honolulu
Waiola Shave Ice
2135 Waiola Ave, 808-949-2269
(plus one other location)
Type: Walk-up stand
Shave ice stand known for its wide range of flavors, from Li Hing Mui to lychee.

Wai'anae
Dave's Hawaiian Ice Cream
85-786 Farrington Hwy.
808-696-9294 (plus eight other locations)
www.daveshawaiianicecream.com
Type: Scoop shop
Ice cream with a Hawaiian twist in such flavors as lychee, *poho*, *ube* and *haupia*.

IDAHO
Boise
Delsa's Ice Cream Parlour
7923 Ustick Rd., 208-375-3495
Type: Old-time parlor
For more than 40 years, Delsa's has served 16-percent butterfat ice cream in flavors such as Swiss Orange Chip and Maple Nut.

Coeur d'Alene
I.C. Sweets
602 E. Sherman Ave.
208-664-1549

www.icsweets.com
Type: Scoop shop/Custard stand
Try the Help Me Make It (Through the Night) sundae with four scoops of custard.

McCall
McCall Drug & Gifts
1001 N. 2nd St., 208-634-2433
Type: Old-fashioned soda fountain
Stop in for a Huckleberry milk shake or a hot fudge sundae at this circa-1940s fountain.

ILLINOIS
Chicago
Margie's Candies
1960 N. Western, 773-384-1035
www.margiescandies.com
Mail-Order: Yes, for hot fudge
Type: Old-time parlor
A Chicago landmark since 1921 that retains its charm and its signature turtle sundaes served in plastic clamshell bowls.

The Original Rainbow Cone
9233 South Western Ave.
773-238-7075 (plus one other location)
Open: Seasonally
Mail-Order: Yes, via www.bestofchicago.com
Type: Scoop shop
Since 1926, they've served up colorful cones, made from chocolate, strawberry, Palmer House and pistachio ice creams and orange sherbet.

Scooter's Frozen Custard
1658 W. Belmont Ave.
773-244-6415
www.scootersfrozencustard.com
Type: Scoop shop/Custard stand
Neighborhood shop with a new flavor each day; try one of their thick concrete shakes.

Zephyr Cafe
1777 W. Wilson Ave.
773-728-6070
Type: Diner
Art Deco-style with creative sundae creations bearing playful names, such as Son of Frankenstein and War of the Worlds.

Downers Grove
Every Day's a Sundae
5150 Main St., 630-810-9155
www.everydaysasundae.net
Type: Parlor
Known for huge sundaes, including the Cookies Lovers and the Pig's Dinner.

Homewood
Mitchell's Ice Cream and Candies
18211 Dixie Hwy., 708-799-3835
Type: Old-time parlor
Since 1931, Mitchell's has been known for its not-too-sweet ice cream and ice cream sodas in such flavors as Green River and peach.

Lebanon
Dr. Jazz Soda Fountain & Grille
230 W. St. Louis St.
618-537-2200
www.drjazzsodafountain.com
Type: Retro parlor
Try a George Bailey sundae (coconut ice cream with fudge and coconut) or, if you're really hungry, try the Ice Cream Overdose.

Moline
Lagomarcino's
1422 5th Ave., 309-764-1814
(plus one other location)
www.lagomarcinos.com
Type: Old-fashioned soda fountain
Pristine 1908 soda fountain known for its delicious hot fudge sauce, which is served on the side in a small pitcher.

Whitey's Ice Cream
2601 41st St., 888-5WHITEY
(plus 11 other locations)
www.whiteysicecream.com
Type: Old-time parlor
Try one of their upside-down candy bar shakes or a scoop of their chocolate chip cookie dough.

Mount Prospect
Capannari Ice Cream
10 S. Pine St., 847-392-2277
www.capannaris.com
Open: March 13–October 30
Type: Parlor
Quaint shop housed in a nineteenth-century building offers some of the richest ice cream in the Chicagoland area.

Oak Park
Petersen's Ice Cream
1100 Chicago Ave.,
708-386-6131
www.petersenicecream.com/default.htm
Type: Old-time parlor
An Oak Park institution for more than 80 years known for its rich, 18-percent butterfat ice cream.

Palos Park
The Plush Horse Ice Cream Parlour
12301 S. 86th Ave.
708-448-0550
www.theplushhorse.com
Type: Old-time parlor
Expect a line on weekends at this popular Chicago-area parlor; while you wait you can mull over the appetizing range of choices.

Peoria Heights
The Spotted Cow
4614 N. Prospect Rd.
309-682-8120
Type: Parlor
Homemade ice cream with clever flavor names, including Chip Happens and Moo-Newer.

Wilmette
Homer's Restaurant & Ice Cream Parlor
1237 Green Bay Rd.
847-251-0477
www.homersicecream.com
Mail-Order: Yes
Type: Old-time parlor
Since 1935, award-winning ice cream in 35 flavors, including Prairie Berry and Burgundy cherry.

INDIANA
Brazil
Lynn's Pharmacy
22 W. National Ave.
812-446-2381
www.lynnspharmacy.com
Type: Refurbished fountain
Old-fashioned soda fountain with an 1890s air and a display of old-time drugs and herbs.

Clarksville
The Widow's Walk
445 Riverside Dr., 812-280-7564
Type: Retro parlor
Right across the river from Louisville, Kentucky, this quaint Victorian-style home offers ice cream with a gorgeous view.

Columbus
Zaharako's
329 Washington St.
812-379-9329
Type: Old-fashioned soda fountain
A plain-Jane storefront hides the jewels inside: two Mexican onyx soda fountains, circa 1905, and intricate wood detailing.

Greenwood
Mrs. Curl Ice Cream Shop
259 S. Meridian St.
317-882-1031
www.mrscurl.com
Open: March 6–November 1
Type: Walk-up stand
Local favorite for soft-serve; bring

a crowd (10 or more people) and receive a 10 percent discount.

Indianapolis
Chris' Ice Cream
1405 E. 86th St., 317-255-2156
Type: Scoop shop
Ice cream made in small batches using 70-year-old rock salt and ice freezers.

Sundae's Homemade Ice Cream & Coffee Co.
9922 E. 79th St., 317-570-0533
(plus four other locations)
Type: Scoop shop
Georgia peach, lemon custard and other creamy flavors.

Lafayette
McCords Candy
536 Main St., 765-742-4441
Type: Old-fashioned soda fountain/Confectionery
Grab a stool at the white marble counter, order a sundae and time-travel back to 1912.

Original Frozen Custard
2319 Wallace Ave., 765-743-8024
(plus two other locations)
www.snowbearfc.com
Open: Seasonally
Type: Walk-up stand
Founded by the Kirkhoff family in 1932, this is believed to be the oldest continuously operated frozen custard stand in the country.

Madison
Mundt's Candy Sales & Soda Fountain
207 W. Main St., 812-265-6171
www.mundtscandies.com
Type: Old-fashioned soda fountain/Confectionery
A local landmark since 1917, Mundt's makes its own ice cream in a vintage 1948 Bastian-Blessing machine.

Rochester
Webb's Family Pharmacy
724 Main St., 574-224-WEBB
www.webbrx.com/fountain/
Fountain.htm
Type: Old-fashioned drug
store fountain
Fountain treats come with a
serving of history; Webb's dates
back to the 1860s.

Shelbyville
Compton Cow Palace
318 N. Harrison St.
317-392-4889 (plus one other
location)
Type: Restaurant/Parlor
Since 1969, customers flock here
for delicious shakes and 30-some
flavors of ice cream daily.

IOWA
Akeny
Blue Sky Creamery
107 NE Delaware #4
515-964-4366
www.blueskycreamery.com
Type: Scoop shop
Watch ice cream made with a flashy
liquid-nitrogen machine; the vapor
that spills out is cool to watch.

Des Moines
Bauder's Pharmacy
3802 Ingersoll Ave.
515-255-1124
Type: Old-fashioned soda fountain
A 1920s-era drugstore known for
its strawberry and peach ice cream
and the signature ice cream sandwiches it serves at the state fair.

Dubuque
**Betty Jane HomeMade
Candies & Ice Cream**
3049 Asbury Rd., 800-642-1254
www.bettyjanecandies.com
Type: Parlor/Confectionery
Super-premium ice cream in such
flavors as coconut almond cherry
and double fudge truffle.

Mason City
Birdsall's Ice Cream Co.
518 N. Federal Ave.
641-423-5365 (plus two
other locations)
Type: Old-style parlor
Not much has changed since it
opened in 1931; the ice cream is
still good and made on-site.

Sidney
Penn Drug Co.
714 Illinois St., 712-374-2513
Type: Old-fashioned soda fountain
Iowa's oldest drugstore fountain
(dating back to the 1890s) serves
up sodas, phosphates and sundaes.

Wilton
Wilton Candy Kitchen
310 Cedar St., 563-732-2278
Type: Old-fashioned soda
fountain/Confectionery
Longtime soda fountain and confectionery (this location dates back
to 1910) offers phosphates and a
rich sense of history.

KANSAS
Greensburg
**Hunter Drugstore & Old
Fashioned Soda Fountain**
121 S. Main St., 620-723-2331
Type: Old-fashioned soda fountain
Vanilla phosphate and chocolate
ice cream sodas served up from
a 1940s fountain in 1917-era
drugstore.

Lawrenceville
Sylas & Maddy's Home Made
1014 Massachusetts St.
785-832-8323
Type: Scoop shop
Forty flavors of ice cream, plus
a special flavor nominated by
customers each month.

Leavenworth
Corner Pharmacy
5th and Delaware, 913-682-1602
Type: Refurbished soda fountain
An 1880s drugstore pristinely
restored to its Victorian-era glory,
with a fountain featuring 43
bentwood mahogany stools
on which to enjoy your treats.

Lee's Summit
Custard's Last Stand
111 S. 291 Hwy., 816-524-7677
(plus four other locations)
Type: Scoop shop/Custard stand
Frozen custard made fresh on the
hour is a favorite among Kansas
City locals.

Topeka
Potwin Drug
Historic Ward-Meade Park
124 NW Fillmore, 785-368-3888
www.washburn.edu/cas/art/cyoho/
archive/AroundTopeka/ward-meade
Type: Old-fashioned soda fountain
Exact replica (using all parts) of
the 1902 fountain from the original
location of Potwin Drug.

WaKeeney
Cleland Drugstore
221 Main St., 785-743-2200
Gibson Health Mart Drug
125 N. Main St., 785-743-5753
Type: Old-fashioned soda fountains
WaKeeney's Main Street still boasts
two soda fountains: Cleland Drug
has a 1957 fountain and grill, and
Gibson's has a 24-foot-long soda
fountain that dates back to 1892.

Wichita
Freddy's Frozen Custard
621 W. 21st N., 316-722-2299
(plus one other location)
Type: Retro parlor
Concretes and turtle sundaes
are the specialties at this retro-feel
restaurant.

Old Mill Tasty Shop
604 E. Douglas Ave.
316-264-6500
Open: Days only
Type: Old-fashioned soda fountain
Since 1936, people have sat at
the 25-foot-long, black marble
counter and enjoyed authentic
sodas and banana splits.

KENTUCKY
Bellevue
Schneider's Sweet Shop
420 Fairfield Ave., 859-431-3545
www.schneiderscandies.com
Type: Parlor/Confectionery
Since 1939, Schneider's has been
serving the greater Cincinnati region
with its 17 flavors of homemade ice
cream and its signature ice balls.

Lexington
Jonathan at Gratz Park
120 W. 2nd St., 859-252-4949
www.jonathanatgratzpark.com
Type: Upscale restaurant
Chef Jonathan Lundy turns out
such flavors as toasted pecan,
pawpaw and strawberry
marscapone.

Louisville
**Homemade Ice Cream
and Pie Kitchen**
2525 Bardstown Rd.
502-459-8184
Type: Parlor/Bakery
For the ultimate indulgence,
pair a scoop of homemade ice
cream with one of their delicious
cakes or pies.

Plehn's Bakery
3940 Shelbyville Rd.
502-896-4438
Type: Bakery/Old-time parlor
Try the peppermint or caramel
ice creams, or a fountain treat.

LOUISIANA

Lafayette

Borden's
1103 Jefferson, 337-235-9291
Type: Old-time parlor
Art Deco-era Borden's store (as in Elsie the cow) still has flips and frappes and sundaes with wet nuts.

New Orleans

Angelo Brocato Ice Cream
214 N. Carrollton Ave.
504-486-0078
Type: Old-time parlor/Bakery
Ice cream with an Italian flair (try the spumoni) and a selection of Italian ices.

Brennan's
417 Royal St., 504-525-9711
www.brennansneworleans.com
Type: Upscale Restaurant
Bananas Foster (banana halves sautéed in brown sugar, butter, banana liqueur and rum and served with vanilla ice cream) was created at this local landmark in 1951.

Hansen's Sno-Bliz Sweet Shop
4801 Tchoupitoulas St.
504-891-9788
Open: Summers with limited hours; call first
Type: Walk-up stand
Local institution where the shave ice machine was invented and the syrups are still homemade.

Herbsaint
701 St. Charles Ave.
504-524-4114
www.herbsaint.com
Type: Upscale restaurant
There's always an ice cream of the day on the menu at this well-regarded and well-reviewed bistro; locals rave it's among the best in town.

Plum Street Snowball Stand
1300 Burdette St., 504-866-7996
Open: March-Early October
Type: Walk-up stand
Since 1935, there's been snowballs in 72 flavors; try one topped with condensed milk, whipped cream and chopped cherries.

Slidell

Old Town Slidell Soda Shop
301 Cousin St., 985-649-4806
www.slidellsodashop.com
Type: Retro parlor
Homemade ice cream sweetens the old-fashioned malts and sodas from the shop's fountain.

MAINE

Bar Harbor

Ben & Bill's Chocolate Emporium
66 Main St, 800-806-3281
(plus four other locations)
www.benandbills.com
Mail-Order: Yes
Type: Scoop shop/Confectionery
More than 50 homemade flavors of ice cream, including lobster with real chunks of lobster meat.

Farmington

Gifford's Dairy Bar
293 Main St., 207-778-3617
(plus three other locations)
www.giffordsicecream.com
Open: Mid-March–End of October
Type: Walk-up stand
Dairy bar for local manufacturer Gifford's, with flavors such as Maine Black Bear and Maine Deer Tracks.

Gray

Cole Farms
Route 100, 207-657-4714
www.colefarms.com
Type: Restaurant
Nearly everything is made from scratch here, including the delicious ice cream.

Newfield

Willowbrook at Newfield
77 Elm St., 207-793-2784
www.willowbrookmuseum.org
Open: May 15–September 30
Type: Old-time parlor
Ice cream lovers should seek out the period ice cream parlor at this nineteenth-century museum.

Crystal Spring Farm
1413 Main St. (Route 26)
207-743-6723
Type: Farm stand
For more than 35 years, the Smedberg's Jersey cows have produced delicious "one-cow ice cream."

Portland

Beal's Old-Fashioned Ice Cream
18 Moulton St., 207-828-1335
Open: Seasonally
Type: Walk-up stand
Some 40 flavors to choose from, plus Swiss cones made fresh on-site each day.

Little Lad's Bakery
482 Congress St., 207-871-1636
Type: Vegan bakery/Restaurant
There's no dairy here (they're vegan), but they do offer homemade "nice cream," made from soy milk, in more than 15 flavors.

Scarborough

Len Libby Candies
419 U.S. Route 1, 207-883-4897
www.lenlibby.com
Open: Ice cream is only available in summer
Type: Confectionery
Ice cream is made in-house, in such flavors as Needham, cashew caramel and coffee toffee.

South Portland

Red's Dairy Freeze
167 Cottage Rd., 207-799-7506
Open: Seasonally

Type: Walk-up stand
Since 1952, this local fixture has served up ice cream in 50 flavors and thick Nor' Easters shakes.

Stow

Stow Corner Store & Bakery
Route 113, 207-697-2943
Type: Scoop shop/Bakery
Grab a stool at the counter and enjoy one of their huge ice cream cones.

Westbrook

Smiling Hill Farm
Route 22 (County Road)
207-775-4818, ext.13
www.smilinghill.com
Type: Dairy bar
There's always 20 farm-fresh flavors to choose from at this longtime working dairy farm.

York

Brown's Old Fashioned Ice Cream
232 Nubble Rd., 207-363-1277
Open: May 1–Columbus Day
Type: Walk-up stand
For more than 40 years, Brown's has served up flavors like mint oreo and blueberry in a picturesque setting by the Nubble Lighthouse.

MARYLAND

Annapolis

Aromi D'Italia
8 Dock St., 410-263-1300
Type: Gelateria
The retail store for the country's largest gelato supplier (to 300 stores nationally).

Baltimore

Note: Snowballs are a popular area treat and in the summer, stands abound. Ask a local for their favorite spot.

Lee's Ice Cream
301 S. Light St., Harborplace's
Light Street Pavilion
410-727-8776
(plus six other locations)
www.leesicecream.com
Type: Scoop shop
Known for its Oreo cookie ice
cream, snowballs and homemade
hot fudge.

Vaccaro's Italian Pastry Shop
222 Albemarle St., 410-685-4905
(plus five other locations)
www.vaccarospastry.com
Type: Gelateria/Pastry shop
A long-time fixture of the Little
Italy neighborhood serves up
gelato and granita.

Bethesda
Bob's Famous Ice Cream & Deli
4706 Bethesda Ave.
301-657-2963
Type: Scoop shop/Deli
Known for flavors such as
Mozambique (made with cinnamon,
nutmeg and cloves) and orange
chocolate chip.

**Gifford's Ice Cream
& Candy Co.**
7237 Woodmont Ave.
301-907-3436
www.giffords.com
Type: Parlor/Confectionery
Homemade since 1938, with flavors
such as honey melon, champagne
sorbet and coconut almond chip.

Bowie
Simple Pleasures Ice Café
6948 Laurel-Bowie Rd.
301-809-5880
www.simplepleasuresicecafe.com
Type: Cafe/Scoop shop
Homemade ice cream in flavors
such as tiramisu, Apple Dapple and
strawberry shortcake, served in
a genteel setting.

Burtonsville
**Seibel's Ice Cream
& Dairy Store**
15540 Old Columbia Pike
301-384-5661
Type: Parlor/Dairy bar
Since 1939, Seibels has churned
out ice cream in classic flavors
from honey to the more modern
Reese's Pieces.

Hampstead
Simmons Store
2841 Snydersburg Rd.
410-374-2310
Type: Country store
There are usually just three flavors
to choose from, but it's ultra-fresh
and scooped directly from tubs
that are wrapped in newspaper to
prevent melting.

Havre de Grace
**Bomboy's Home Made
Ice Cream**
322 Market St., 410-939-2924
www.bomboycandies.com
Open: Easter–Early Fall
Type: Parlor
Local favorite confectionery
expanded into ice cream–making
in 2001 with such flavors as Hokey
Pokey and Duck Duck Goose.

Ocean City
Dumser's
4901 Coastal Hwy., 410-524-1588
(plus three other locations)
www.beach-net.com/dumsers
Type: Old-fashioned parlor
A boardwalk fixture since 1939 with
a large selection of flavors and sundaes like Gorilla's Treat and the
Dieter's Revenge.

Rock Hall
Durding's Store
5742 Main St., 410-778-7957
www.sailingemporium.com/
durdings.htm
Type: Old-fashioned soda fountain

A town fixture for more than 80
years, known for its milk shakes
and quaint charm.

Silver Spring
York Castle Tropical Ice Cream
9324 Georgia Ave., 301-589-1616
Type: Scoop shop
Known for their fruity flavors, such
as piña colada, papaya, soursop
and mango.

Timonium Maryland
Jay's Shave Ice
2046 York Rd., 410-561-0405
www.jaysshaveice.com
Type: Walk-up stand
Hawaiian-style shave ice in
such flavors as Tiger Blood
and Whiskey Sour.

Towson
Moxley's Ice Cream Parlor
25 W. Allegheny Ave.
410-825-2544
(plus two other locations)
www.moxleys.com
Mail-Order: Yes
Type: Scoop shop
Named for the owner's dog,
Moxley's is known for its smooth
ice cream in flavors such as Funky
Monkey and Mojo.

Westminster
**Hoffman's Home Made
Ice Cream**
934 Washington Rd.
410-857-0824
www.hoffmansicecream.com
Type: Parlor
Expect a long line of hungry fans in
summer, waiting to sample ice
cream that's still made according
the original 1947 recipe.

MASSACHUSETTS
Amherst
Barts Homemade
103 N. Pleasant St., 413-253-
9371 (plus one other location)

www.bartshomemade.com
Type: Scoop shop
Favorite of area college students,
Barts is known for fun flavors
like French Toast and Choca-
chew-setts.

Boston/Cambridge
J.P. Licks
352 Newbury St., 617-236-1666
(plus six other locations)
Type: Scoop shop
Mind-boggling array of flavors,
from Sam Adams Cream Stout
and cranberry-and-vodka to maple
butter walnut and vanilla hazelnut.

**Christina's Homemade
Ice Cream**
1255 Cambridge St.
617-492-7021
Type: Scoop shop
Creative, gourmet ice cream in
such flavors as carrot cake, lemon
verbena and blood peach. Rated
Boston's best by several local
media outlets.

Toscanini's Ice Cream
899 Main St.
617-491-5877
(plus three other locations)
www.tosci.com
Type: Scoop shop
Nationally awarded and recognized
for its exotic and sublime ice cream
in flavors such as cardamom, burnt
caramel and Guinness.

Centerville
Four Seas Ice Cream
360 S. Main St., 508-775-1394
www.fourseasicecream.com
Open: Saturday before Memorial
Day–Sunday after Labor Day
Type: Scoop shop
A lively Cape Cod landmark
since 1934, drawing crowds for
delicious ice cream in such flavors
as penuche pecan and lemon.

Carlisle
Great Brook Farm State Park
984 Lowell Rd.
978-369-6312
www.state.ma.us/dem /parks/gbfm.htm
Open: April–October
Type: Farm stand
A state park that's a working dairy farm, too. Try one of the 68 flavors of ice cream in a lovely pastoral setting.

Haverhill
England's Microcreamery
109 Washington St.
978-373-6400
www.microcreamery.com
Type: Scoop shop
Homemade ice cream with your choice of mix-ins, hand-folded on a granite slab.

Hyde Park
Ron's Gourmet Homemade Ice Cream & Bowling
1231 Hyde Park Ave.
617-364-5274
Type: Parlor/Bowling alley
Try one of 32 flavors of ice cream (like baked brownie), before or after you've bowled a few games.

Middleton
Richardson's Ice Cream
156 S Main St.
978-774-5450
www.richardsonsicecream.com
Type: Dairy bar
There are 55 flavors of farm-fresh ice cream and an array of activities at this lively farm stand.

Newtonville
Cabot's
743 Washington St.
617-964-9200
www.cabots.com
Type: Parlor/Restaurant
The ice cream menu alone is six pages long. Create your own treat or choose from one of their 16 signature sundaes.

Northampton
Herrell's Ice Cream
8 Old South Street (in Thorne's Market), 413-586-9700
(plus two Boston locations)
www.herrells.com
Type: Scoop shop
Steve Herrell invented the mix-in slab concept. His ice cream flavors are famous, too; the chocolate pudding is top-notch.

Sharon
Crescent Ridge Dairy
355 Bay Rd., 800-660-2740
www.crescentridge.com
Type: Dairy bar
The dairy store offers milk and 31 flavors of ice cream, including toasted walnut fudge and orange pineapple.

South Hadley
McCray's Farm and Country Creamery
55 Alvord St., 413-533-0775
www.mccraysfarm.com
Open: Mid-April–Mid-November
Type: Farm stand
Petting farm, sugar house and fresh and creamy homemade ice cream.

Yarmouthport
Hallet's
139 Main St. (Route 6A)
508-362-3362
www.hallets.com
Open: Seasonally
Type: Old-fashioned soda fountain
An 1889 drugstore with a soda fountain that serves treats and bottles its brand of soda.

Waltham
Lizzy's Homemade Ice Cream
367 Moody St., 781-893-6677
www.lizzysicecream.com
Type: Parlor
Homemade hot fudge and 35 homemade flavors, from Mocha Chocolate Lace to Chocolate Orgy.

Westford
Kimball Farm Ice Cream & Restaurant
400 Littleton Rd., 978-486-3891
(plus two other locations)
www.kimballfarm.com
Type: Walk-up stand
Since 1939, this local favorite offers 40 flavors of ice cream, bumper boats rides, pitch-and-putt and more.

Vineyard Haven
Mad Martha's
20 Union St., 508-693-5883
(plus two other locations)
Open: May–October
Type: Parlor
Local institution since 1971, serving up 26 flavors and a 12-scoop Pig's Delight sundae.

MICHIGAN
Stucchi's
302 S. State St., 734-662-1700
(plus two other locations)
Type: Scoop shop
Features 16 flavors of ice cream, to which you can add toppings to make their signature Smushins.

Washtenaw Dairy
602 S. Ashley, 734-662-3244
Type: Old-time parlor/Dairy bar
A local fixture since the 1930s known for their homemade doughnuts and generous scoops of ice cream.

Dowagiac
Caruso's Candy Kitchen
130 S. Front St., 269-782-6001
(plus one other location)
www.carusoscandy.com
Type: Old-fashioned soda fountain/Confectionery
Have a Pink Lady at their vintage 1929 soda fountain with marble top and a mirrored back bar.

Lincoln Park
Calder Brothers Dairy
1020 Southfield Rd.
313-381-8858
(plus a location in Carleton)
Type: Parlor/Dairy bar
At this almost 60-year-old dairy, they've made ice cream since 1970 in small batches with the dairy's milk and the same recipe.

Northville
Guernsey Farms Dairy
21300 Novi Rd., 248-349-1466
guernseyfarmsdairy.com
Type: Scoop shop/Dairy bar
Family-owned since 1940, the shop sells ice cream in 48 flavors.

Petoskey
American Spoon Foods Gelato Café
413 E. Lake, 231-347-1739
www.spoon.com
Mail-Order: Yes
Type: Gelateria
Located next to the factory store of fine foods purveyor American Spoon, you'll find gelato and sorbetto in 24 flavors.

Rochester
Red Knapp's Dairy Bar
304 N. Main St., 248-651-4545
Type: Old-fashioned soda fountain/Diner
For more than 50 years, this diner has served up Boston coolers, Brown Cows and malts.

Royal Oak
Ray's
4233 Coolidge Hwy.
888-549-5256
www.raysicecream.com
Mail-Order: Yes
Type: Parlor
Sample their ice cream (try the lemon or cinnamon) and ask about their beautiful, molded ice cream creations.

Saugatuck
Saugatuck Drugstore
201 Butler St., 269-857-2300
Open: Seasonally
Type: Old-fashioned soda fountain
A 1920s fountain that still serves pineapple creamed sodas and Mount Baldhead sundaes with four scoops of ice cream and four toppings.

Saint Clair Shores
Stroh's Ice Cream
31359 Harper Ave.
586-294-2440
Type: Parlor
Founded during Prohibition when the Stroh's brewery got into the ice cream business, Stroh's ice cream continues to be Detroit's best-selling brand. Sample it at this sweet-looking parlor.

Shelby Township
Erma's Original Frozen Custard
6451 Auburn Rd., 586-254-3080
www.ermascustard.com
Open: April 1–October 31
Type: Custard stand/Walk-up stand
When it opened in 1942, there was only vanilla custard served in bowls. Now there are custard puffs and frozen tea infusions.

South Haven
Sherman's Finest
1601 Phoenix Rd., 269-637-8251
www.shermanicecream.com
Open: March–October
Type: Dairy bar
Sample six mini-scoops of Sherman's 40 flavors in its Tour of Sherman's bowl.

Traverse City
Moomer's
7263 N. Long Lake Rd.
231-941-4122
Type: Farm stand/Scoop shop
Have a turtle sundae or a Vernor's float on the deck and watch the cows graze below.

MINNESOTA
Duluth
PortLand Malt Shoppe
716 E. Superior St., no phone
www.portlandmaltshoppe.com
Open: April 1–October 19
Type: Scoop shop/Walk-up stand
Charming lakeside shop, housed in an old gas station, that serves up fountain treats and ice cream.

Excelsior
Adele's Frozen Custard
800 Excelsior Blvd.
952-470-0035
Open: Seasonally
Type: Custard stand
Frozen custard with a featured flavor each day and luscious turtle sundaes, right across from Lake Minnetonka.

Minneapolis
Crema Café
3403 Lyndale Ave. S.
612-824-3868
Open: Year-round, with limited hours in winter
Type: Parlor/Cafe
Owned by the makers of Sonny's Ice Cream, try the Crema, grapefruit Campari sorbet, green tea or Cabernet chocolate chip.

Edina Creamery
5055 France Avenue S.
612-920-2169
Type: Retro fountain
Grab a stool at the counter and sample Nut Goodie Cream or triple chocolate in a fresh-baked cone.

Livingston's
2037 Riverside Ave.
612-333-5692
Type: Cafe/Scoop shop
Owner Melody Livingston makes just two flavors but she makes them with organic cream and dresses them up in heavenly floats and sundaes.

Pumphouse Creamery
4754 Chicago Ave. S.
612-825-2021
www.pumphousecreamery.com
Open: Seasonally
Type: Scoop shop
This newcomer shows promise with such flavors as malted vanilla with Turtle Bread Company's chocolate bread and oatmeal cookie.

Sebastian Joe's Ice Cream Cafe
1007 W. Franklin Ave.
612-870-0065 (plus one other location)
Type: Scoop shop
Full-flavored ice cream, including a cayenne-peppered Chocolate Coyote, raspberry chocolate chip and vanilla made with real vanilla beans.

St. Paul
Grand Ole Creamery
750 Grand Ave., 651-665-0094
Type: Scoop shop
Homemade waffle cones are filled first with a malted milk ball to keep them from dripping and then topped with their rich ice cream.

Izzy's Ice Cream Café
2034 Marshall Ave., 651-603-1458
www.izzysicecream.com
Type: Scoop shop
All scoops, in flavors like fig tart, red Zinfandel and cherries jubilee, come with a small, "Izzy" scoop on top.

Snuffy's Malt Shop
1125 Larpenteur Ave. W.
651-488-0241 (plus one other location)
Type: Diner/Retro fountain
Well, they're named for their malts, and locals swear they're the best around.

MISSISSIPPI
Hattiesburg
Walnut Square Pharmacy and Ice Cream Parlor
124 Walnut St., 601-543-0111
Type: Retro fountain/Deli
There's an old-fashioned feel with a wood bar, stools and tables. Blue Bell ice cream is served up in milk shakes and banana splits.

Hernando
Velvet Cream
2290 Hwy. 51 S., 662-429-6540
Type: Walk-up Stand/Parlor
Known to locals as "The Dip," this greater Memphis stand has been serving up Mule Slobbers and Orange Orangutans since 1947.

Waveland
Waveland Pharmacy
112 Auderer Blvd., 228-463-1055
Type: Retro fountain
New Orleans nectar sodas, cream cheese ice cream and gelato.

MISSOURI
Ferguson
Whistle Stop Depot
1 Carson Rd., 314-521-1600
www.whistlestopdepot.com
Open: Mid–January–Mid–December
Type: Parlor
Located in an historic train depot, the frozen custard creations all have a train theme (such as Fast Tracks or End of the Line).

Florissant
Fritz's Frozen Custard
1055 St. Catherine St.
314-839-4100 (plus other locations)
Type: Parlor/Custard stand
Custard shop known for its
turtle sundae.

Independence
Clinton's Soda Fountain
100 W. Maple, 816-833-2046
Type: Old-fashioned soda fountain
See where Harry Truman earned
his first paycheck and sample
Harry's favorite sundae, too —
chocolate with butterscotch
topping.

Kansas City
Foo's Fabulous Frozen Custard
6235 Brookside Plaza
816-523-2520
Type: Scoop shop/Custard stand
Known for its thick milk shake-like
creations called cements, available
in 20 flavors.

Murray's Ice Creams & Cookies
4120 Pennsylvania Ave.
816-931-5646
Open: March–December
Type: Scoop shop
Try one of their 16 homemade
flavors, or order a Lumpy, a milk
shake that's blended with a spoon.

Jefferson City
Central Dairy
610 Madison St., 573-635-6148
Type: Old-time parlor
A local landmark since 1933 with
wooden booths, a marble counter
and the four-scoop Rock 'n Roll
banana split.

Liberty
The Hardware Cafe
5 E. Kansas St., 816-792-3500
Type: Refurbished fountain
Featuring a 1930s soda fountain

rescued from another store; it still
serves Brown Cows, ice cream
sodas and homemade cherry
limeades.

Osceola
Scott's Iconium Store
12770 C Highway, 417-646-2221
www.scottsiconiumstore.com
Mail-Order: Yes, for Nehi soda only
Type: General store/Walk-up stand
Known for their floats made with
hard-to-find Peach Nehi soda;
they sell some 12,000 of them
each year.

Springfield
Andy's Frozen Custard
3147 E. Sunshine St., 417-881-
2820 (plus two other locations)
Type: Walk-up stand/Custard stand
Popular items include a turtle con-
crete and a Woody P.
Snowmonster concrete.

St. Louis
Crown Candy Kitchen
1401 St. Louis Ave.
314-621-9650
www.crowncandykitchen.com
Type: Old-fashioned soda
fountain/Confectionery
A St. Louis institution since 1913,
offering butterscotch malts, fruit
salad sundaes and Johnny Rabbit
shakes.

Ted Drewes' Frozen Custard
6726 Old Chippewa Rd. (Route
66), 314-481-2652 (plus one
other location)
www.teddrewes.com
Mail-Order: Yes, via telephone
Open: Closed January
Type: Walk-up stand/Custard stand
Legendary Ted Drewes has been
serving up its signature frozen custard in sundaes and thick upside-
down concretes since 1929.

MONTANA
Big Timber
Cole Drug
136 McLeod, 406-932-5316
Type: Old-fashioned soda fountain
Huckleberry sundaes, bitterroot
floats and the huge, nine-scoop Big
Timber sundae.

Conrad
Olson's Drug
5 Fourth Ave., 406-278-3261
Type: Old-fashioned soda fountain
This all-original 1927 fountain with
a marble counter, mahogany back
bar and brass lights is the oldest
operating fountain in the state.

Ennis
Ennis Pharmacy/Yesterday's
Restaurant & Soda Fountain
124 Main St., 406-682-4246
Type: Refurbished fountain
Early 1900s pink marble fountain
serves up treats in equally authen-
tic antique dessert glasses.

Helena
The Parrot Confectionery
42 N. Last Chance Gulch
406-442-1470
Type: Confectionery/Old-fashioned
soda fountain
A 1922 landmark candy shop
and soda fountain where you can
still get cherry phosphates and
caramel cashew sundaes.

Missoula
Big Dipper Ice Cream
631 S. Higgins, 406-721-8713
www.bigdippericecream.com
Type: Walk-up stand
Dip into some of the stand's
intriguing flavors, such as
cardamom, black licorice,
honey Porter or Irish whiskey.

Goldsmith's Premium
Ice Cream
809 E. Front St., 406-549-8826
Type: Parlor
Homemade ice cream available
with your choice of mix-ins, all
incorporated slabbery-style on
a cold stone.

Superior
Superior Drugstore
105 Mullan Rd. E., 406-822-4242
Type: Old-fashioned soda fountain
A step back to 1918, with an
original soda fountain and period
decor.

Townsend
The Creamery Café
108 N. Front St., 406-266-5254
Type: Restaurant/Parlor
Family-style restaurant also serves
up 24 flavors of Montana-made
Wilcoxson's ice cream.

West Yellowstone
Eagle's Store
3 Canyon St., 406-646-9300
www.eaglecompany.com
Type: General store/Old-fashioned
soda fountain
A 1910 mahogany and gray
marble soda fountain with 20
stools still serves up treats topped
with Mom Eagle's original
chocolate sauce.

NEBRASKA
Atkinson
R.F. Goeke Variety and
Old-Fashioned Soda Fountain
110 S. Main St., 402-925-2263
(plus a location with fountain
in Bassett)
www.geocities.com/goekevariety/
index.html
Type: Refurbished fountain/
Variety store
Have a black cow or a haystack
sundae at this 1950s-era fountain.

Louisville

**Blake's Old Fashioned
Soda Fountain**
213 Main St., 402-234-4095
Type: Old-fashioned soda fountain
All-original 1930s fountain serves
up such treats as a Dream (vanilla
ice cream, orange sherbet and
orange soda).

Omaha

Lafata's Caffe Italiano
2304 N. 72nd St., 402-397-1347
Type: Restaurant/Gelateria
Authentic gelato and granita made
by Italian natives in such fresh
flavors as pistachio, strawberry
and lemon.

**Ted and Wally's
Ice Cream Store**
1120 Jackson St., 402-341-5827
Type: Parlor
Since 1986, homemade ice cream
(Dutch chocolate, lemon ginger,
chamomile) has been served up
alongside live music in Omaha's
Old Market.

Springfield

Springfield Drug
205 Main St., 402-253-2000
Type: Old-fashioned soda fountain
This 1935 fountain, with four back
bars, serves up foamy Pink Clouds
made from 7 UP and strawberry
ice cream.

NEVADA

Ely

Steptoe Drug
504 Aultman St., 775-289-2671
Type: Old-fashioned soda fountain
Originally in the Hotel Nevada,
it was moved across the street
in 1926. Today, it offers shakes,
sundaes and Lime Rickeys.

Las Vegas

**Danielle's Chocolates
& Ice Cream**
6394 W. Sahara Ave.
702-259-7616
Type: Parlor/Confectionery
More than 38 homemade flavors
on the menu, from maple nut to
caramel coconut.

Luv-It Frozen Custard
505 E. Oakey Blvd.
702-384-6452
www.luvitfrozencustard.com
Type: Walk-up stand/Custard stand
Local favorite for custard. Try a
Western sundae or one of their
best-selling flavors of the day:
banana nut, tart lemon or butter
pecan.

Virginia City

Red's Old-Fashioned Candies
68 South C St., 775-847-0404
www.redscandies.com
Type: Confectionery/Old-time
parlor
Nevada's oldest candy store has a
parlor that serves Breyers ice
cream and homemade waffle
cones and bowls.

NEW HAMPSHIRE

Concord

Arnie's Place
64 Loudon Rd., 603-228-3225
www.arniesplace.com
Open: Late February–
Columbus Day
Type: Diner/Walk-up stand
Located in a converted Dairy
Queen, Arnie's draws crowds for
its hard ice cream made with
quality ingredients.

Hillsboro

Central Square Ice Cream
5 W. Main St., 603-464-3881
Type: Retro parlor
Old-fashioned charm with black
and white tiled floors and soda
fountain glassware. Have a shake,
or sample their bestselling flavor,
ginger.

Hopkinton

**Beech Hill Farmstand
and Ice Cream Barn**
107 Beech Hill Rd., 603-224-7655
Open: Seasonally
Type: Farm stand/Parlor
At this 110-year-old dairy farm,
the Kimball family serves up some
55 flavors of ice cream in a
pastoral setting.

Manchester

Cremeland Drive In
250 Valley St., 603-641-6663
Open: Seasonally
Type: Drive-in/Walk-up stand
A landmark since 1947, they
started offering homemade ice
cream in the 1980s known for
its high butterfat and generous
amounts of add-ins.

Goldenrod Restaurant & Drive In
1681 Candia Rd., 603-623-9469
Type: Drive-in/Restaurant
Long lines flock here for generous
scoops of ice cream and events
like line dancing and antique car
shows.

Merrimack

King Kone
Route 3, 603-424-6848
Open: Seasonally
Type: Roadside Stand
A local favorite for soft-serve ice
cream in flavors beyond the usual
chocolate and vanilla

Nashua

Hayward's Ice Cream
7 Daniel Webster Hwy. S
603-888-4663 (plus a location
in Milford)
www.haywardsicecream-nh.com
Open: Valentines Day–Columbus Day
Type: Walk-up stand
Open for more than 60 years,
Hayward's spends three hours
training new employees on proper
scooping techniques.

Portsmouth

**Annabelle's Natural Ice Cream
and Frozen Yogurt**
49 Ceres St., 603-436-3400
(plus other locations)
www.annabellesicecream.com
Type: Scoop Shop
Since Annabelle's is known
for super-premium ice cream,
made chunky with lots of added
ingredients.

Rye

Lago's Lone Oak Ice Cream
U.S. Route 1, 603-964-9880
(plus a location in Rochester)
www.lagos-lone-oak.com/
Open: Spring–early Fall
Type: Scoop shop
Try one of their 70 homemade
flavors or one of their signature
Polar Joes.

Weirs Beach

Kellerhaus
Route 3, 603-366-4466
www.kellerhaus.com
Type: Parlor/Confectionery
The oldest candy makers (since
1906) and the oldest ice cream
makers (since the 1920s) in the
Granite State.

NEW JERSEY

Beach Haven

Show Place Ice Cream Parlour
Center Street and Beach Avenue,
609-492-0018
www.lbinet.com/surflight/
showplac.htm
Open: Memorial Day–Labor Day
Type: Cabaret/Parlor
Huge sundaes delivered up during
nightly performances where the
waitstaff sings and dances and the
customers get in on the act, too.

Freehold

Jersey Freeze
120 Manalapan Ave.
732-462-3008

Type: Walk-up stand
For more than 50 years, Jersey Freeze has been serving up its creamy soft serve in 20 flavors.

Highland Park
Corner Confectionary Shop
248 Raritan Ave., 732-246-7373
www.cornerconfectionary.com
Type: Old-time parlor/Confectionery
There are egg cream and scoops of Sedutto's ice cream sold from this vintage 1924 soda fountain.

Ledgewood
Cliff's Dairy Maid
1475 Route 46, 973-584-9721
http://cliffsdm.home.att.net/
Type: Walk-up stand
A local fixture since the 1940s, Cliff's serves homemade ice cream in flavors such as caramel nut cluster, cotton candy and Dutch apple crumble.

Mount Laurel
Lollypops
200 Larchmont Blvd.
856-231-7677
www.lollypopsicecream.com
Mail-Order: Yes, via telephone
Type: Scoop shop/Parlor
Lollypops is sugar-sweet, with bright murals on the walls and a kid-friendly atmosphere.

Newark
Nasto's Olde World Desserts
236-40 Jefferson St.
973-589-3333
Type: Bakery/Parlor
Since 1939, Nasto's has been serving up cherry vanilla and 20 some other flavors of homemade ice cream and Italian ice.

New Brunswick
Thomas Sweet
55 Easton Ave., 732-828-3855
(plus two other locations)

Type: Parlor/Confectionery
Known for their delicious homemade ice cream blend-ins, where you can pick from a range of ingredients to be mixed in.

Rahway
Piece of Cake
62 W. Inman Ave., 732-382-0281
Type: Ice cream pie bakery
There are no cones or scoops on the menu here, just slices of scrumptious, made-from-scratch ice cream pie.

Spring Lake
Susan Murphy's Homemade Ice Cream
601 Warren Ave., 732-449-1130
www.icecreamhomemade.com
Type: Scoop shop
Super-premium ice cream, apple crisp sundaes, and, on its website, a guide to eating a cone.

Stone Harbor
Springer's Homemade Ice Cream
9420 Third Ave., 609-368-4631
www.springersicecream.com
Type: Old-time parlor
Since Prohibition, folks have visited Springer's. Try the Potpourri flavor, a mixture of leftover flavors available for half price.

Upper Montclair
Applegate Farms
616 Grove St., 973-744-5900
(plus three other locations)
www.applegatefarm.com
Mail-Order: Yes, via 800-784-3848
Type: Farm stand/Parlor
Set on a farmstead dating back to 1848, Applegate has been dishing up ice cream since the 1920s.

NEW MEXICO
Arroyo Seco
Taos Cow
482 NM 150, 505-776-5640

Type: Scoop shop
All-natural, artisanal ice cream in such flavors as lavender, ginger chocolate chip and cherry ristra.

Las Cruces
Caliche's Frozen Custard
590 South Valley Dr.
505-521-1161 (plus other locations)
Type: Walk-up stand/Custard stand
Frozen custard served up with a choice of 60-some toppings, including green chile.

Sante Fe
Delectables
720 St. Michaels Dr.
505-438-8152
Type: Cafe/Parlor
Pick from such homemade flavors as pumpkin ice cream or scarlet wine sorbet.

NEW YORK
Aurora
Dorie's
283 Main St., 315-364-8818
Type: Old-fashioned soda fountain
A 1900s soda fountain serving up brownie sundaes and other treats.

Bedford
La Crémaillère Restaurant
46 Bedford-Banksville Rd.
914-234-9647
www.frenchicecream.com
Mail-Order: Yes
Type: Restaurant
The restaurant's well-regarded Crème Crémaillère ice cream is served here in such flavors as crème brûlée, fraises des bois and chocolat Suzette.

Brooklyn
Brooklyn Ice Cream Factory
Fulton Ferry Landing (between Old Fulton and Water streets)
718-246-3963
Type: Scoop shop

Much like the Brooklyn Bridge that shadows over this shop, the ice cream is classic, well-made and a landmark in its own right.

Spumoni Gardens
2725 86th St., 718-449-6921
www.spumonigardens.com
Type: Restaurant/Walk-up stand
Since 1939, delicious pizza and paper cups full of lemon ice or their signature sherbet-like spumoni ice cream.

Buffalo
Parkside Candy Co.
3208 Main St, 716-833-7540
Type: Old-time parlor/Confectionery
Have a sundae in grand style at this elegant 1930s-era parlor.

Colonie
Kurver Kreme
1349 Central Ave., 518-459-4120
Open: Seasonally
Type: Walk-up stand
Albany landmark known for its towering soft-serve cones.

Greece
Buckman's Bakery and Ice Cream
2576 Ridge Rd. W., 585-225-7720
Type: Bakery/Parlor
Handmade ice cream that's still made according to a 1914 recipe.

Kenmore
Anderson's Frozen Custard
2235 Sheridan Dr., 716-875-5952
(plus eight other locations)
www.andersonscustard.com
Mail-Order: Yes
Type: Walk-up stand/Custard stand
Buffalo-area fixture since the 1940s serves up chocolate, vanilla and a flavor of the day.

Lido Beach

Marvel's Dairy Whip
258 Lido Blvd., 516-889-4232
Open: Seasonally
Type: Walk-up stand
For more than 50 years, Long Islanders have come for coffee soft-serve, hand-dipped vanilla Brown Bonnets and Flying Saucer cookie sandwiches.

Massapequa

Krisch's Restaurant and Ice Cream Parlour
11 Central Ave., 516-797-3149
www.krischs.com
Type: Old-time parlor
Locals flock here for the authentic 1950s atmosphere, complete with a soda fountain, 10 stools and homemade ice cream.

New York City

Bespeckled Trout
422 Hudson St., 212-255-1421
Type: Retro Parlor/Confectionery
Sweet as can be shop that serves up authentic fountain treats. Don't miss the egg cream.

Chinatown Ice Cream Factory
65 Bayard St., 212-608-4170
www.chinatownicecream
factory.com
Type: Scoop shop
Try one of the signature Asian-inspired flavors: almond cookie, red bean, taro or lychee.

Cones
272 Bleeker St., 212-414-1795
Type: Gelateria
Argentinian-style gelato in flavors such as *dulce de leche*, blueberry and dark chocolate.

Il Laboratorio Del Gelato
95 Orchard St., 212-343-9922
www.laboratoriodelgelato.com
Mail-Order: Yes, via www.
manhattanfruitier.com

Type: Scoop shop
Owner Jon Snyder is a true master. All of his flavors — from *fromage blanc* to green grape to black sesame — are ice cream at its absolute best.

Otto Enteca Pizzeria
One Fifth Ave., 212-995-9559
www.ottopizzeria.com
Type: Restaurant/Gelateria
Make sure you leave room for dessert here. The gelati and sorbetti are exquisite, with flavors such as olive oil, campari-grapefruit and ricotta.

Ronnybrook Farm Dairy
75 Ninth Ave. (Chelsea Marketplace), 518-398-6455
www.ronnybrook.com
Mail-Order: Yes, via www.icecream
source.com
Type: Stand
Ronnybrook Farm is based in upstate New York, but they have this retail outlet in the Big Apple.

Serendipity 3
225 E. 60th St., 212-838-3531
www.serendipity3.com
Mail-Order: Yes, for Frrrozen Hot Chocolate mix
Type: Parlor
You'll want to get a reservation at this landmark parlor, known for its overflowing sundaes and Frrrozen Hot Chocolate.

Oxford

Hoppie's Ice Cream Parlor
19 E. State St., 607-843-2663
Open: Seasonally
www.hoppies.com
Type: Old-fashioned soda fountain
Their vintage fountain turns out an array of sundaes from the 25-scoop Kitchen Sink to the PB&J to the Candy Bar.

Queens

Eddie's Sweet Shop
105-29 Metropolitan Ave.
718-520-8514
Type: Old-time parlor
A century-old parlor with metal stools and lots of wood and charm, where they still make the ice cream and toppings.

Jahn's
117-03 Hillside Ave.
718-847-2800
www.jahnsicecream.com
Type: Old-time parlor
Parlor dates back to 1897, with Tiffany-style lamps, a Nickelodeon and an extensive fountain menu.

Lemon Ice King of Corona
52nd Avenue and 108th Street
718-699-5133
Type: Walk-up stand
For more than 60 years Pete Benfaremo has been serving up Italian ice. Try the lemon or orange, made with fresh fruit, or the peanut.

Max & Mina's
71-26 Main St., 718-793-8629
Type: Scoop Shop
There's ice cream in unusual flavors (ketchup and Nova lox), but the good news is that they aren't just weird; they actually taste good. Plus, tasty traditional flavors, too.

Riverhead

Snowflake Ice Cream Shoppe
1148 W. Main St., 631-727-4394
Type: Parlor
Homemade ice cream in traditional and not-so-traditional flavors (cannoli, Baseball Nuts and cantaloupe sorbet).

Rochester

Abbott's Frozen Custard
4791 Lake Ave., 585-865-7400

(plus 19 other locations)
www.abbottscustard.com
Mail-Order: Yes, via
www.NYDeli.com
Type: Scoop shop/Custard stand
A Rochester institution and one of the nation's longest-running custard stands.

Rye

Longford's Own-Made Ice Cream
4 Elm Street, 914-967-3797
(plus one other location)
Type: Scoop shop
Fifty homemade flavors such as Oreo Bomb and carrot cake.

Slingerlands

Tollgate Ice Cream & Coffee Shop
1569 New Scotland Rd.
518-439-9824
Type: Old-time parlor
In the 1900s, travelers passing by had to pay a nickel toll; since 1959, travelers come to pay for huge sundaes made with homemade ice cream.

Valley Stream

Walt Itgen's Ice Cream Parlor
211 Rockaway Ave.
516-825-7444
Type: Old-time parlor
For almost 40 years, Itgen's has offered freshly made ice cream and the whopping, 15-scoop Sock-It-To-Me sundae.

West Seneca

Antoinette's on the Hill
1203 Union Rd., 716- 675-3981
Type: Old-time parlor/Confectionery
Longtime local favorite serves homemade ice cream and a lengthy fountain menu.

Williamson

The Original Candy Kitchen
4069 West Main St., 315-589-9085
www.originalcandykitchen.com
Type: Confectionery/Old-fashioned
soda fountain
In business since 1890, the
Original Candy Kitchen features a
1950s soda fountain that serves
up malts, sundaes and the like.

NORTH CAROLINA
Asheville

Kamm's Frozen Custard
Grove Arcade, 1 Page Ave., #111,
828-225-7200 (plus a location in
Greenville, South Carolina)
www.kammscustard.com
Type: Scoop shop/Custard stand
Specials include a flavor of the
day, ice cream sandwiches and
ice cream pies.

Sweet Heaven Ice Cream
& Music Café
35B Montford Ave., 828-259-9848
www.sweetheavenicecream.com
Type: Scoop shop/Cafe
Homemade ice cream (including an
organic line and soy cream, too) in
some 18 flavors, served up alongside live music on the weekend.

Cary

Ashworth Drugs
105 W. Chatham St.
919-467-1877
Type: Old-fashioned soda fountain
Egg creams, ice cream sodas and
other classics can be had
at this 1903 fountain.

Goodberry's Frozen Custard
1146 Kildaire Farm Rd.
919-467-2386 (plus eight other
locations and two in Australia)
www.goodberrys.com
Type: Custard stand
A local favorite for fresh,
creamy custard and thick
Carolina Concretes.

Chapel Hill

The Inside Scoop
764 Airport Rd. (Midtown Market),
919-933-6366
Type: Parlor
Homemade ice cream (including
soy and rice creams and sorbets)
in a zany setting, complete with
funhouse mirrors and a kids'
play area.

Charlotte

Pike's Old Fashioned Soda Shop
1930 Camden Rd., 704-372-0092
Type: Retro parlor/Restaurant
Retro feel with old pharmacy
antiques and old-fashioned
items like ice cream sodas on
the menu, too.

Conover

Udderly Delicious Ice Cream
1006 W. Conover Blvd.
828-465-1070 (plus a location
in Hickory)
www.udderlydelicious.com
Type: Scoop shop
Flavors like snow cream, brownie
crunch and banana pudding and
Moo-oon Pie sundaes.

Gastonia

Tony's Ice Cream Shop
604 E. Franklin Blvd.
704-867-7085
Type: Diner/Old-time parlor
Local landmark diner that serves
ice cream that Charlotte's city-
search.com site calls "Gastonia's
answer to Ben & Jerry's."

Greensboro

Yum Yum Better Ice Cream
1219 Spring Garden St.
336-272-8284
Type: Old-time parlor
A local fixture since the 1920s
known for its homemade ice
cream served straight-up; there's
no toppings, no fancy creations,
just honest ice cream.

Hillsborough

Maple View Ice Cream Store
3109 Dairyland Rd.
919-960-5535
www.mapleviewfarm.com
Type: Dairy bar/Scoop shop
Come before sunset, grab a cone
of homemade ice cream, sit on the
front porch in a rocking chair and
watch the sun go down.

Huntersville

Dolce Gelato
16916-A Birkdale Commons Pkwy.,
704-892-3116
(plus one other location)
Type: Gelateria/Cafe
Try the limoncello (a lemon liqueur
flavor), the crema pera (creamed
pear) or green apple.

Pittsboro

S & T Soda Shoppe
85 Hillsboro St., 919-545-0007
Type: Refurbished soda fountain
While the shop is new (just three
years old), the decor feels like
the real deal, with an early 1900s
fountain back bar and a 1941
jukebox.

Raleigh

Cream and Bean
2010 Hillsborough St.
919-828-CONE
Type: Parlor/Cafe
Quaint parlor with homemade
ice cream and homemade
waffle cones.

Person Street Pharmacy
Soda Fountain
702 N. Person St.
919-832-0432
Type: Old-fashioned soda
fountain/Diner
Lovely historic building with
fountain dating back to 1910;
it's currently outfitted in a 1950s
theme and serves malteds
and other fountain fare.

Rock Hill

P W'S Gourmet Ice Cream
491 S. Herlong, 803-366-7777
Type: Roadside stand
Known for turtle sundaes in
summer; hot fudge brownie
sundaes come winter.

Roxboro

Cole's Pharmacy
117 N. Main St.
336-599-2171
Type: Old-fashioned soda fountain
Cole's has been in this location
since the 1960s, but its original
1920s equipment is still used to
make fountain treats.

Salisbury

Spanky's Homemade
Ice Cream
101 N. Main St.
704-638-0780
Type: Parlor
Located in a 150-year-old building
on the town square, Spanky's has
some 50 flavors to choose from.

Winston-Salem

Blue Ridge Ice Cream
135 S. Stratford Rd.
336-724-5454
Type: Parlor
Homemade waffle cones and
homemade ice cream in some
50 flavors.

NORTH DAKOTA
Mandan

Mandan Drug and
Soda Fountain
316 W. Main St., 701-663-5900
www.mandandrug.com
Type: Retro parlor/Confectionery
Quaint atmosphere with antiques,
a jukebox and a player piano.
Sit at the counter and have a
Purple Cow.

Stanley
Dakota Drug Co
118 Main St., 701-628-2255
www.stanleynd.com/dakotadrug
/whirlawhip.htm
Type: Old-fashioned soda fountain
The only place in the world where
you can get Whirla Whip cones
(where your choice of flavors is
whipped into the ice cream and
dispensed into a cone soft-serve
style) on an original circa-1949
Whirla Whip machine.

OHIO
Akron
Strickland's Frozen Custard
1809 Triplett Blvd.
866-478-7425 (plus five other
locations; some open year-round)
www.stricklands.info
Open: Seasonally
Type: Walk-up stand
Since 1936, Strickland still makes
custard on its custom-built 1930s
machines and still dips scoops
using its signature tall, conical
dipper.

Canton
Taggarts
1401 Fulton Rd. N.W.
330-452-6844
Type: Old-fashioned soda fountain
Try a Bittner, a thick milk shake
drink that has vanilla ice cream,
chocolate sauce and pecans. It
dates back to 1931 when the
store was just six years old.

Cincinnati
Aglamesis Brothers
3046 Madison Rd., 513-531-5196
(plus one other location)
www.aglamesis.com
Mail-Order: Yes
Type: Old-time
parlor/Confectionery
Quaint-as-can-be 1913 parlor
where the rich French-style ice
cream is still made on-site in
small batches.

Circleville
Wittich's Fine Candies & Ice
Cream Soda Fountain
117 W. High St., 740-474-3313
Type: Old-fashioned soda
fountain/Confectionery
In business since 1840, there's a
1946 Bastian-Blessing soda fountain
serving up classic fountain treats.

Cleveland
Honey Hut Ice Cream Shoppe
4674 State Rd., Cleveland
216-749-7077
(plus three other locations)
Open: Seasonally
Type: Walk-up stand
Famous for its honey-sweetened
ice cream in such flavors as
orange blossom and honey pecan.

Weber's Premium Custard
& Ice Cream
20230 Lorain Rd., 440-331-0004
www.weberscustard.com
Type: Old-time parlor
Their 73-year-old vintage frozen
custard machines continue to
churn out long-time favorites such
as frosted malt, lemon and
banana.

Columbus
Jeni's Fresh Ice Creams
59 Spruce St. (inside the North
Market), 614-228-9960
www.jenisicecream.com
Mail-Order: Yes, via telephone
Type: Walk-up stand
Inventive and bold flavors from Jeni
Britton that are as gourmet and fine
as any you will find on either coast.

Mardi Gras Homemade
Ice Cream & Cakes
1947 Hard Rd., 614-766-2020
(plus one other location)
Type: Scoop shop
Traditional flavors, but also exotic
offerings like Indian kulfi, sweet
rose, fennel and *kaju draksh*
(cashew raisin).

Deersville
Deersville General Store
212 W. Main, 740-922-0831
Type: General store/Scoop shop
The store's been standing for 100
years, and equally timeless is the
homemade ice cream that's sold
alongside fishing lures and firewood.

Findlay
Dietsch Brothers
400 W. Main Cross St.
419-422-4474
(plus one other location)
Type: Old-fashioned soda
fountain/Confectionery
A local institution since 1926,
there's homemade ice cream in
nearly three dozen flavors and a
1950s soda fountain offering
sundaes and milk shakes.

Hudson
Saywell's Drugs
160 N. Main St., 330-653-5411
Type: Old-fashioned soda fountain
Locals gather at this 1909 soda
fountain for neighborhood news
and sodas and egg creams made
with homemade chocolate syrup.

Lakewood
Malley's Chocolates
14822 Madison Ave.
216-529-6262 (plus other
locations, three of which are ice
cream parlors)
www.malleys.com
Type: Old-time parlor/
Confectionery
Charming soda fountain known for
its handmade chocolates, rich hot
fudge sauce and ice cream in such
flavors as Nut Mallow and Big Boy.

Lyndhurst
East Coast Frozen Custard
5618 Mayfield Rd., 440-461-7690
(plus five other area locations)
www.eastcoastcustard.com
Type: Scoop shop/Custard stand
A Cleveland favorite. Flavors of the

day include chocolate marshmallow coconut, Whitehouse (cherries
in vanilla) and butter pecan.

New Middletown
Giering's Homemade
Ice Cream Shoppe
10829 Main St., 330-542-3670
Type: Parlor/Walk-up stand
Just two years old, Giering's has
found a following with its strawberry cheesecake, butter pecan and
chocolate pecan ice creams.

Reynoldsburg
Johnson's Real Ice Cream
7113 E. Main St., 614-577-1916
Type: Parlor
Longtime favorite of Columbus's
East Side (in business since
1950), there are 50 flavors
of homemade ice cream to
choose from.

Sandusky
Toft's Dairy
3717 Venice Rd. (Route 6)
419-625-5490 (plus two
other locations)
www.toftdairy.com
Type: Dairy bar
Toft's has been in the dairy
business for more than a century;
they serve up gigantic scoops
in more than 50 flavors.

Uniontown
Menches Brothers
3700 Massillon Rd.
330-896-2288 (plus one
other location)
www.menchesbros.com
Type: Parlor/Restaurant
Ice cream with cones baked fresh
according to the recipe Frank and
Charles Menches developed at
the 1904 World's Fair.

Wooster
Hartzler Family Dairy
5454 Cleveland Rd. (Route 3)
330-345-8190

www.hartzlerfamilydairy.com
Type: Dairy bar/Parlor
Their chemical-free, cream-on-top milk is used to make such farm-inspired flavors as Heifer Trails, Ditch Tea Delight and Chicken Feed.

Cafe Woo
17 W. Liberty St., 330-262-2435
(plus one other location)
www.woocity.com
Mail-Order: Yes
Type: Scoop shop/Cafe
Hand-crafted Woo City ice cream and sorbets with an emphasis on organic ingredients and Woo-Fu, their frozen vegan tofu dessert.

Westlake
Mitchell's
26161 Detroit Rd., 440-250-0952
(plus two other locations)
Type: Scoop shop
Mitchell's serves up dense, super-premium ice cream in such flavors as double chocolate chunk and caramel fudge brownie.

Wilmington
Gibson's Goodies
718 Ohio Ave., 937-383-2373
Type: Parlor
Gibson's claims to use the same recipe for their banana split as Doc Hazard (one of the claimants to the split's invention).

Vermilion
Ednamae's Gourmet
Honey Ice Cream
5598 Liberty Ave.
440-967-7733
www.ednamaes.com
Open: Seasonally
Mail-Order: Yes
Type: Parlor
Located in a renovated 1850s Victorian funeral parlor, and featuring ice cream that's sweetened with honey.

Yellow Springs
Young's Jersey Dairy
6880 Springfield Xenia Rd.
(Route 68), 937-325-0629
www.youngsdairy.com
Type: Dairy bar/Parlor
There's plenty to do at this 135-year-old dairy — pet the goats or play miniature golf, to name a few — but the reason to come is for the ice cream, especially their famous milk shakes.

Zanesville
Tom's Ice Cream Bowl
532 McIntire Ave., 740-452-5267
Type: Old-fashioned soda fountain
Not much has changed since 1948 at Tom's: the male servers wear white caps and bow ties and the overflowing sundaes are served in bowls with saucers.

OKLAHOMA
Meers
Meers Store and Restaurant
26005 St. Hwy. 1115
580-429-8051
www.meersstore.com
Type: Restaurant
Rambling 102-year-old restaurant has homemade vanilla ice cream on the menu.

Oklahoma City
Grateful Bean Café/Kaisers
Old-Fashioned Ice Cream Parlor
1039 N. Walker, 405-236-3503
www.okclive.com/bean/Index.htm
Type: Old-fashioned soda fountain/Cafe
Home to an old-fashioned 1918 fountain where ice cream treats live on, thanks to the efforts of the non-profit Grateful Bean organization.

Tulsa
Freckles Frozen Custard
5138 S. Harvard, 918-749-5663
(plus one other location)
www.frecklesfrozencustard.com

Type: Walk-up stand/Custard stand
There's always a flavor of the day on the menu, from Nutty Waffle to banana cream pie to bubblegum.

Merritt's Bakery
3202 E. 15th, 918-747-2301
www.merrittsbakery.com
Type: Bakery/Gelateria
Esteemed Tulsa bakery has added gelato in a range of flavors to the menu.

OREGON
Eugene
Prince Pückler's Gourmet
Ice Cream
1605 E. 19th Ave., 541-344-4418
Type: Scoop shop
Inventive flavors include chai, chocolate raspberry and Black Tiger with ground up espresso beans.

Independence
Taylor's Ice Cream Fountain
296 S. Main St., 503-838-1124
Type: Old-fashioned soda fountain
Since 1945, Taylor's has kept its turn-of-the-century soda fountain in use. In summer, try a milk shake made with local fruits.

Portland
Roberto's Homemade Ice Cream
921 SW Morrison St.
503-224-4234
Type: Scoop shop
There are 30 kinds of tempting ice cream, from gingersnap to fresh banana.

Paley's Place
1204 NW 21st Ave.
503-243-2403
www.paleysplace.citysearch.com
Type: Upscale restaurant
There's always house-made selections of sorbets and ice creams on the menu, and they're always delectably good.

Scooter's
3312 SE Belmont St.
503-235-0032
Type: Scoop shop/Toy shop
Quaint shop serves Oregon's Cascade Glacier and Noris ice creams in such flavors as white licorice and caramel blackberry.

Staccato Gelato
232 NE 28th Ave., 503-231-7100
Type: Gelateria
Vibrantly colored shop with vibrant flavors: torrone, Bosc pear, honey lavender and chocolate orange.

Sunriver
Goody's
57100 Mall Dr., 541-593-2155
(plus two other area locations and two in Idaho)
www.goodysgoodies.com
Type: Confectionery/Retro fountain
Homemade ice cream made into milk shakes or a sundae topped with homemade hot fudge.

Tillamook
Tillamook Cheese
Visitor's Center
4175 Highway 101 N.
503-815-1300
www.tillamookcheese.com
Type: Scoop shop
Tillamook draws one million visitors each year to learn about cheese-making. Ice cream lovers will enjoy the ice cream counter, which features 40 homemade flavors.

PENNSYLVANIA
Analomink
Mary Ann's Dairy Bar
Route 447, 570-828-2457
Open: Seasonally
Type: Walk-up stand
Wooden stand nestled in the Pocono Mountains has served up soft-serve cones and dense Flurries since 1968.

Barto

Longacre's Modern Dairy Bar
1445 Route 100, 610-845-7551
Type: Dairy bar
Homemade ice cream from the dairy next door, plus fountain service offering sundaes and floats.

Bethlehem

Nuts About Ice Cream
1124 Linden St., 610-861-7733
www.nutsabouticecream.com
Mail-Order: Yes
Type: Scoop shop
Try one of their exotic flavors: fig, rose, saffron pistachio, or coconut mango.

Bensalem

Nifty Fifty's
2555 Street Rd., 215-638-1950
(plus three other locations)
www.niftyfiftys.com
Type: Retro parlor
The decor is retro 1950s and the fountain serves up thick milk shakes, egg creams and a hundred flavors of sodas.

Butler

Cummings Candy & Coffee Shop
146 N. Main St., 724-287-3287
Type: Confectionery/Old-fashioned soda fountain
A 1915 confectionery that's stood the test of time, complete with a custom-made white marble fountain.

Chambersburg

Kenny's Drive-In & Ice Cream Shoppe
2342 Philadelphia Ave.
717-264-8351
www.kennysdrivein.com
Type: Custard stand
Kenny's uses vintage 1950s machines to churn out fresh frozen custard in such flavors as lemon and peanut butter.

Chester Springs

Chester Springs Creamery/Milky Way Farm
521 Uwchlan Ave., 610-363-8500
www.chesterspringscreamery.com
Open: Seasonally
Type: Dairy bar
Serving up ice cream named after the Milky Way Farm's cows, such as Abby's apple cinnamon and Belle's blueberry cheesecake.

Cranberry

Cranberry Creamery Homemade Ice Cream
20635 Rte. 19, 724-742-1313
Open: Seasonally
Type: Scoop shop
Eye-catching building (painted in cow-spotted black and white) with flavors like Bananas Foster and Mud Pie.

Duncannon

Jimmy's Old-Time Penny Arcade & Soda Fountain
The Old Sled Works,
722 North Market St.
717-834-9333
www.sledworks.com
Open: Weekends only
Type: Refurbished fountain/Antique mall
Have a birch beer float or a fresh banana milk shake at this 1950s soda fountain with lots of retro atmosphere.

Hatboro

Shanna's Cafe & Ice Cream Factory
332 S. York Rd., 215-293-0375
www.worldwidecompusave.com/Shannaicecream.htm
Open: Seasonally
Type: Cafe/Scoop shop
Featuring 36 flavors of homemade ice cream, including cinnamon caramel swirl and chocolate marshmallow.

Kittanning

Mulberry Street Creamery
103 Mulberry St., 724-548-7328
www.mulberrystreetcreamery.com
Open: Seasonally
Type: Gelateria/Scoop shop
Italian ices, frozen custard and gelato made in flavors like coconut mango, chocolate meringue and caramel apple.

Millvale

Regis Steedle Candies
1149 Evergreen Ave.
412-821-9850
Type: Confectionery/Parlor
Serving up homemade ice cream treats since the 1930s.

Yetter's Candies
504 Grant Ave., 412-821-1387
www.yetterscandies.com
Type: Confectionery/Parlor
Since 1950, Yetter's has served up homemade ice cream and homemade toppings.

New Holland

Lapp Valley Farm
244 Mentzer Rd., 717-354-7988
(plus one other location)
Type: Farm stand
Tour the farm and sample some homemade ice cream. You can also buy it from their shop at Kitchen Kettle Village in Intercourse.

Newtown

Goodnoe Farm Dairy Bar
298 N. Sycamore St.,
215-968-3875
www.goodnoe.com
Type: Dairy Bar/Restaurant
Since 1955, locals and visitors have come to the dairy bar to sample homemade ice cream in flavors such as Butterscotch Ripple and banana chip.

North Huntingdon

Kerber's Dairy
1856 Guffy Rd., 724-863-6930
(plus one other location)
www.kerberdairy.com
Type: Dairy bar
Ice cream fresh from the dairy with creative flavors such as Plantation Peach Cobbler, Cow Patty and Le Blanc.

Philadelphia

Bassett's
Reading Terminal Market
45 N. 12th St., 215-925-4315
www.bassettsicecream.com
Type: Counter stand
An institution since 1861, they use a paddle to dip their ice cream. Order your ice cream in a dish and have them slide it to you down the counter.

Capogiro
119 S. 13th St., 215-351-0900
Type: Gelateria
More than 25 artisanal flavors offered daily, ranging from rosemary goat's milk to black walnut and baked heirloom apple.

Maron Chocolates/Scoop de Ville Ice Cream
107 S. 18th St., 215-988-9992
www.maronchocolates.com
Type: Confectionery/Old-time parlor
Longtime confectioner (in business since 1850, in this location since 1913) offers 12 base flavors of ice cream and a choice of almost 100 mix-ins to create your own custom flavor.

More Than Just Ice Cream
1119 Locust St., 215-574-0586
Type: Restaurant/Parlor
A large range of choices for sundaes and fountain drinks (featuring Richmond Ice Cream), set in a retro-cool atmosphere.

Pittsburgh
Boulevard Ice Cream
719 Brookline Blvd.
412-561-9982
Type: Parlor
Kid-friendly parlor with homemade flavors like White Cliffs of Dover and the Unbelievable Milk Shake made with a full pint of ice cream.

Dave and Andy's Homemade Ice Cream
207 Atwood St., 412-681-9906
Type: Scoop shop
Grab a seat on a milk can and have a cone of chocolate chip cookie dough, honey apple cinnamon granola or Golden Ale Espresso Chip.

Klavon's
2801 Penn Ave., 412-434-0451
www.klavonsicecream.com
Type: Old-fashioned soda fountain
Pristine 1925 Art Deco soda fountain still serves up fountain treats (try a pecan ball or a Martha Sunday) featuring locally made Reinhold ice cream and three different flavors of whipped cream.

South Tamaqua
Leiby's Ice Cream House and Restaurant
848 W. Penn Pike, 570-386-4389
www.leibys.com
Type: Restaurant
Serving up almost 20 types of pie and 44 kinds of ice cream, frozen yogurt and sherbet since 1965.

Sprindale
Glen's Frozen Custard
400 Pittsburgh St.
724-274-5510
Open: March–November
Type: Walk-up stand/Custard stand
Vintage Electro-Freeze machines serve up three fresh flavors of frozen custard daily. Try some warm apple crisp topped with vanilla custard.

RHODE ISLAND
Adamsville
Gray's Store
4 Main St., 401-635-4566
Type: General store/Old-fashioned soda fountain
In business since 1788, Gray's may be the oldest continuously operating store in the country.

Narragansett
Brickley's Ice Cream
921 Boston Neck Rd.
401-789-1784
Open: Seasonally
Type: Scoop shop
Almost 50 flavors of homemade ice cream, from maple walnut and Grape Nuts to lemon and peanut butter cup.

Newport
Gelati Per Tutti
21 Brown and Howard Wharf
401-849-6777
Type: Gelateria
The owner went to Rome to learn the art of gelato-making, and the result is an authentic rendition, using Italian machines, ingredients and recipes.

North Kingstown
The Inside Scoop
30 Ten Rod Rd., 401-294-0091
www.insidescoopri.com
Open: Call to confirm during off-season
Type: Scoop shop
Homemade ice cream in more than 50 flavors, including blueberry pie, orange pineapple and chocolate brownie.

Providence
Maxmillian's Ice Cream Cafe
1074 Hope St., 401-273-7230
Type: Parlor
Super-rich, 17-percent butterfat ice cream in 34 rotating flavors.

Newport Creamery
673 Smith St., 401-351-4677
(plus twelve other locations)
www.newportcreamery.com
Type: Restaurant/Parlor
A local landmark since 1940 (look for the golden cow), the creamery is known for its trademark shake, the Awful Awful.

Tiverton
Gray's Ice Cream
16 East Rd., 401-624-3576
(plus one other location)
www.graysicecream.com
Mail-Order: Yes
Type: Walk-up stand/Grocery store
Eighty-year-old landmark that serves up nationally recognized homemade ice cream.

Warren
Delekta's Pharmacy
496 Main St., 401-245-6767
Type: Old-fashioned soda fountain
A pharmacy and soda fountain has been here since 1854. Order a coffee cabinet made with homemade coffee syrup.

Watch Hill
St. Clair Annex
141 Bay St., 401-348-8407
Type: Walk-up stand
Open: Seasonally
They've been perfecting the art of homemade ice cream for more than a century; it's no wonder there are usually lines waiting for a scoop.

SOUTH CAROLINA
Anderson
Water Wheel Ice Cream
29624 Perdairy Rd., 864-224-9999
(plus four other locations)
www.waterwheelicecream.com
Type: Scoop shop/Mill
Sample the only ice cream in the world that's made from freezers powered by a water wheel.

Beaufort
Berry Island Ice Cream Cafe
1 Merchant, Ste. 102
843-524-8779
Type: Scoop shop/Cafe
Try the Kahlúa Fudge or Prince of Tides (coffee ice cream with almonds and fudge), a flavor created for the movie.

McCormick
Strom's Drugstore
124 S. Main St., 864-465-2011
Type: Old-fashioned soda fountain
Offering sundaes, Lemon Sours and milk shakes since 1911.

North Myrtle Beach
Original Painter's Homemade Ice Cream
2408 Hwy. 17 S., 843-272-6934
Open: March–November
Type: Walk-up stand
Since 1954, this beach town fixture has served up ice cream and other treats, including a Vanna Banana sundae.

Ravenel
Wholly Cow
Food Court at Citadel Mall
6400 Savannah Hwy. (State Route 17) and Sam Rittenberg Blvd.
843-556-7708
www.whollycowicecream.com
Type: Walk-up food court stand
Super-premium ice cream in flavors such as Killa Vanilla, Southern praline, Key lime sherbet and Margarita Grande sorbet.

Santee
Santee General Store
8932 Old Number 6 Hwy.
803-854-2105
Type: General store
Ice cream and milk shakes served up whenever you get a craving — the 27-old store is open 24 hours.

Summerville
Guerin's Pharmacy
140 S. Main St., 843-873-2531
Type: Old-fashioned soda fountain
The state's oldest pharmacy
(founded in 1871) features a
fountain that serves up malted
milk shakes and fresh-squeezed
lemonade.

SOUTH DAKOTA
Elk Point
Pioneer Drug — Edgar's
I-29 Business Loop, 605-356-3336
www.edgarssoda.com
Type: Refurbished soda fountain
The centerpiece is a lovingly
restored 1906 fountain that serves
up treats using equally vintage
fountain recipes.

Rapid City
Fjord's Ice Cream Factory
3606 Canyon Lake Dr.
605-343-6912
(plus one other location)
Type: Parlor
Serving up homemade ice cream
in such flavors as black licorice,
peanut butter Oreo and Black Hills
Gold for more than 20 years.

Soda Falls at Zandbroz Variety
209 S. Phillips Ave.
605-331-5137 (plus a Fargo,
North Dakota, location)
Type: Refurbished fountain/
Gift shop
In the back of the store, you'll find
a handsome 1920s fountain with
green marbled countertop and
10 stools.

TENNESSEE
Chattanooga
Clumpies
26 Frazier Ave. # B, 423-267-5425
Type: Scoop shop
Well-regarded homemade ice
cream in such flavors as peanut
butter, chai and mango sorbet.

Knoxville
Fountain City Creamery
114 Hotel Rd., 865-688-4607
www.fountaincitycreamery.com
Type: Restaurant
Homemade ice cream in such
flavors as chocolate raspberry
truffle, After Dinner Mint and Irish
cream are on the menu.

Memphis
Capriccio's Cafe
149 Union Ave., 901-529-4164
Type: Cafe
Located inside the tony Peabody
Hotel, this dessert spot also
serves up homemade ice cream
and hot fudge.

Wiles-Smith Drugstore
1635 Union Ave., 901-278-6416
Type: Old-fashioned soda fountain
Since 1944, shakes and sodas have
been enjoyed at the counter. Order
an extra-thick "Joe" milk shake.

Nashville
Bobbie's Dairy Dip
4109 Utah Ave., 615-292-2112
Open: March–November
Type: Walk-up stand
Fifty-year-old stand known for
its extra-creamy soft-serve and
thick milk shakes.

Elliston Place Soda Shop
2111 Elliston Pl., 615-327-1090
Type: Old-fashioned soda fountain
One of the city's oldest
restaurants, locals have come
here since 1939 to sit a booth
and enjoy a shake or a sundae.

Sevierville
**Bellacino's/Cranky's
Homemade Ice Cream**
716 Dolly Parton Pkwy.
865-774-7072
(plus other locations)
Type: Pizzeria/Scoop shop
Inside Bellacino's Pizzeria, there's
a Cranky's Homemade Ice Cream
stand featuring such flavors
as bubble gum, eggnog and
cotton candy.

TEXAS
Austin
Amy's Ice Creams
1012 W. Sixth St., 512-480-0673
(plus nine other locations)
www.amysicecream.com
Type: Scoop shop
First opened in 1984, Amy's
has become an area favorite for
delicious homemade ice cream
and a playful scooping staff
behind the counter.

Dolce Vita
4222 Duval St., 512-323-2686
Type: Gelateria
Have one of the 14 flavors of
gelato with a pizzelle cookie
or with a shot of liqueur.

Sandy's Hamburgers
603 Barton Springs Rd.
512-478-6322
Type: Custard stand
Known for its burgers, its frozen
custard and its too-thick-for-a-
straw shakes.

Bedford
**Milwaukee Joe's Gourmet
Ice Cream**
201 Harwood Rd., 817-581-1953
(plus two other locations)
www.milwaukeejoes.com
Type: Scoop shop
There are usually about 15
homemade flavors to choose from,
including a flavor of the day.

Corsicana
Dee's Place
125 N. Beaton St., 903-874-5891
www.pflash.net/~deesplace/
Type: Old-fashioned soda fountain
One of Texas' oldest soda
fountains, this location has been
in operation since 1927 and
still serves splits and floats.

Dallas
Paciugo Gelato
Renaissance Tower, 1201 Elm St.
214-658-1160
(plus nine other locations)
www.paciugo.com
Type: Gelateria
Gelati made with either a milk, dairy
or soy base and offered in a rotating menu of some 200 flavors.

Wild About Harry's
3113 Knox St., 214-520-3113
(plus two other locations)
www.wildaboutharrys.com
Type: Custard stand
Frozen custard made according
to a recipe from owner Harry
Coley's mom.

Denton
Beth Marie's
117 W. Hickory St., 940-384-1818
www.bethmaries.com
Type: Refurbished fountain/
Scoop shop
Eighty-two flavors of homemade
ice cream (made on a 1926 Henry
Thompson machine), waffle cones
made on demand, and a lovely
1927 oak soda fountain.

Forth Worth
Paleteria La Flor de Michoacan
2201 W. Berry St., 817-207-0333
Type: Mexican paleteria
Rice, tamarind, cucumber with
chile, coconut and other flavors
of Mexican-style popsicles.

Hemphill
Hank's Ice Cream Parlor
9291 Main St., 713-665-5103
Type: Scoop shop
The signature flavor at this
well-regarded shop is butter
pecan, and it's loaded to the
brim with pecan halves.

AN EDUCATION IN GOOD ICE CREAM: UNIVERSITY CREAMERIES

Many of the nation's agriculture schools have their own dairy herds and processing plants. Much to the students' delight, most make ice cream, too. Here are a few places worth studying:

Brigham Young University
Provo, Utah
BYU Creamery
North end of campus near Deseret Towers, (plus 3 other locations around campus)
801-422-2581
www.byu.edu/creamery/
Mail-Order: Yes, call
800-313-3559
On the Menu: Brigham's Beehive Crunch, Ernestly Chocolate and LaVell's Vanilla Bean.

California State University
Fresno
Farm Market
Barstow and Chestnut
559-278-4511
On the Menu: Toasted almond, Tahitian vanilla and black cherry.

University of Connecticut
Storrs, Connecticut
UConn Dairy Bar
3636 Horsebarn Rd.
(off Route 195), 860-486-2634
www.canr.uconn.edu/ansci/dairybar/dbar.htm
Mail-Order: 888-UC-ALUM-1;
www.uconnalumni.com
On the Menu: Jonathan's Supreme, strawberry cheesecake and coffee espresso crunch.

Cornell University
Ithaca, New York
Cornell Dairy Bar
Stocking Hall on Tower Road,
607-255-3272
www.foodscience.cornell.edu/dairy-store/location.htm

On the Menu: Sticky Bunz, Concord and Bavarian raspberry fudge.

Kansas State University
Manhattan, Kansas
Call Hall Dairy Bar
Call Hall 144
Mid Campus Drive and Claflin
785-532-1292
www.oznet.ksu.edu/dp_ansi/Sales/DairyMain.htm
On the Menu: Swiss chocolate almond and K-State Purple Pride.

Louisiana Tech University
Ruston, Louisiana
Tech Farm Salesroom
Corner of West California and Hull avenues, 318-257-3550
www.techfarmsales.latech.edu/
On the Menu: Fresh peach, praline pecan and Butterfinger.

Michigan State Unversity
East Lansing, Michigan
Dairy Store
1140 South Anthony Hall
517-355-8466
www.dairystore.msu.edu/
On the Menu: Black cherry, Blue Moon and lemon custard.

University of Minnesota
St. Paul, Minnesota
The Dairy Products Store
Room 166 Andrew Boss Lab of Meat Science, 1354 Eckles Ave.
612-624-7776
www.fsci.umn.edu/pilotplant/salesroom.html
On the Menu: Chocolate peanut butter truffle and Gopher Gold.

Mississippi State University
Starkville, Mississippi
MAFES Sales Store
Room 160 Herzer Food Science Building, Stone Boulevard
662-325-2338
msucheese.com
On the Menu: Muscadine ripple, butter pecan and chocolate almond.

University of Missouri
Columbia, Missouri
Buck's Place
Eckles Hall, 573-882-1088
www.fse.missouri.edu/bucks/
On the Menu:: Tiger Stripe and MIZZOU Gold.

University of Nebraska
Lincoln
The UNL Dairy Store
The Food Processing Center,
143 Food Industry Complex,
East Campus, 402-472-2951
www.dairystore.unl.edu/
On the Menu: Amaretto raspberry, Karmel Kashew and Bavarian mint.

Pennsylvania State University
University Park, Pennsylvania
University Creamery
Corner of Shortlidge and Curtin roads, 814-865-7535
www.foodscience.psu.edu/creamery/creamery.html
Mail-Order: 877-778-7467
or via website
On the Menu: Peachy Paterno, Death By Chocolate and butter pecan.

South Dakota State University
Brookings, South Dakota
Dairy Plant and Sales Bar
Dairy Microbiology Building
605-688-5420, 605-688-4116
dairysci.sdstate.edu/
On the Menu: Butter brickle, root beer and peppermint bonbon.

Utah State University
Logan, Utah
Dairy Bar/Aggie Ice Cream
750 N. 1200 East, 435-797-2109
www.usu.edu/univinn/agicecrm.htm
On the Menu: Lemon custard, Jam'in Peanut Butter Boogie and USU Centennial.

Washington State University
Pullman, Washington
Ferdinand's Ice Cream Shoppe
Food Quality Building,
509-335-4014
www.wsu.edu/creamery/
On the Menu: Tin Lizzy, blackberry ripple and Grabber's ice cream sandwiches

University of Wisconsin
Madison
Babock Hall Dairy Store
1605 Linden Dr., 608-262-3045
www.wisc.edu/foodsci/store/
Mail-Order: 877-947-6233,
www.wisconsinmade.com, or
920-495-1668, www.icecream source.com
On the Menu: Orange custard chocolate chip and seasonal flavors often named after campus landmarks (Bo's Express, Union Utopia).

Jefferson
Jefferson General Store
113 E. Austin St., 903-665-8481
www.jeffersongeneralstore.com
Type: General Store/Refurbished
fountain
Charming general store soda
fountain serves up Coke floats
and ice cream cones.

Marble Falls
Michel's Drugstore
211 Hwy. 281., 830-693-2344
Type: Old-fashioned soda fountain
There's been a drugstore at this
site since 1891 (it's the state's
oldest) and a 1927 fountain still
serves up treats.

Plano
Henry's Ice Cream
2909 W. 15th St., 972-612-9949
www.henryshomemadeicecream.com
Type: Scoop shop
Henry's makes creamy, 16-percent
butterfat ice cream. Try a scoop
of cinnamon.

San Antonio
Justin's Ice Cream Company
510 Riverwalk St.
210-222-1457
Type: Scoop shop
Well-regarded microcreamery known
for such flavors as mango
(President Clinton's favorite),
chili caramel and sweet onion.

UTAH
Brigham City
Idle Isle
24 S. Main St., 435-734-2468
Type: Old-time parlor/
Cafe/Confectionery
A town landmark since 1921. Have
a sundae or shake at the marble
and onyx soda fountain.

Cedar City
Bulloch's Drug
91 N. Main St., 435-586-9651

Type: Refurbished soda fountain
A 1942 Bastian-Blessing beauty
that serves up such treats as
chocolate Cokes.

Heber City
Granny's Drive In
511 S. Main St., 435-654-3097
Type: Walk-up stand
Well-known for its milk shakes,
which come in 59 flavors.

Holladay
Iceberg Drive Inn
3906 S. 900 E., 801-262-0652
(plus 11 other locations)
www.icebergdriveinn.com
Type: Walk-up stand/Parlor
For more than 40 years, the
Iceberg has been known for its
thick shakes that stand two inches
over the rim of the cup.

Logan
The Bluebird Restaurant
19 N. Main St., 435-752-3155
Type: Old-fashioned soda fountain
In business since 1914, the green
marble soda fountain still serves up
an array of fountain treats.

Ogden
Farr Better Ice Cream
286 21st St., 801-393-8629
Type: Old-time parlor
Snowballs and generous cones
in flavors such as Willard Bay
Blackberry and Lime Rickey
sherbet have made this a local
favorite since 1929.

Richmond
Casper's Retail Malt Shoppe
11805 North 200 E.
435-258-2477
www.fatboyicecream.com
Mail-Order: Yes
Type: Dairy Bar
Try the Casco Nut Sundaes and Fat
Boy ice cream sandwiches this
company has made since 1925.

Salt Lake City
Hires Big H
425 S. 700 E., 801-364-4582
(plus four other locations)
www.hiresbigh.com
Type: Drive-in/Diner
There are shakes and sundaes on
the menu, but, naturally, a favorite
is the Hires root beer float.

Nielsen's Frozen Custard
3918 S. Highland Dr.
801-277-7479 (plus other locations)
Type: Custard stand/Parlor
Family-run for more than 20 years,
their frozen custard concretes made
with nuts are especially popular.

VERMONT
Bennington
Vermont Confectionery
Route 9 West Road, 888-669-7425
www.vermontcandy.com
Type: Confectionery/Scoop shop
They serve up 30 flavors of ice
cream; rum raisin, ginger and
pineapple are popular.

Rochester
**Rochester Cafe and
Country Store**
Route 100 (Main St.)
802-767-4302
Type: Old-fashioned soda fountain
A 1930s soda fountain with Italian
marble countertop serves up maple
milk shakes.

Manchester
**Mother Myrick's Confectionery
& Ice Cream Parlor**
Route 7A, 802-362-1560
www.mothermyricks.com
Mail-Order: Yes, for hot fudge
Type: Confectionery/Parlor
Be sure to have a hot fudge
sundae made with their
signature sauce.

Rutland
Seward Family Restaurant

& Ice Cream
224 N. Main St., 802-773-2738
Type: Restaurant/Walk-up stand
A 50-year-old landmark with a dairy
store, a walk-up window or a restaurant in which to enjoy their ice
cream.

Woodstock
Billings Farm & Museum
Route 12 and River Road
802-457-2355
www.billingsfarm.org
Open: May–October
Type: Dairy bar
Have a cone of Mountain Creamery
ice cream at the dairy bar at
this living museum to Vermont's
dairy history.

VIRGINIA
Alexandria
Del Ray Dreamery
2310 Mount Vernon Ave.
703-683-7767
www.delraydreamery.com
Type: Frozen custard shop
Freshly made custard (you can even
watch it being made via a webcam)
in flavors like chocolate Frango mint
and pineapple upside-down cake.

Pop's Old Fashioned Ice Cream
109 King St., 703-518-5374
Type: Retro parlor
Egg creams, banana splits and
sundaes all served up in the style of
classic old-time parlors. As a plus,
the ice cream is made on-site.

**Scoop Grill & Homemade
Ice Cream**
110 King St., 703-549-4527
Type: Parlor/Grill
New ice creams and frozen cus-
tards are churned out daily, from
Cherry Blossom to peanut butter.

Arlington
Lazy Sundae
2925 Wilson Blvd., 703-525-4960

Type: Parlor
Whimsical parlor where ice cream is scooped with style (tossed in the air and caught in a dish) and the ice cream is made with equal finesse.

Chantilly
Milwaukee Frozen Custard
13934 Lee Jackson Memorial Hwy., 703-263-1920
(plus three other locations)
www.milwaukeefrozencustard.com
Type: Scoop shop/Parlor/Custard stand
Frozen custard shop that features a flavor of the day, including the cleverly titled Good Bye Marion Berry.

Charlottesville
Timberlake's Drugstore
322 E. Main St., 434-295-9155
Type: Old-fashioned soda fountain
This 1890s-era drugstore serves up egg creams, milk shakes and sundaes.

Chesapeake
Bergey's Dairy Farm
1128 Battlefield Blvd. N.
757-547-7360
Type: Dairy bar/Farm stand
A working farm since 1933, see Bergey's Jersey and Guernsey cows and taste the ice cream they helped make.

Chincoteague Island
Mister Whippy
6201 Maddox Blvd.,757-336-5122
www.misterwhippy.com
Type: Scoop shop/Drive-thru
Soft-serve ice cream, homemade waffle cones and a choice of dips ranging from orange to espresso to peanut butter.

Fredericksburg
Carl's
2200 Princess Anne St., no phone
Open: Mid–February–

Mid–November
Type: Walk-up stand
An institution since 1947 that draws crowds for its vanilla, chocolate and strawberry frozen custard made on 1940s Electro-Freeze machines.

Goolrick's Modern Pharmacy
901 Caroline St., 540-373-9878
www.goolricks.com
Type: Old-fashioned soda fountain
The fountain here's been in business since 1912, serving up vanilla Cokes, sundaes with wet nuts and thick malts.

Front Royal
Royal Dairy Ice Cream Bar & Restaurant
241 Chester St.
540-635-5202
Type: Old-fashioned soda fountain
Have an old-fashioned milk shake at this well-preserved 1947 eatery.

Manassas
Kline's Freeze
8200 Centreville Rd.
703-368-2013
Open: Seasonally
Type: Scoop shop/Walk-up stand
Since 1965, soft-serve, shakes and red raspberry Italian ice.

Norfolk
Doumar's Cones & Barbecue
1919 Monticello Ave.
757-627-4163
www.doumars.com
Type: Drive-in/Parlor
Full fountain menu, but don't miss the waffle cones made fresh using the same recipe that Abe Doumar invented at the St. Louis Fair.

Richmond
Bev's Homemade Ice Cream
2911 W. Cary St., 804-204-2387
Type: Scoop shop/Cafe
Well-regarded parlor churns out

homemade flavors like Dirty Chocolate, Almond Joy and piña colada.

Gelati Celesti
8906-A W. Broad St. (Gold's Gym Plaza), 804-346-0038
Type: Gelateria
Almost 40 flavors to choose from each day, including Chocolate Decadence and cookie dough.

Staunton
Wright's Dairy-Rite
346 Greenville Ave.
540-886-0435
Type: Drive-in/Restaurant
A town fixture since 1952, you can still order from your car and get hot fudge ice cream cake or a banana milk shake delivered curbside.

WASHINGTON
Artic
Clarks Restaurant
734 U.S. Hwy. 101
360-538-1487
www.clarksrestaurant.com
Type: Restaurant
Since 1962, they've been serving up homemade ice cream and their signature dome shakes.

Bellingham
Mallard Ice Cream
207 E. Holly St., 360-734-3884
Type: Scoop shop
Brightly colored shop serves up homemade ice cream in flavors like chocolate raspberry and mint Oreo.

The Malt Shop
1135 Railroad Ave., 360-676-5156
Type: Retro diner/Parlor
There are usually 48 flavors on the menu, from Rocky Road to seasonal favorites like eggnog.

Longview
Scoops Ice Cream Parlor
1339 Commerce Ave. #103
360-423-4986
Type: Retro fountain
A 1940s fountain from Iowa with a mahogany back bar and large mirror and recipes from a 1952 soda fountain formulary.

Lynnwood
Snoqualmie Gourmet Ice Cream
2100 196th St. SW, Ste. 121
425-771-0944
Type: Scoop shop
Super-premium ice cream with 18-percent butterfat and flavors such as Mukilteo Mud.

Ocean Shores
Murphy's Candy & Ice Cream
172 W. Chance A La Mer NW
360-289-0927
Type: Parlor
Serving up homemade ice cream in such flavors as Bailey's Irish Cream and spumoni.

Port Townsend
Elevated Ice Cream Co.
627 Water St., 360-385-1156
www.elevatedicecream.com
Mail-Order: Yes
Type: Scoop shop
In business since 1977, there's always 29 freshly made flavors on the menu, from Swiss orange chocolate chip to amaretto hazelnut.

Redmond
Theno's Dairy
12248 156th Ave. NE
425-885-2339
Type: Dairy Bar
Theno's has been around since 1944, and the ice cream is still homemade using old-fashioned recipes.

Seattle

Husky Deli
4721 California Ave. SW
206-937-2810
Type: Deli/Parlor
A local landmark, Husky's been making its popular ice cream since 1932.

Mix Ice Cream Bar
4507 University Way NE
206-547-3436
Type: Scoop shop
House-made ice cream and frozen yogurt can be mixed with a range of ingredients on a cold slab.

Spokane Valley

Mary Lou's Milk Bottle
802 W. Garland Ave
509-325-1772
(plus one other location)
Type: Parlor
A vintage landmark, the building resembles a two-story milk bottle. Go inside for ice cream treats and huckleberry milk shakes.

Steilacoom

Bair Restaurant
1617 Lafayette St.
253-588-9668
Type: Old-fashioned soda fountain
Part museum with displays pertaining to this 1895 hardware and drugstore, and part vintage fountain, with a 1906 model still serving up treats.

WASHINGTON, D.C.

Coppi's
1414 U St. NW
202-319-7773
Type: Italian restaurant/Pizzeria
Well-regarded pizzeria also makes its own ice cream. You can even order an apple pie pizza with vanilla on top.

Dickey's Frozen Custard
1710 I St., 202-861-0669
(plus other locations)
Open: Weekdays only
Type: Walk-up stand
Dickey's makes it simple. You have two choices: chocolate or vanilla.

Max's Best Homemade Ice Cream
2416 Wisconsin Ave. NW
202-333-3111
Type: Scoop shop
There are always at least 25 flavors to choose from, out of some 250 in rotation.

Patisserie Poupon
1645 Wisconsin Ave. NW, 202-342-3248 (plus one location in Baltimore)
Type: Cafe/Bakery
A serene cafe serving up French pastries and its own *glacé* in such flavors as white peach and pear.

WEST VIRGINIA

Cairo

The Scoop
Main Street, 304-628-3796
Type: Old-time parlor
Classic 1949 shop still serves hand-dipped cones, sodas and malts.

Ceredo

Austin's Homemade Ice Cream & Yogurt Shop
1103 C St. (U.S. Route 60)
304-453-2071
Open: Seasonally
Type: Parlor
Fifty-year-old shop serves up home-made ice cream, fountain treats and frozen yogurt.

Huntington

Smith's Midway Drive-In
445 W. Sixth Ave., 304-523-4844
Type: Drive-In
Let the carhop bring you a milk shake at this landmark 60-year-old drive-in.

Kanawha City

Trivillian's Pharmacy Sandwich and Gift Shop
215 35th St. SE, 304-343-8621
Type: Old-fashioned soda fountain
Ice cream sodas, sundaes and even some non-fat milk shakes are on the menu at this 1950 fountain.

Martinsburg

Patterson's Old Fashion Drugstore
134 South Queen St.
304-267-8903
www.martinsburg.com/patter-sons/pds.html
Type: Old-fashioned soda fountain
A 70-year-old soda fountain serves up Jo-Jo sundaes and local commentary from the regulars of the Coffee Club.

WISCONSIN

Appleton

Vande Walle's Candies
400 Mall Dr., 920-738-7799
Type: Confectionery
Sixteen flavors of homemade ice cream daily, which often incorporate their homemade chocolates and bakery.

Cedarburg

The Chocolate Factory
W62 N577 Washington Ave.
262-377-8877
(plus seven other locations)
www.subsandicecream.com
Type: Parlor/Deli
Features Bloomer's ice cream, a longtime local maker, and an unusual "double-dare" flavor each month.

Chippewa Falls

Olson's Ice Cream Parlor and Deli
611 N. Bridge St., 715-723-4331
Type: Old-time parlor
You can watch through a window as they make their 20 flavors of "Homaid" ice cream, a local tradition since 1923.

Ephraim

Wilson's Restaurant
9990 Water St., 920-854-2041
Open: May–Mid–October
Type: Old-time parlor
A Door County fixture since 1906 known for their towering cones, with a jelly bean on the bottom.

Green Bay

Hansen's Dairy & Deli
620 Gray St., 920-494-1090
(plus four other locations)
www.hansenfoods.com
Mail-Order: Yes, via www.ice creamsource.com
Type: Scoop shop/Deli
In the dairy business since 1912, Hansen's serves up thick shakes and ice cream in flavors like Frozen Tundra and Mackinac Island Fudge.

Lake Delton

Cheese Factory Restaurant
521 Wisconsin Dells Pkwy.
608-253-6065
www.cookingvegetarian.com/Ice_cream.htm
Type: Restaurant/Retro parlor
Try an espresso float or a Black Narcissus sundae.

Madison

Chocolate Shoppe Ice Cream
468 State St., 608-255-5454
(plus two other locations)
www.chocolateshoppeice cream.com
Mail-Order: Yes, via www.icecream source.com
Type: Scoop shop
Chocolate raspberry truffle, Blue Moon and other super-premium flavors from this more than 40-year-old micro-creamery.

Ella's Kosher Deli & Ice Cream
2902 E. Washington Ave.
608-241-5291
Type: Parlor/Deli
This zany, kinetic parlor (think flying objects and decorated tables) with a carousel out front still makes its vanilla, chocolate, strawberry on site.

Michael's Frozen Custard
2531 Monroe St., 608-231-3500
(plus three other locations)
www.ilovemichaels.com
Mail-Order: Yes, via www.icecream source.com
Type: Walk-up stand/ Custard stand/Grill
A Madison favorite since 1986, known for its fresh custard in flavors like French Silk and caramel cashew.

Manitowoc
Beerntsen's Confectionery
108 N. Eighth St., 920-684-9616
(plus one other location in Cedarburg)
www.beerntsens.com
Type: Confectionery/Old-time parlor
This quaint shop hasn't changed much since 1932. It's still lined with gleaming wood and the ice cream and toppings are homemade.

Cedar Crest Ice Cream Parlor
2000 S. 10th St., 920-682-5577
www.cedarcresticecream.com
Type: Dairy bar
Attached to the company's plant, there are 26 flavors on the menu and a giant cow out front.

Milwaukee
Gilles Frozen Custard Drive-In
7515 W. Bluemound Rd.,
414-453-4875
www.gillesfrozencustard.com
Type: Custard stand/Grill
Since 1938, Gilles has been

serving up fresh custard. Try one of their specialty sundaes such as the Lalapalooza or a Razzanna.

Leon's Frozen Custard
3131 S. 27th St., 414-383-1784
(plus a location in Osh Kosh)
Type: Custard stand
Said to be the inspiration for Arnold's on the TV show Happy Days, this stand is classic, both for its neon looks and its old-school custard.

Kitt's Frozen Custard Drive-In
7000 W. Capitol Dr., 414-461-1400
Type: Walk-up stand
This 1950s neon-beauty of a stand still uses vintage machines to crank out some of the town's creamiest custard.

Kopp's Frozen Custard
7631 W. Layton Ave.
414 282-4080
(plus two other locations)
www.kopps.com
Mail-Order: Yes
Type: Custard stand/Grill
Frozen custard doesn't get much creamier or indulgent than here, and their flavors of the day are loaded with goodies.

Sheboygan
Randall's Frozen Custard
3827 Superior Ave.
920-458-9699
Type: Custard stand
Flavors of the day include caramel fudge pecan, amaretto cherry cheesecake and Chocolate Naughty.

Sister Bay
Door County Ice Cream Factory & Sandwich Shop
Hwy. 42 at Beach Road
920-854-9693
Mail-Order: Yes, via www.ice creamsource.com
Type: Parlor

Homemade ice cream with locally inspired flavors, including Door County Cherry and Chamber Island Fudge.

Stevens Point
Belts Soft Serve
2140 Division St.
715-344-0049
Type: Walk-up stand
Its sign says "Home of the Large Cone," and indeed they are quite tall. They also offer free puppy cups for the dairy-loving canines in your life.

Wales
Le Duc's
S17 W31884 Hwy. 18
(at Route 83)
262-968-2894
www.explorewisconsin. com/leducs/
Type: Walk-up stand/Custard stand
Creamy custard that's rich and fresh. It sounds boring, but you can't go wrong with their vanilla.

Washington Islands
The Albatross Drive-In Restaurant
1 Main Rd., 920-847-2203
(plus one other location)
www.explorewisconsin.com /AlbatrossDriveInRestaurant
Open: Memorial Day– Columbus Day
Type: Walk-up stand/Grill
Door County institution known for their Alby burgers and thick shakes.

Waterford
Uncle Harry's Frozen Custard & Ice Cream
100 S. Jefferson St.
262-534-4757
Type: Scoop shop/Custard stand
A local favorite for 20 years with 100 flavors in rotation

and 15 kinds of ice cream cakes and pies.

Watertown
Mullen's Dairy Bar & Eatery
212 W. Main St., 920-261-4278
(plus two other locations)
Type: Old-time parlor
Serving up homemade ice cream and fountain treats since 1932. The Bigger Than Bill sundae has seven scoops of ice cream and three toppings.

Waukesha
Divino Gelato Cafe
227 West Main St., 262-446-9490
www.divinogelatocafe.com
Type: Gelateria/Cafe
Offers more than 24 flavors of fresh and smooth gelati and sorbetti daily. Get a Bambino, a sampler of five mini-scoops.

WYOMING
Chugwater
Chugwater Soda Fountain
314 First Street, 307-422-3222
Type: Old-fashioned soda fountain
Dating back to the early 1900s, they still use a counter that was hauled in by horse and wagon.

Shoshoni
Yellowstore Drugsture
127 Main St., 307-876-2539
Type: Old-fashioned soda fountain
This 1909 drugstore is renowned for its milk shakes, serving up some 65,000 of them a year.

Thayne
Lower Valley United Drug & Soda Fountain
190 S. Main St., 307-883-4600
Type: Retro soda fountain
Wire parlor chairs, marble soda fountain counter and 32-ounce milkshakes named for hometown Olympic wrestler Roulon Gardner. ∎

WE ALL SCREAM FOR

HOMEMADE ICE CREAM: GREAT RECIPES TO MAKE YOURSELF

There is a seemingly endless array of recipes for great homemade ice cream. Everyone has his or her own way of making it. Some people swear by evaporated milk. Others insist on whole vanilla bean over extract. Sweeteners range from sugar to honey to Splenda. Eggs are used in every form — whole, just the whites or yolks — and in quantities ranging from two to eight eggs. There's isn't necessarily a right way to make ice cream; what's important is finding your favorite way to make it. My hope is that you will have fun with these recipes and experiment so that the ice cream you make at home becomes your favorite brand.

Very, Very Vanilla

Easy Vanilla Ice Cream

The great thing about no-cook recipes is that you're less than a half-hour away from licking fresh ice cream off the dasher. This recipe is the perfect backdrop for adding mix-ins. (See sidebar on page 162 for ideas.)

Makes 1 Quart

1 cup whole milk, chilled
3/4 cup sugar
2 cups heavy whipping cream
  or half-and-half, chilled
2 teaspoons vanilla extract

1. Whisk sugar into milk until completely dissolved.
2. Stir in cream and vanilla extract.
3. Add mixture to ice cream maker and freeze according to manufacturer's directions. If a firmer consistency is desired, transfer to an airtight container and ripen in freezer for two or more hours.

Rich Vanilla Custard-Based Ice Cream

This ice cream is delicious, and the effort of using real vanilla beans makes all the difference in terms of flavor. This recipe is from a July/August 1993 *Cook's Illustrated* recipe by Jack Bishop. You'll need a candy thermometer, but the technique is foolproof.

Makes 1 Quart

2 cups whole milk
1/2 vanilla bean
3/4 cup sugar
4-6 egg yolks
1 cup heavy whipping cream

1. Add milk to a medium saucepan.

2. Slit vanilla bean lengthwise. Scrape the seeds from the pod with the edge of a paring knife into the saucepan, and then place the vanilla pods into the saucepan. Heat mixture over medium heat until a candy thermometer reads 175 degrees, stirring occasionally.
3. Meanwhile, beat sugar and egg yolks with an electric mixer on medium speed until pale yellow in color and the egg mixture falls off the beaters in ribbon-like strands.
4. Once milk is hot with bubbles forming around edges, take 1/2 cup of the milk mixture and add it to the beaten egg yolks, whisking constantly.
5. Then, stirring constantly with a wooden spoon, add the egg yolk mixture into the saucepan.
6. Continue to stir constantly until the thermometer reads 180 degrees.
7. Remove from heat and pour custard through a strainer into a bowl. Add cream. Retrieve vanilla bean pods and return to mixture.
8. Place in airtight container and chill thoroughly for at least four hours.
9. Stir mixture and remove vanilla pods.
10. Add mixture to ice cream maker and freeze according to manufacturer's instructions. If a firmer consistency is desired, transfer to an airtight container and ripen in freezer for two or more hours.
■ If you don't have a vanilla bean you can substitute 2 teaspoons of vanilla extract. Add along with cream in Step 7.

Crazy for Chocolate

Easy Chocolate Ice Cream

This is chocolate ice cream you can make in a jiffy. The result is a lighter chocolate taste that children, in particular, seem to love, and it's equally good eaten soft directly out of the maker or after it has hardened in the freezer for a few hours.

Makes 1 Quart

1 cup whole milk
1/2 cup sugar
2 tablespoons unsweetened
  cocoa powder
1/2 cup canned chocolate syrup
2 cups heavy whipping cream
1 teaspoon vanilla extract

1. Whisk milk, sugar and cocoa until completely dissolved.
2. Add chocolate syrup and whisk to combine.
3. Stir in cream and vanilla extract.
4. Chill in freezer for about 10 minutes to cool mixture slightly.
5. Add mixture to ice cream maker and freeze according to manufacturer's instructions. If a firmer consistency is desired, transfer to an airtight container and ripen in freezer for two or more hours.

Rich Chocolate Custard-Based Ice Cream

This recipe is a chocoholic's dream. It's adapted from a recipe in *The New Basics Cookbook* by Julee Rosso and Sheila Lukins. The buttermilk brings out the chocolate's flavor perfectly.

Makes 1 Quart

1 cup whole milk
4 ounces bittersweet
  chocolate, coarsely chopped
3 ounces semisweet
  chocolate, coarsely chopped
4 egg yolks
3/4 cup sugar
1 cup heavy whipping cream
3/4 cup buttermilk
1 teaspoon vanilla
Pinch of salt

1. Heat milk and chocolate in a medium saucepan over medium heat and stir constantly until bubbles form around the edges, or a candy thermometer reads 175 degrees. Do not boil.
2. Beat sugar and egg yolks with an electric mixer on medium speed until pale yellow in color and the egg mixture falls off in ribbons. Set aside.
3. Once milk mixture is ready, add 1/2 cup of it to the egg yolks and whisk constantly to incorporate.
4. Then, stirring constantly with a wooden spoon, add the egg yolk mixture into the saucepan.
5. Continue to stir constantly until the mixture thickens and coats the back of a wooden spoon, or a candy thermometer reads 180 degrees. Do not boil.
6. Remove from heat and pour custard into a bowl. Add cream, buttermilk and vanilla. Place in airtight container and chill thoroughly for at least four hours.
7. Stir mixture before adding to ice cream maker. Freeze according to manufacturer's instructions. If a firmer consistency is desired, transfer to an airtight container and ripen in freezer for two or more hours.

Fruit Flavors

Strawberry Ice Cream

This recipe is adapted from the friend of a friend. In this case, my friend, Candace Hartzler, shared her friend Sharon Endicott's recipe with me. Sharon, in turn, got the recipe from her mother-in-law, who made it in an old hand-crank. You can substitute almost any ripe summer fruit in this recipe (peaches, raspberries, blueberries), and it tastes just as good.

Makes 1 Generous Quart

3 egg yolks
1 cup sugar
1½ heaping teaspoons of flour
1½ cups of milk
¾ cup heavy whipping cream
3 cups pureed strawberries, fresh or thawed from frozen
2 teaspoons freshly squeezed lemon juice

1. Beat the eggs with an electric mixer on medium speed until pale yellow and egg mixture falls off in ribbons.
2. Mix the sugar and flour in a saucepan, and then add the milk. Heat on medium until bubbles form around the edges, or a candy thermometer reads 175 degrees. Do not allow mixture to boil.
3. Once milk mixture is ready, add ½ cup of it to the egg yolks and whisk to incorporate.
4. Pour the eggs into saucepan, stirring constantly. Cook until the mixture thickens and coats the back of a wooden spoon, or a candy thermometer reads 180 degrees. Do not boil.
5. Remove from heat and add cream, pureed strawberries and lemon juice.
6. Seal in an airtight container and chill for at least four hours.
7. Add mixture to ice cream maker and freeze according to manufacturer's directions. If a firmer consistency is desired, transfer to an airtight container and ripen in freezer for two or more hours.

Lemony Lemon Ice Cream

The lemon shines through in this easy recipe. The consistency is more like sherbet, but the flavor is ice-cream rich.

Makes 1 Quart

1 cup milk, chilled
1 cup heavy whipping cream, chilled
1 cup sugar
¼ cup freshly squeezed lemon juice
2 teaspoons finely grated lemon zest

1. Whisk sugar into milk until dissolved.
2. Add cream, lemon juice and lemon zest.
3. Add mixture to ice cream maker and freeze according to manufacturer's instructions. If a firmer consistency is desired, transfer to an airtight container and ripen in freezer for two or more hours.

Going All-Out: Gourmet Ice Cream

Basil Ice Cream

My friend, Virginia-based chef Elizabeth Brigham, is a big fan of infusing ice cream with spices and herbs. (She especially loves mint and cardamom.) She suggested I make ice cream with basil, and it works surprisingly well. It's reminiscent of licorice, but mellower and earthier. Try serving this with fresh strawberry slices.

Makes 1 Quart

1 cup milk
½ vanilla bean*
1 cup tightly packed basil leaves (stems removed)
4 egg yolks
¾ cup sugar
2 cups heavy cream

1. Add milk to a medium saucepan.
2. Slit vanilla bean lengthwise. Scrape the seeds from the pod with the edge of a paring knife into the saucepan, and then place the vanilla pods and basil into the saucepan.
3. Heat mixture over medium heat and stir occasionally until bubbles form around the edges, or a candy thermometer reads 175 degrees. Do not allow mixture to boil.
4. Remove from heat, cover and allow mixture to steep for 30 minutes. Strain mixture to remove basil leaves. Retrieve vanilla bean pods and return to mixture. Return basil-infused milk to saucepan.
5. Meanwhile, beat egg yolks and sugar with an electric mixer on medium speed until pale yellow in color and the egg mixture falls off in ribbons.
6. Once milk mixture is ready, add ½ cup of it to the egg yolks and whisk constantly to incorporate.
7. Then, stirring constantly with a wooden spoon, add the egg yolk mixture into the saucepan.
8. Continue to stir constantly until mixture coats the back of a spoon, or a candy thermometer reads 180 degrees.
9. Remove from heat and pour custard through a strainer into a bowl. Add cream; whisk well to combine.
10. Place in airtight container and chill thoroughly for at least four hours. Remove vanilla pods and stir mixture well.
11. Add mixture to ice cream maker and freeze according to manufacturer's instructions. If a firmer consistency is desired, transfer to an airtight container and ripen in freezer for two or more hours.
▪ If you don't have a vanilla bean, you can substitute 2 teaspoons of vanilla extract. Add along with cream in Step 9.

Butter Pecan

This recipe is adapted from the Cuisinart Flavor Duo maker's recipe booklet. It tastes even better after it's had the chance to firm up for a few hours in the freezer. Use the leftover pecan butter on waffles and pancakes with slices of fresh banana or over pasta with gorgonzola, sun-dried tomatoes and freshly ground pepper.

Makes 1 Quart

½ stick salted butter
½ – ⅔ cup coarsely chopped pecans
¼ teaspoon salt
¾ cup whole milk
¾ cup sugar
1½ cups heavy whipping cream
2 teaspoons vanilla extract

1. Place butter in large skillet over medium-low heat. Add pecans and salt. Stir until pecans are golden brown.
2. Pour butter and pecan mixture through a strainer into a bowl. Reserve ½ teaspoon of the

pecan-flavored butter. (Save remainder of butter for another use.) Set aside the strained pecans in a bowl to cool.

3. Heat milk in medium saucepan over medium-low heat until bubbles form around the edges. Do not boil. Remove from heat and add sugar. Whisk vigorously until sugar has dissolved.

4. Pour mixture into a bowl. Stir in cream and $1/2$ teaspoon of the pecan-flavored butter.

5. Cover and thoroughly chill in refrigerator for at least four hours.

6. Stir in vanilla. Transfer mixture to ice cream maker and freeze according to manufacturer's directions.

7. Add chopped pecans during last five minutes of freezing process.

8. Place in an airtight container and ripen in freezer at least four hours before serving.

Espresso Frozen Custard

Terese Allen, a Wisconsin-based cookbook author and regional food-ways expert, shares this intensely flavored and super-rich recipe.

Makes 1 Quart

$2/3$ cup espresso coffee beans
$1/2$ vanilla bean*
2 cups heavy whipping cream
1 cup milk
3 large egg yolks
$2/3$ cup sugar
1 tablespoon flour
$1/4$ teaspoon salt

1. Place espresso beans in a plastic ziploc bag; pound with heavy instrument to coarsely chop them. Split vanilla pod lengthwise; scrape out seeds with edge of a paring knife.

2. Combine espresso beans, vanilla beans and pod, cream and milk in heavy saucepan. Bring to simmer,

or until a candy thermometer reads 175 degrees. Turn off heat immediately, cover pan and let stand 30-60 minutes.

3. Whisk egg yolks in bowl. Gradually whisk in sugar until mixture is thickened and pale yellow and egg mixture falls off in ribbons.

4. Stir in flour and salt.

5. Gradually whisk in coffee-cream mixture. Return mixture to pan and cook, stirring constantly and without boiling, until custard thickens and coats the back of a wooden spoon, or a candy thermometer reads 180 degrees, usually six to eight minutes.

6. Pour through a fine mesh strainer into clean bowl. Let cool, stirring occasionally.

7. Place in an airtight container and chill thoroughly.

8. Stir mixture. Transfer mixture to ice cream maker and freeze according to manufacturer's directions. If desired, ripen in freezer for at least four hours before serving.

■ If you don't have a vanilla bean, you can substitute 2 teaspoons of vanilla extract. Add in Step 6.

Honey Lavender Ice Cream

Bea Delpapa ran the popular Riverside Cooking School in Cleveland, Ohio, and the Inn at Willow Pond in Lisbon, Ohio. Bea's cooking is famous for its fresh flavors and elegant presentation, and this recipe is no exception.

Makes 1 Generous Quart

$1/2$ cup sugar
$1 1/2$ teaspoons dried lavender flowers
3 cups half-and-half*
3 whole eggs*
1 teaspoon vanilla
$1/4$ cup honey

Candied violets or mint leaves for garnish (optional)

1. Place the sugar and lavender flowers in blender; pulse at high speed until lavender is pulverized and blended with the sugar. Set aside.

2. Place the half-and-half in the top of a double boiler; whisk in the eggs and lavender sugar. Cook over simmering — but not boiling — water and stir constantly until mixture coats the back of a spoon, or until a candy thermometer reads 180 degrees.

3. Strain mixture through a fine mesh strainer into a bowl. Stir in the vanilla and honey.

4. Place in an airtight container in the refrigerator overnight. (To chill quickly, place the pan in a bowl of ice water and whisk until mixture is cold.)

5. Freeze according to manufacturer's instructions. If a firmer consistency is desired, transfer to an airtight container and ripen in freezer for two or more hours. To serve, garnish with candied mint leaves or violets.

■ Note: For a richer ice cream, replace part or all of the half-and-half with heavy whipping cream, and use 6 egg yolks instead of 3 whole eggs.

Stracciatella Gelato

This is the Italian version of chocolate chip ice cream. Serve slightly softened to get the full flavor.

Makes 1 Quart

2 cups whole milk
$1/2$ vanilla bean*
$1 1/4$ cups sugar
6 egg yolks
1 cup heavy whipping cream
2 ounces best-quality semisweet chocolate, finely chopped

1. Add milk to a medium saucepan.

2. Slit vanilla bean lengthwise. Scrape the seeds from the pod with the edge of a paring knife into the saucepan, and then place the vanilla pods into the saucepan. Heat mixture over medium heat until bubbles form around edges, or a candy thermometer reads 175 degrees, stirring occasionally.

3. Meanwhile, beat sugar and egg yolks with an electric mixer on medium speed until pale yellow in color and the egg mixture falls off the beaters in ribbon-like strands.

4. Once milk mixture is ready, add $1/2$ cup of it to the egg yolks and whisk constantly to incorporate.

5. Then, stirring constantly with a wooden spoon, add the egg yolk mixture into the saucepan.

6. Continue to stir constantly until the thermometer reads 180 degrees.

7. Remove from heat and pour custard through a strainer into a bowl. Add cream. Retrieve vanilla bean pods and return to mixture.

8. Place in airtight container and chill thoroughly for at least four hours.

9. Stir mixture and remove vanilla pods.

10. Add mixture to ice cream maker and freeze according to manufacturer's instructions. Add chopped chocolate during last five minutes of freezing. If a firmer consistency is desired, transfer to an airtight container and ripen in freezer for two or more hours. Serve slightly softened.

■ If you don't have a vanilla bean, you can substitute 2 teaspoons of vanilla extract. Add along with cream in Step 7.

GREAT THINGS TO ADD TO YOUR ICE CREAM

Sweet Cream: Make a vanilla ice cream base, but omit vanilla flavoring. Great for fruit bases or when adding cookies or candies to your ice cream.

Almond: Heat oven to 250 degrees and roast 3/4 cup almonds for a few minutes until lightly browned. Cool completely. Add to mixture about five minutes before freezing is complete.

Apple Cinnamon: Add one 14.5 ounce can of apple pie filling and 1 to 2 teaspoons of cinnamon, to taste, to vanilla base before freezing.

Brownie Chunk: Place two or three regular-size brownie squares in refrigerator for 30 minutes to chill thoroughly. Then, chop into bite-size pieces and add to mixture about five minutes before freezing is complete

Chocolate Candy (M&M'S candies, Heath bar, Reese's Peanut Butter Cup, Kit Kat, Reese's Pieces, Twix bars, malted milk balls): Add 1/3 to 1/2 cup of your favorite small, whole candy (or coarsely chopped larger candy) to mixture about five minutes before freezing is complete. Note: If chopping chocolate-based candy, freeze before chopping.

Carob Chip: Add 1/2 cup of carob chips to mixture about five minutes before freezing is complete. Great with toasted coconut and nuts or with granola.

Chocolate Chip: Add 1/2 cup of chocolate chips to mixture about five minutes before freezing is complete.

Chocolate Chunk: Coarsely chop about 3 ounces of your favorite chocolate candy bar and add to mixture about five minutes before freezing is complete.

Cinnamon: Add 2 teaspoons cinnamon to mixture before freezing.

Coconut: Reduce sugar to 1/2 cup and omit vanilla. Add one cup of Coco Lopez Cream of Coconut to mixture and stir well before freezing. Then, add 1/3 cup of toasted coconut to mixture about five minutes before freezing is complete. If desired, also add 1/3 cup of chocolate chips along with the toasted coconut.

Coffee: Add 3 tablespoons instant coffee to mix before freezing and blend well. Chopped Heath Bars pair nicely with coffee.

Cookies and Cream: Add about 15 crushed cream-filled chocolate cookies (such Oreo brand) to mixture about five minutes before freezing is complete.

Honey Vanilla: Add 1/2 cup of honey in place of sugar. Almonds, coconut and pineapple are all good additions to this mixture; add to mixture during last five minutes of freezing process.

Malted: Stir in 1/3 to 1/2 cup malted milk powder to mixture before placing into ice cream maker. Tastes best with custard-based recipes.

Maple Walnut: Make the No-Cook Vanilla base, omitting the vanilla extract and reducing the sugar to 1/2 cup. Add 1/3 cup maple syrup to mixture before freezing. Then, add 1/2 cup coarsely chopped, toasted walnuts about five minutes before freezing is complete.

Mint Chocolate Chip: Replace vanilla extract with 1 to 2 teaspoons pure peppermint extract (to taste), and add a few drops of green food coloring (if desired) before freezing. Then, pour 1/2 cup of chocolate chips into mixture about five minutes before freezing is complete.

Peanut Butter: Remove one cup of ice cream mixture to a separate bowl. Stir in 1/2 cup smooth peanut butter until well-blended. Add to rest of mixture and freeze according to manufacturer's instruction.

Pecan-Coconut Chip: Add 3 tablespoons each of chopped pecans, toasted coconut and chocolate chips to mixture about five minutes before freezing is complete.

Peppermint Candy: Add 1/2 cup of coarsely chopped peppermint candy into mixture about five minutes before freezing is complete.

Rocky Road: Add 1/2 cup miniature marshmallows, 1/2 cup chocolate chips and 1/4 cup chopped walnuts or pecans to chocolate base about five minutes before freezing is complete.

Rum Raisin: Steep 1/2 cup of raisins in 1/4 cup dark rum for 30 minutes. Strain and add 2 teaspoons of rum to mixture before freezing. Add raisins to mixture about five minutes before freezing is complete.

Sensational Sherbets, Sorbets and Granitas

Orange Sherbet

The freshness of the orange juice and the zest gives this sherbet a full flavor. This recipe loses its creaminess when stored in a freezer, however, so it's best enjoyed right out the ice cream maker.

Makes 1 Quart

2 1/2 cups orange juice
1/3 cup sugar
3/4 cup half-and-half
1/2 teaspoon orange zest
1/4 teaspoon vanilla extract

1. Cook sugar and orange juice in a saucepan over medium heat until sugar is dissolved.
2. Transfer mixture to a bowl and place in refrigerator for an hour to thoroughly chill.
3. Whisk in half-and-half, orange zest and vanilla to mixture.
4. Add mixture to ice cream maker and freeze according to manufacturer's instructions. Serve immediately.

Chocolate Sorbet

It's worth seeking out Dutch-processed cocoa for this recipe; it has a velvety smooth taste without any bitterness.

Makes 1 Quart

1 1/2 cups sugar
3/4 cup unsweetened, Dutch-processed cocoa
1 teaspoon instant coffee
2 cups water
1 teaspoon vanilla extract

1. Combine sugar, cocoa, coffee granules and water in a saucepan and heat over medium heat until sugar is dissolved. Do not allow to boil.
2. Stir in vanilla extract.
3. Place in airtight container and chill thoroughly for at least four hours.
4. Add mixture to ice cream maker and freeze according to manufacturer's instructions. If a firmer consistency is desired, transfer to an airtight container and ripen in freezer for two or more hours.

Berry Sorbet

Jeni Britton of Jeni's Fresh Ice Creams in Columbus, Ohio, is a master at bold and unique combinations that capture the fresh essence of whatever ingredients she's using. In this simple recipe, the berries give the sorbet vibrant color and vibrant flavor. For best results, choose fresh berries at the peak of ripeness.

Makes 1 Generous Quart

2 cups sugar
2 cups water
Zest of one lemon, cut from lemon with a vegetable peeler in large pieces
5 cups (2 1/2 pints) raspberries, gooseberries, blackberries or a combination
Juice of 1/2 lemon

1. Heat sugar, lemon zest and water in a saucepan. Bring to a boil until liquid is perfectly clear. Remove from heat. Remove lemon zest. Chill.
2. Puree raspberries, put through a food mill or sieve to remove seeds. Add lemon and two cups of sugar syrup, or more to taste.
3. Chill, and then freeze in an ice cream machine according to manufacturer's instructions. If a firmer consistency is desired, transfer to an airtight container and ripen in freezer for two or more hours.

Lime Granita

Granitas are wonderfully light and refreshing, and they don't require an ice cream maker. These are nothing like a snow cone; the ice ends up in glistening flakes and the flavors are bright, not syrupy. Granita is best eaten the day it is made.

Serves 4-6

3 cups water
1 1/2 cup sugar
Zest of 1 lime
1 1/2 cups freshly squeezed lime juice

1. Combine water, sugar and lime zest in a medium saucepan. Boil over medium-high heat until sugar is dissolved and liquid is clear.
2. Stir in the lime juice.
3. Place in an airtight container and place in the refrigerator until chilled.
4. Pour granita into a shallow metal baking pan, cover with foil and place in freezer for one hour.
5. Remove granita from freezer. With the tines of a fork, scrape and mix granita to remove any lumps. Cover and return to return to freezer.
6. Repeat process every 30 minutes (for about two more hours), until granita is frozen into small, puffy flakes of ice.
7. Serve immediately. If not eating right away, you'll need to set mixture out for 10-15 minutes and scrape with fork before serving.

Coffee Granita

This is delicious when served with a dollop of freshly made whipped cream on top.

Serves 4 to 6

4 cups strong, dark-roast coffee or espresso, freshly made
1 teaspoon lemon zest
1 cup sugar
Whipped cream for garnish, optional

1. Make coffee, and stir in sugar and lemon zest while still hot. Allow coffee to cool to room temperature.
2. Pour granita into a shallow metal baking pan, cover with foil and place in freezer for one hour.
3. Remove granita from freezer. With the tines of a fork, scrape and mix granita to remove any lumps. Cover and return to return to freezer.
4. Repeat process every 30 minutes (for about two more hours), until granita is frozen into small, puffy flakes of ice.
5. Serve immediately. If not eating right away, you'll need to set mixture out for 10-15 minutes and scrape with fork before serving.

Yummy Yogurt

Peach Frozen Yogurt

This simple, low-fat recipe is adapted from the recipe booklet for the Cuisinart Flavor Duo maker. Custard-style yogurt, which contains gelatin, makes all the difference. The result is tasty, easy and quite creamy, even though it's low in fat.

Makes 1 Quart

1 14.5-ounce can of peaches, packed in juice
2 cups low-fat, custard-style vanilla yogurt
$1/2$ cup brown sugar
1 teaspoon freshly squeezed lemon juice

1. Drain peaches and reserve $1/4$ cup of the juice. Take 4 peach slices (about $1/3$ cup) and coarsely chop by hand. Set aside. Chop the remaining peaches using a food processor or blender.
2. Add the yogurt, brown sugar, lemon juice and reserved peach juice to blender or food processor and blend until smooth and sugar is dissolved.
3. Transfer mixture to ice cream maker and freeze according to manufacturer's directions. Add reserved chopped peaches during last five minutes of freezing. If a firmer consistency is desired, transfer to an airtight container and ripen in freezer at least four hours before serving.

ICE CREAM FOR SPECIAL DIETS

Everybody, regardless of dietary restrictions, can still love ice cream. Here are ways, with just a few simple modifications, to adapt ice cream recipes for any eating style.

Low-Carb Diets

■ Increase the amount of cream to 2 cups and use half-and-half or water for remaining liquid.
■ Replace sugar with a sugar substitute (such as Splenda, Nutrasweet, Stevia, or, my favorite, maltitol). You can use the same amount of granular Splenda and maltitol for sugar in any recipe cup for cup, but Stevia and sugar substitute packets require experimenting to get the right mix.
■ Egg yolks add richness and creaminess without adding many carbs, so look for frozen custard recipes, or add 4 to 6 egg yolks to a favorite no-egg recipe. (Use only recipes that call for heating the egg yolks.)
■ Good low-carb additions for your ice cream base include: pureed raspberries, strawberries and blackberries; sugar-free, low-carb fruit spreads made from raspberries or strawberries; spices like cinnamon, cardamom and ginger; unsweetened cocoa powder and chocolate; unsweetened coconut milk and shredded coconut; nuts; and sugar-free, low-carb chocolates and candies.

Low-Fat/Weight Watchers

■ Most sorbets, ices and granitas are non-fat and have two points for a $1/2$ cup serving. (All of the sorbets and granitas recipes in this book are two-point recipes.)
■ Sherbets average about three points per a serving. The orange sherbet included here is a two-pointer.

■ Use a sugar substitute (like Splenda or maltitol) in place of sugar to reduce points, and alter recipes to use more milk than cream.
■ Substitute milk for cream and use an egg substitute to replace egg yolks in recipes.

Diabetics

■ A combination of milk, evaporated milk and nonfat milk powder adds creaminess without the fat of heavy whipping cream.
■ Gelatin adds body and creaminess to ice cream without adding any fat or carbohydrates.
■ Substitute $1/4$ cup egg substitute, such as Egg Beaters, for eggs in recipes.
■ Sugar substitutes like those mentioned above for low-carb diets can add sweetness without affecting blood sugar levels.

Lactose Intolerant/Milk Allergic/Vegan

■ Rice and soy milks can be substituted cup-for-cup for milk in recipes. Soy creamer can stand in for half-and-half.
■ Consider adding eggs (if part of your diet) to non-dairy recipes for additional richness and creaminess.
■ Blend in silken tofu for a mousse-like texture.
■ Substitute maple syrup, honey, date sugar or Sucanat for refined sugar.
■ Add fruits or nuts to give body and flavor to mixture.

Low-Carb, Non-Dairy and No-Sugar Ice Creams

Low-Carb Vanilla Ice Cream
This makes for a creamy and tasty ice cream. My husband couldn't even tell it was made with a sugar substitute. You'll need a candy thermometer, but the perfect results are worth it.

Makes 1 Quart

3 carbs per $\frac{1}{2}$-cup serving

2 cups heavy whipping cream
4 egg yolks
1 cup powdered maltitol, such as Nature Sweet brand*
1 cup half-and-half
2 tablespoons vanilla extract

1. Add cream to a medium saucepan. Heat over medium heat, stirring occasionally.
2. Meanwhile, beat maltitol and egg yolks with an electric mixer on medium speed until pale yellow in color and the egg mixture falls off the beaters in ribbon-like strands.
3. Once cream reads 175 degrees on a candy thermometer, take $\frac{1}{2}$ cup of the cream mixture and add it to the beaten egg yolks, whisking constantly.
4. Then, stirring constantly with a whisk, add the egg yolk mixture into the saucepan.
5. Continue to stir constantly with a wooden spoon until the thermometer reads 180 degrees.
6. Remove from heat and add half-and-half or water and vanilla extract.
7. Place in an airtight container and chill thoroughly for at least four hours.
8. Add mixture to ice cream maker and freeze according to manufacturer's instructions. If a firmer consistency is desired, transfer to an airtight container and ripen in freezer for two or more hours.

◼ I prefer taste and resulting texture of maltitol for making ice cream; however, please note that excessive consumption of maltitol, a polyol or sugar alcohol, can have a laxative effect. A serving or two of maltitol-sweetened ice cream should be fine, but don't overindulge. You can purchase maltitol online or at most natural food stores. If desired, you can substitute another sweetener. See Ice Cream for Special Diets sidebar on opposite page for other suggestions.

Variations:
Blackberry Ginger (3.5 carbs per $\frac{1}{2}$ cup): Add 2 teaspoons ground ginger to mixture before freezing. Then, add $\frac{1}{2}$ cup fresh blackberries about five minutes before freezing is complete.
Cheesecake (3 carbs per $\frac{1}{2}$ cup): Substitute an 8-ounce brick of cream cheese for the half-and-half. Beat on the medium speed of an electric blender until smooth. For serving, top with heated sugar-free raspberry or strawberry fruit spread that's been thinned slightly with water. Or spread on low-carb crust to make frozen cheesecake.
Coconut (3 carbs per $\frac{1}{2}$ cup): Substitute 1 cup unsweetened coconut milk for half-and-half and add 2 teaspoons coconut extract. Then, add $\frac{3}{4}$ cup unsweetened, toasted coconut to mixture about five minutes before freezing is complete.
Maple Nut (3.5 carbs per $\frac{1}{2}$ cup): Add 2 teaspoons maple extract before freezing and $\frac{1}{2}$ cup toasted, coarsely chopped walnuts about five minutes before freezing is complete.

White Chocolate Macadamia Nut (3.5 carbs per $\frac{1}{2}$ cup): Coarsely chop two 1.6-ounce low-carb, white chocolate bars (with less than 2 net carbs for the whole bar) and $\frac{1}{3}$ cup of macadamia nuts. Add to mixture about five minutes before freezing is complete.

Low-Carb Chocolate Ice Cream
This is quite luscious and rich, with a velvety smooth texture. If desired, add $\frac{1}{2}$ cup toasted pecans or hazelnuts about five minutes before mixture is frozen.

Makes 1 Quart

4 carbs per $\frac{1}{2}$ cup serving

2 cups heavy whipping cream
3 tablespoons Atkins brand chocolate syrup
$\frac{1}{4}$ cup, plus 1 tablespoon, unsweetened cocoa, preferably Dutch-processed
4 egg yolks
1 cup maltitol, such as Nature Sweet brand*
1 cup half-and-half or water
2 teaspoons vanilla extract

1. Add cream, chocolate syrup and cocoa to a medium saucepan. Heat over medium heat, whisking to fully combine cocoa. Then, stir occasionally until heated.
2. Meanwhile, beat maltitol and egg yolks with an electric mixer on medium speed until pale yellow in color and the egg mixture falls off the beaters in ribbon-like strands.
3. Once cream reads 175 degrees on a candy thermometer, take $\frac{1}{2}$ cup of the cream mixture and add it to the beaten egg yolks, whisking constantly.

4. Then, stirring constantly with a whisk, add the egg yolk mixture into the saucepan.
5. Continue to stir constantly with a wooden spoon until the thermometer reads 180 degrees.
6. Remove from heat and add half-and-half or water and vanilla extract.
7. Place in an airtight container and chill thoroughly for at least four hours.
8. Add mixture to ice cream maker and freeze according to manufacturer's instructions. If a firmer consistency is desired, transfer to an airtight container and ripen in freezer for two or more hours.
◼ See note about maltitol below low-carb vanilla recipe.

Sugar-Free, Reduced-Fat Ice Cream For Diabetics
The gelatin and nonfat dry milk give this recipe richness without the fat. You can make this recipe chocolate by whisking $\frac{1}{3}$ cup unsweetened cocoa into mixture before freezing.

Makes 1 Quart

$1\frac{1}{2}$ cups whole milk
1 teaspoon gelatin
$\frac{2}{3}$ cup Splenda
1 can evaporated milk
$\frac{1}{2}$ cup heavy whipping cream
$\frac{3}{4}$ cup nonfat dry milk
2 teaspoons vanilla

1. Combine gelatin and milk in a saucepan. Warm over low heat until gelatin is completely dissolved.
2. Remove from heat. Add Splenda, evaporated milk, cream, nonfat dry milk and vanilla. Whisk until Splenda is dissolved.

3. Place in an airtight container and chill thoroughly for at least two hours.

4. Add mixture to ice cream maker and freeze according to manufacturer's instructions. If a firmer consistency is desired, transfer to an airtight container and ripen in freezer for two or more hours.

Banana Walnut Non-Dairy Ice Cream

This is quite yummy and a great substitute for anyone who can't handle dairy. If desired, you can substitute soy milk for the rice milk.

Makes 1 Quart

1 12.3-ounce box of silken firm tofu (such as Nori Mu brand), undrained and chilled
1 cup of vanilla rice milk, chilled
$3/4$ cup Sucanat granulated cane juice or sugar
$1/4$ cup date sugar
1 small banana
1 teaspoon lemon juice
2 teaspoons vanilla
$1/2$ cup roasted, chopped walnuts

1. In a food processor or a blender, combine first six ingredients (tofu through lemon juice) and blend until completely smooth.
2. Add vanilla and blend to combine.
3. Add mixture to ice cream maker and freeze according to manufacturer's instructions.
4. During last five minutes of freezing, add walnuts to mixture.
5. When freezing is finished, transfer to an airtight container and ripen in freezer for two or more hours before serving.

Chocolate Tofu Ice Cream

This recipe is adapted from one submitted by Annette Ooyevaar on www.vegweb.com. It's just as good (and maybe even better) than traditional chocolate ice cream.

Makes 1 Quart

1 12.3-ounce box of silken firm tofu (such as Nori Mu brand), undrained and chilled
1 12-ounce bag vegan semisweet chocolate chips, such as Tropical Source
$3/4$ cup unrefined or vegan sugar
1 cup rice milk
1 tablespoon vanilla extract

1. Place the chocolate chips in a small saucepan on low heat until melted. Remove from heat and cool to room temperature.
2. Remove tofu from box. Do not drain. Place tofu in a blender or food processor and puree until smooth.
3. Add melted chocolate to tofu and process until combined. Stop to scrape the sides of the blenders so that everything is incorporated.
4. Add the rice milk a little at a time and process until incorporated.
5. Add sugar and vanilla and process until sugar is dissolved and mixture is smooth.
6. Place mixture in airtight container and chill mixture in refrigerator for at least one hour.
7. Add mixture to ice cream maker and freeze according to manufacturer's instructions. If a firmer consistency is desired, transfer to an airtight container and ripen in freezer for two or more hours.

Fun Ice Cream

Plastic Bag Ice Cream

This is perhaps the quickest and easiest way to make ice cream without a maker. The result is very soft, but very quick. For a crowd, consider getting enough plastic bags, ice and rock salt for each person to make their own, then increase the recipe proportionately.

Makes 1 serving ($1/2$ cup)

2 one-quart freezer plastic bags (such as Ziploc)
1 one-gallon, freezer plastic bag (such as Ziploc)
$1/2$ cup half-and-half or milk
2 tablespoons sugar
$1/2$ teaspoon vanilla
4 cups crushed ice
$1/4$ cup rock salt
Gloves or a towel

1. Place half-and-half, sugar and vanilla in a one-quart plastic bag. Squeeze out excess air and seal tightly. Shake vigorously to ensure sugar is completely dissolved.
2. Double-bag with another quart-size bag.
3. Put these bags inside a gallon-size bag. Add salt and ice to the outer gallon-size bag. Squeeze out excess air and seal tightly. Place the bag inside a towel or put on gloves and then shake and massage the bag to work the ice around the ice cream mixture. When mixture firms up (five to 10 minutes), remove quart bag from salt and ice and serve.
■ Note: Dispose of salt and ice solution outside, away from grass or tender plantings.

Coffee Can Ice Cream

A great way to occupy the kids; they'll love getting involved in making their own ice cream. If the cans are tightly sealed, they can even kick the can back and forth.

Makes about a Pint

3 pound coffee can
1 pound coffee can
$3/4$ cup whole milk
1 cup cream
$1/3$ cup plus 2 tablespoons sugar
1 teaspoon vanilla
2-3 pounds crushed ice
$3/4$ cup rock salt
Duct tape

1. Whisk sugar and milk in a bowl until completely dissolved. Stir in cream and vanilla. Pour mixture into one-pound coffee can. Seal can securely by placing duct tape around edges of lid.
2. Put one-pound coffee can into three-pound can. Place a one to two-inch layer of crushed ice in the bottom of three-pound coffee can, then add about $1/4$ cup of salt. Continue to alternate layers of ice and salt until you reach the top of the three-pound can. Seal three-pound can securely by placing duct tape around edges of lid.
3. Roll, or kick, the can back and forth for 10 minutes.
4. After 10 minutes check on the mixture. If it's not frozen enough, scrape down the sides and reseal. If necessary, drain water out of three-pound can, and add ice and salt as necessary to refill can. Reseal and roll can for another five minutes or so.
5. Once mixture has the consistency of soft serve, scoop out of can and enjoy. If a firmer consistency is desired, ripen in freezer for two hours before eating.
■ Note: Dispose of salt and ice solution outside, away from grass or tender plantings.

TOPPING IT OFF

RECIPES FOR SUNDAES, SODAS AND OTHER ICE CREAM TREATS

It's fine to enjoy ice cream plain in a dish. But the beauty of ice cream is that it doesn't take much effort to add a few ingredients and create something memorable. Some caramel and hot fudge sauce over coffee ice cream makes a sundae to savor. A quart of vanilla becomes a dessert show stopper when transformed into an ice cream pie. The following recipes highlight some classic combinations that can serve as a starting point for dreaming up new formulas of your own. You can make all — or none — of the ingredients from scratch. Homemade is grand, but store-bought ice creams and toppings are delicious, too.

Sensational Sauces

Hot Fudge Sauce
A homemade hot fudge sauce is best served on its own with a good-quality vanilla. It's so rich and gooey and substantial that you really don't need anything else.

Makes 2 cups

3/4 cup heavy whipping cream
3 tablespoons butter
1/2 cup sugar
3 tablespoons light corn syrup
6 ounces bittersweet chocolate, chopped
1 teaspoon vanilla extract

1. Combine cream through corn syrup in a medium saucepan and heat over medium heat, stirring until butter is melted and sugar is dissolved. Add chocolate and stir until melted. Bring sauce to a boil.
2. Reduce heat to medium-low and simmer for 10 minutes, stirring occasionally, until the sauce has thickened
3. Remove from heat and stir in the vanilla extract.
4. Cool slightly and serve. Or place in an airtight container and refrigerate. To reheat, microwave at 70 percent power for one to two minutes or until warm. Stir before serving.

Variations:
Mocha Fudge Sauce: Add 1 tablespoon instant coffee granules at beginning of process.
Chocolate Mint Sauce: Reduce vanilla to 1/4 teaspoon and add 1 teaspoon peppermint extract.

Chocolate Sauce
Chocolate sauce is similar to hot fudge, but it's thinner in consistency and less rich- tasting.

Makes about 2 cups

3/4 cup heavy whipping cream
1/2 cup sweetened condensed milk
6 ounces semisweet chocolate, chopped, or chocolate chips
1/2 teaspoon vanilla extract
Pinch of salt

1. Combine cream, condensed milk and chocolate in a medium-size saucepan over medium-low heat. Stir until smooth and chocolate is melted.
2. Stir in vanilla and salt.
3. Serve immediately. Or place in an airtight container and refrigerate. To reheat, microwave at 70 percent power for one to two minutes or until warm. Stir before serving.

Caramel Sauce
You need to keep a close eye on caramel so it doesn't burn, and take extra care when mixing so you don't splatter any on yourself.

Makes 2 cups

1 cup heavy whipping cream
1 1/2 cups sugar
1/3 cup water
1 teaspoon lemon juice
2 tablespoon light corn syrup
Pinch of salt
2 tablespoons unsalted butter
1 teaspoon vanilla extract

1. Place cream in a small saucepan over medium-low heat. Keep warm while you prepare the caramel.
2. In a 3-quart saucepan, combine sugar, water, lemon juice and corn syrup. (Choose a saucepan that has an interior light enough to see when the sugar caramelizes.) Cook over medium-high heat, and whisk constantly until sugar is dissolved and mixture is boiling.

3. Boil without stirring for about five to eight minutes until mixture is golden amber in color. (Do not overcook.) You can use a wet pastry brush to incorporate any sugar crystals that form on the sides of the pan.
4. Remove pan immediately from heat, and carefully and slowly whisk in heated cream mixture. (Don't splatter any on yourself; it will burn.)
5. Return pan to heat and cook over medium-low heat, whisking sauce until smooth. Whisk in salt, butter and vanilla until smooth.
6. Cool slightly and serve. Or place in an airtight container and refrigerate. To reheat, microwave at 70 percent power for one to two minutes or until warm. Stir before serving.

Butterscotch Sauce
Butterscotch is a close cousin to caramel sauce, except that brown sugar and more butter is used in butterscotch, giving the sauce a rich buttery flavor.

Makes 2 cups

3 tablespoons unsalted butter
1 cup brown sugar, packed
1 cup heavy cream
Pinch of salt

1. Combine all the ingredients in a medium saucepan over medium heat. Whisk constantly until sugar is dissolved and mixture is boiling.
2. Reduce heat to medium-low and simmer for three to five minutes more or until mixture thickens a bit.
3. Serve immediately. Or place in an airtight container and refrigerate. To reheat, microwave at 70 percent power for one to two minutes or until warm. Stir before serving.

Marshmallow Topping
Marshmallow topping was quite popular during World War II when sugar was rationed. Today, it provides a special touch to any scoop of ice cream, especially when combined with some hot fudge sauce.

Makes 2 cups

16 large marshmallows
2 tablespoons corn syrup
1/3 cup milk
Pinch salt

1. Combine all ingredients in the top half of a double boiler over simmering water. Stir until marshmallows have melted and sauce is smooth.
2. Serve immediately. Or place in an airtight container and refrigerate. To reheat, microwave at 70 percent power for one to two minutes or until warm. Stir before serving.

Macerated Strawberries
In summer, keep a container of these in your refrigerator. They're great on ice cream, over shortcakes or angel food cake or on oatmeal. For an adult twist, add a tablespoon of orange liqueur or Modena balsamic vinegar to the mix.

2 cups sliced fresh strawberries
2–3 tablespoons sugar, to taste

1. Combine strawberries and sugar in a bowl. Stir well.
2. Cover and return to refrigerator to sit for one to three hours. Serve cold, or heat in the microwave for one to two minutes.

Whipped Cream

When making homemade whipped cream, avoid buying cream that's been ultra-pasteurized. It doesn't whip as well. You can also flavor your whipped cream with $1/4$ teaspoon of cinnamon, instant coffee granules, cocoa powder or vanilla extract.

Makes about 2 cups

$1/2$ pint (1 cup) heavy whipping cream, not ultra-pasteurized
5–6 tablespoons powdered sugar, to taste

1. A half-hour before making whipped cream, place mixing bowl and beaters in freezer to chill.
2. In the chilled mixing bowl, place the whipping cream and whip on high speed of an electric mixer. Add powdered sugar, one tablespoon at a time, to desired sweetness. Beat until whippy and peaks form. (Do not overbeat.) Serve immediately.

Cool Cones

Homemade Waffle Cones

You'll need a pizzelle or waffle maker and a cone form for these cones. Cone-rolling can be a little tricky at first, but it gets easier with practice. You can also forgo the cone-rolling altogether and make an edible cup instead; just place warm cone on top of an upside-down ramekin.

Makes 6-8 cones

3 tablespoons butter, melted and cooled
1 egg
2 egg whites
$1/2$ teaspoon salt
$2/3$ cup sugar
1 cup flour
1 teaspoon vanilla
Wooden cone mold

1. Spray pizzelle or waffle maker with nonstick cooking spray and preheat according to manufacturer's directions.
2. Combine eggs and salt with a whisk. Add sugar and whisk until smooth. Stir in the flour, and then the butter and vanilla. (Mixture will be thick.)
3. Place about 2 tablespoons (or more depending on size of maker) of mixture in center of iron and cook for one to two minutes or until golden. Gently remove pizzelle or waffle from maker with a fork. Using a kitchen towel to protect your hands, wrap pizzelle or waffle around a wooden cone mold. Gently pinch to seal bottom shut. Hold for a minute or two to set. Cool on a baking sheet, a cone holder or a rectangular baking pan filled with sugar.
4. Repeat steps with remaining batter.
5. Serve filled with ice cream. Or store in an airtight container up to a week.
■ Note: If the cone's point isn't sealed fully, you can place a mini-marshmallow or a small piece of soft candy in the bottom to catch drips before adding ice cream.

EVERYBODY SCREAMS FOR EGG CREAMS (OR WHY THEY SHOULD)

If you're not from New York, you might not have heard of an egg cream. But for native New Yorkers, egg creams are as much a part of the town's culinary heritage as bagels and coney dogs. The name is bit of a misnomer; there are no eggs and no cream in it. (There are at least a dozen stories about the origin of the name. One theory is that the chocolate syrup originally included eggs.) The key to a great egg cream is the right balance of chocolate taste (many purists insist on Brooklyn-made Fox's U-Bet chocolate syrup) and perfect visual appearance (chocolate cream below and a clean, white foam on top).

Craig Bero of the Bespeckled Trout in New York City made me my first egg cream. He explained it was like the Gatorade of its time, the drink of choice for thirsty athletes after a tough game. I can see why; it's filling and satisfying but not too heavy. He makes his delicious egg creams with fresh soda water and the practiced flourish and finesse of a true soda jerk. When in the Big Apple, be sure to order one. The Bespeckled Trout, 422 Hudson St., 212-255-1421; Junior's, 386 Flatbush Ave. in Brooklyn, 718-852-5257; and the Gem Spa newsstand, 131 Second Ave., 212-529-1146, are good choices. To make one at home, follow the recipe below. Fox's U-Bet Syrup is available from several retailers online.

New York Egg Cream

Serves 1

$1/2$ cup whole milk, well-chilled
1 cup seltzer water or club soda, well-chilled
2–3 tablespoons chocolate syrup (preferably Fox's U-Bet)

1. Pour milk into a tall, well-chilled soda glass. Add seltzer to milk while stirring vigorously with a long spoon. The head should rise just to the top of the glass. Keep the spoon in the glass and drizzle in syrup, stirring with small wrist motions to leave the head undisturbed. The resulting drink should have a brown bottom and a one-inch head of clean white foam on top.

Every Day is for Sundaes

Hot Fudge Sundae

You can use store-bought hot fudge sauce, but it's so easy — and so tasty — to make your own. The variations on this classic are endless, but that's part of the fun.

Serves 1

2–4 tablespoons hot fudge sauce (recipe on page 168), warmed and divided
1–2 scoops ice cream
1–2 teaspoons chopped nuts, optional
Whipped cream, optional
Cherry or sliced strawberry, optional

1. Place $1/2$ tablespoon of hot fudge sauce in bottom of a shallow bowl or tulip-shaped glass cup.
2. Add 1 to 2 scoops of your favorite flavor of ice cream. (Vanilla is always a good bet.)
3. Pour remaining hot fudge over top. Add chopped nuts, whipped cream, and cherry, if desired.

20 More Sundae Variations

Here are a few more ways to enjoy a sundae. Vanilla is always a good base for a sundae, but experiment with your favorite flavors. Recipes for sauces can be found on page 168. And don't forget to finish it off with whipped cream and a cherry.

Affogato al Caffe: An Italian classic. Pour one shot of espresso over ice cream.
Apple Maple: Ice cream topped with 2 to 3 tablespoons each of warmed canned apple pie filling and maple syrup. Top with 1 to 2 teaspoons chopped walnuts.
Black and White: Ice cream (usually a scoop each of vanilla and chocolate) topped with 2 to 3 tablespoons each of chocolate sauce and marshmallow topping.
Black and Tan: Ice cream topped with 2 to 3 tablespoons chocolate sauce and 2 to 3 tablespoons butterscotch or caramel topping.
Brownie: Put one square slice of brownie on bottom of dish. Add ice cream, 2 to 3 tablespoons hot fudge or caramel sauce (or even better, both) and 1 to 2 teaspoons chopped nuts.
Candy: Chop your favorite candy into bite-sized pieces and sprinkle 2 to 3 tablespoons over top of ice cream. (If using a chocolate-based candy, freeze before chopping.) If desired, add a sauce or topping.
Cookie: Ice cream topped with 2 to 3 tablespoons coarsely crushed cookie (chocolate chip, gingersnaps, chocolate wafers or a chocolate sandwich cookie, such as Oreos). Add 2 to 3 tablespoons hot fudge or caramel sauce, depending on ice cream and cookie flavors, and whipped cream.
Dirty Worm: A favorite for kids. Ice cream topped liberally with $1/4$ cup finely ground chocolate wafers (the dirt). Place 3 gummy worms on top.
Dusty Miller/Dusty Road: Ice cream topped with 2 to 3 tablespoons hot fudge and 1 to 2 teaspoons malted milk powder.
Honey Almond: Ice cream topped with 2 to 3 tablespoons honey and 1 to 2 teaspoons chopped toasted almonds.

Liqueur: For an adult twist, top ice cream with 1 to 2 ounces of liqueur. **A few ideas:** Bailey's Irish Cream, Cassis, Chambord, Godiva, Grand Marnier, Kahlúa or Kirsch.
Maple Granola: Ice cream topped with 2 to 3 tablespoons maple syrup, warmed. and 1 to 2 teaspoons granola. Garnish with toasted coconut or chopped toasted almonds if desired.
PB&J: Ice cream with 2 to 3 tablespoons peanut butter topping and 2 to 3 tablespoons blueberry, raspberry or strawberry topping.
Peach Melba: Add two peach halves (either freshly poached at home or from a can, drained of juice or syrup) to bottom of shallow bowl or a tulip-shaped glass cup. Add 2 scoops of ice cream. Top with 2 to 3 tablespoons raspberry sauce.
Pineapple: Ice cream topped with 2 to 3 tablespoons crushed pineapple. If desired, add 1 to 2 teaspoons dark rum over ice cream. Top with toasted coconut and garnish with a whole pineapple slice, if desired.
Red, White & Blue: Ice cream topped with 1 tablespoon each of macerated strawberries, marshmallow topping and fresh blueberries.
S'mores: Vanilla or Rocky Road ice cream topped with 3 tablespoons of hot fudge sauce and 2 tablespoons marshmallow topping. Sprinkle 2 tablespoons graham cracker crumbs on top.
Tin Roof: Ice cream with 2 to 3 tablespoons chocolate sauce and 1 to 2 teaspoons roasted Spanish peanuts.
Turtle: Ice cream topped with 2 to 3 tablespoons each of caramel topping, and hot fudge topping and 1 to 2 teaspoons roasted pecans.

White Mountain: Ice cream topped with 2 to 3 tablespoons of marshmallow topping and 1 to 2 teaspoons toasted coconut. Garnish with white chocolate shavings, if desired.

Banana Split

This is the classic version of the banana split. You, of course, can use any combination of flavors or toppings that you like. Try butterscotch, chocolate and marshmallow, or all-fruit toppings (raspberry, pineapple and strawberry).

Serves 1-2

1 banana, sliced lengthwise
1 scoop each of chocolate, strawberry and vanilla ice cream
2 tablespoons chocolate sauce (recipe on page 168)
2 tablespoons macerated strawberries (recipe on page 168)
2 tablespoons crushed pineapples
Whipped cream
3 maraschino cherries
Chopped nuts

1. Place banana in bottom of an oval-shaped, shallow banana split dish.
2. Add ice cream scoops in a row between banana halves.
3. Pour chocolate sauce over chocolate ice cream; strawberries on strawberry ice cream; and pineapple over vanilla ice cream.
4. Top with a generous amount of whipped cream, and a maraschino cherry on top of each scoop of ice cream. Sprinkle with nuts.

EASY ICE CREAM SANDWICHES

An easy alternative to making ice cream sandwiches from scratch is to use store-bought cookies and smoosh a scoop of your favorite (slightly softened) ice cream inside. You can't go wrong using such standbys as chocolate chip or soft Dutch cocoa cookies (try Archway brand). For added indulgence, spread a layer of hot fudge or caramel on the cookie before adding the ice cream and then roll the sandwich in nuts, chocolate chips or coconut. Here are some more ideas:

- Gingersnaps with lemon ice cream or sorbet
- Oatmeal-raisin cookies with apple pie ice cream
- Macaroons with vanilla ice cream and hot fudge sauce
- Pizzelles with raspberry sorbet
- Snickerdoodles with vanilla ice cream and caramel sauce
- Shortbread with butter pecan or honey lavender ice cream
- Vanilla wafers with banana ice cream and caramel sauce
- White chocolate macadamia nut cookies with coconut ice cream

Perfect Parfaits

Simple Parfait

Use this recipe as a base to create your own masterpiece, keep in mind that contrasting colors but complementary flavors are key to a great parfait.

Serves 1

$1/3$ cup hot fudge sauce
$1/2$ cup sliced strawberries or raspberries
2 scoops of ice cream
Whipped cream
Berries for garnish

1. In a tall glass, layer in order: 2 tablespoons each of hot fudge and 3 tablespoons raspberries. Add one scoop of ice cream.
2. Repeat layers again, beginning with hot fudge. Add remaining 2 tablespoons of berries and remaining hot fudge.
3. Top with whipped cream and put a berry on top for garnish.

Variations:
Lemon Raspberry Gingersnap: Layer crushed gingersnaps, raspberry sauce and lemon sorbet.

Garnish with mint leaves.
Mint: Layer chocolate sauce, chopped mint cookies or candies (such as Thin Mints or After 5 Dinner Mints) with mint chocolate chip or vanilla ice cream. Garnish with whipped cream and chopped cookies or candies.

Shake It Up with Milk Shakes

Classic Milk Shake

The key to a great milkshake is keeping everything as cold as possible. I sometimes put the milk in the freezer for 15 or 20 minutes before blending to get it as cold as possible.

Serves 1-2

3 generous scoops of ice cream, or about $1^{1}/2$ cups*
1 cup milk, 2 percent or whole, well-chilled
3–4 tablespoons flavored syrup of choice, to taste
Whipped cream, optional

1. Place ingredients in a blender, or a large tumbler if using a

milkshake machine or a handheld immersion blender. Blend to desired consistency. If needed, transfer to a tall chilled drink glass. Top with whipped cream, if desired. Serve with a straw and a long spoon.
■ Note: if you like a thicker milkshake, increase ice cream to 4 scoops and reduce milk to $1/2 – 3/4$ cup.

Variations:
Malted: Add 1 tablespoon of malted milk powder to shake before blending.
Strawberry Banana: Use strawberry ice cream as the base and add $1/2$ a banana, sliced, before blending
Sorbet Cooler: A dairy-free shake. Combine 3 scoops of sorbet and $1^{1}/2$ cups of seltzer water and blend.

Fountain Favorites: Sodas and Floats

Classic Chocolate Ice Cream Soda

Sodas are at their best when made with fresh seltzer. If you love

sodas, a siphon with a CO_2 charger is worth the investment.

Serves 1

3 tablespoons chocolate syrup
2 tablespoons half-and-half
$1/2$ cup seltzer water, well-chilled
$1^{1}/2$ generous scoops vanilla ice cream, divided
Whipped cream
Maraschino cherry for garnish

1. In a chilled, tall glass, add syrup and half-and-half. Stir well to combine. Add $1/2$ scoop of ice cream. Mash in to combine. Stir in seltzer to create a nice head of foam. Add final scoop of ice cream, placing it on the edge of the glass. If needed, add more seltzer to fill glass. Top with whipped cream and cherry. Serve with straw and a long spoon.

Variations:
Broadway: Substitute coffee ice cream in place of vanilla.
Double-Chocolate: Substitute chocolate ice cream in place of vanilla.

Strawberry: Substitute strawberry syrup and strawberry ice cream in place of chocolate syrup and vanilla.

Root Beer Float

Also called a Brown Cow, this is a classic. Use the best vanilla ice cream you can buy (or make) and the coldest root beer.

Serves 1

$1^1/_2$ cups (12 ounces) root beer
3 scoops, about 1 cup, of vanilla ice cream

1. In a chilled, tall glass, pour in about $^1/_3$ of root beer and a half scoop of ice cream. Stir to combine. Pour in remaining root beer until glass is about $^3/_4$ full. Add remaining ice cream. Serve with straw and a tall spoon.

Variations:
Black Cow: Vanilla ice cream with cola-flavored soda.
Champagne Float: An adult version with one scoop of raspberry sorbet and 6 ounces of champagne in place of the root beer and vanilla.
Ginger Float: Vanilla ice cream with ginger ale.
Orange Dream: Vanilla ice cream with orange-flavored soda.

Bombe-shell of a Dessert: Pies and Bombes

Ice Cream Pie

I usually buy a premade crumb crust (choose from graham cracker, chocolate, shortbread, or, my favorite, Oreo cookie), but you can make your own. I like pies best when they are made with a chunky flavor of ice cream; the mix-ins add to the look — and the taste — of the pie. Be generous with the whipped cream; you want the layers to look substantial when sliced.

Serves 6-8

1 crumb pie crust
$1^1/_4$ cup of hot fudge sauce, divided
1 quart (4 cups) of ice cream
4-6 cups of whipped cream (recipe on page 169)
Maraschino cherries for garnish, optional

1. Spread $^1/_2$ to $^3/_4$ cup of room temperature hot fudge sauce evenly over bottom of crust. Place in freezer to set for 30 minutes. Meanwhile, set ice cream out for about 20 minutes or until just soft enough to spread. (If needed, microwave on 50 percent power for 30 seconds to one minute to speed up softening process.) With a spatula or an ice cream spade, spread ice cream on top of hot fudge layer. If making whipped cream, return ice cream to freezer while it's being made.
2. When whipped cream is ready, retrieve pie from freezer. Spread on a generous layer of whipped cream. If desired, decorate with cherries.
3. Freeze for at least two hours to harden. Before serving, set pie in refrigerator for 15 minutes to soften slightly. Warm remaining hot fudge; pass around in a small pitcher to drizzle over slices of pie.

Variations:
Caramel Banana: Vanilla or banana ice cream, caramel sauce, sliced bananas, chopped walnuts and whipped cream.
Cherries Jubilee: Vanilla ice cream, hot fudge sauce, cherry pie filling and whipped cream.
Mocha Fudge: Coffee ice cream, hot fudge or mocha fudge sauce, Oreo cookie crumb crust and whipped cream. Decorate with chocolate-covered espresso beans.

Basic Ice Cream Bombe

To make a bombe, you'll need a metal bowl, loaf pan, tubular cake pan or a gelatin mold and some advance planning time. (I like using a springform pan for easy release.) Bombes are best made at least a day in advance. You can customize the recipe below to suit your tastes; keep in mind you may need more or less ice cream depending on the size of the mold or pan used. You can also add a layer of sauce between the ice cream layers; freeze as you would for a layer of ice cream.

Serves 4-6

3 pints of ice cream in two or three different flavors
6-cup ($1^1/_2$-quart) metal pan, bowl or mold
Sauce and toppings for garnish, optional

1. Line pan with plastic wrap, making sure that some of the wrap hangs over the edge (you may have to crisscross two pieces of wrap to get full coverage). Set out one pint of ice cream for 20 minutes or until soft enough to spread. (If needed, microwave on 50 percent power for 30 seconds to one minute to speed up the softening process.) Use a spatula or ice cream spade that's been dipped in warm water to spread ice cream into bottom of pan. (Dip utensil into warm water as needed to easily spread ice cream.)

Return to freezer for an hour to harden.
2. Set out second flavor of ice cream for 20 minutes until soft enough to spread. Use a spatula or ice cream spade that's been dipped in warm water to spread ice cream into pan. Return to freezer for about an hour to harden.
3. Set out third flavor of ice cream for 20 minutes until soft enough to spread. Use a spatula or ice cream spade that's been dipped in warm water to spread ice cream into pan, making sure it's even to create a smooth bottom for the bombe. Cover with plastic wrap and return to freezer for about three hours until frozen solid.
4. Before serving, remove bombe from pan by covering with a warm, wet towel and turning over to release. If needed, pull gently on plastic wrap. Discard plastic wrap. Run a spatula that's been dipped in warm water along tops and sides of bombe to smooth out edges if necessary. If not serving immediately, cover and return to freezer until ready to eat.
5. Serve bombe by bringing intact to table (for maximum visual effect) and slicing in front of guests. Add toppings and sauces as desired.

Variations:
Heath Bar: Vanilla, Heath Bar and caramel ice creams, topped with hot fudge sauce and chopped Heath bars.
Raspberry Chocolate: Vanilla ice cream, raspberry sorbet, hot fudge sauce, chocolate ice cream, topped with raspberry sauce and fresh raspberries.
Tropical: Coconut ice cream, mango sorbet and strawberry ice cream, topped with whipped cream, chopped pineapple and toasted coconut. ◼

During the 1940s, milk shakes were all the rage, thanks to the popularization of the so-called "Hollywood Lunch" and ice cream's image as a wholesome and nutritious food.

SELECTED BIBLIOGRAPHY

History

Butko, Brian. *Klondikes, Chipped Ham & Skyscraper Cones: The Story of Isalys.* Mechanicsburg, PA: Stackpole Books, 2001.

Chr. Hansen's Laboratory. *The Junket Book.* Hanson Falls, NY: Chr. Hansen s Laboratory, 1935.

David, Elizabeth. *Harvest of the Cold Months: The Social History of Ices and Ice.* Edited by Jill Norman. New York: Viking, 1994.

Dickson, Paul. *The Great American Ice Cream Book.* New York: Galahad Books, 1972.

Funderberg, Anne Cooper. *Chocolate, Strawberry and Vanilla: A History of American Ice Cream.* Bowling Green, OH: Bowling Green State University Popular Press, 2002.

———. *Sundae Best: A History of Soda Fountains.* Bowling Green, OH: Bowling Green State University Popular Press, 2002.

Herbst, Sharon Tyler. *The New Food Lover's Companion.* 3rd ed. Hauppauge, NY: Barron's Educational Series, 2001.

Liddell, Caroline and Robin Weir. *Frozen Desserts: The Definitive Guide to Making Ice Creams, Ices, Sorbets, Gelati, and Other Frozen Delights.* New York: St. Martin's Griffin, 1995.

Marks, Ed. *Ice Cream Collectibles.* Atglen, PA: Schiffer Publishing Ltd., 2003.

Smith, Wayne. *Ice Cream Dippers.* Walkersville, Maryland: self-published, 1986.

Turback, Michael. *A Month of Sundaes.* New York: Red Rock Press, 2002.

Visser, Margaret. *Much Depends on Dinner: The Extraordinary History and Mythology, Allure and Obsessions, Perils and Taboos of an Ordinary Meal.* New York: Grove Press, 1986.

Ice Cream Science and Culture

Marshall, Robert T. and W.S. Arbuckle. *Ice Cream.* 5th ed. Gaithersburg, MD: Aspen Publishers, 2000.

Robbins, Carol T. and Herbert Wolff. *The Very Best Ice Cream and Where to Find It.* New York: Warner Books, 1985.

An Ice Cream Show. 1999. Produced and directed by Rick Sebak. 60 min. videocassette. PBS Home Video.

Stern, Jane and Michael. *Road Food: The Coast-to-Coast Guide to 500 of the Best Barbeque Joints, Lobster Shacks, Ice Cream Parlors, Highway Diners and Much More.* New York: Broadway Books, 2002.

Wardlaw, Lee. *We All Scream for Ice Cream!: The Scoop on America's Favorite Dessert.* New York: Harper Trophy, 2000.

Recipes

Cohen, Ben and Jerry Greenfield with Nancy J. Stevens. *Ben & Jerry's Homemade Ice Cream and Dessert Book.* New York: Workman Publishing, 1987.

Cuisinart. *Cuisinart Instruction and Recipe Booklet for Flavor Duo Yogurt-Ice Cream and Sorbet Maker.* East Windsor, NJ: Cuisinart, 2002.

Damerow, Gail. *Ice Cream! The Whole Scoop.* Lakewood, CO: Glenbridge Publishing Ltd., 1995.

Farmer, Fannie Merritt. *The Boston Cooking-School Cook Book.* Boston: Little, Brown, and Company, 1929.

Johns, Pamela Sheldon *Gelato!: Italian Ice Creams, Sorbetti & Granite.* Berkeley, CA: Ten Speed Press, 1999

Kelly, Patricia M., ed. *Luncheonette: Ice-Cream, Beverage, and Sandwich Recipes from the Golden Age of the Soda Fountain.* New York: Crown Publishers, 1989.

Longbotham, Lori. *The Scoop: How to Change Store-Bought Ice Cream into Fabulous Desserts.* New York: Villard, 2003.

Pappas, Lou Seibert. *Sorbets and Ice Creams.* San Francisco: Chronicle Books, 1997.

Petersen-Schepelern, Elsa. *Soda Fountain Classics: Ice Cream, Sundaes, Milkshakes and More.* New York: Ryland Peters & Small, 2000.

Roden, Nadia. *Granita Magic: 55 Ices for Every Reason and Every Season — Always the Perfect Thing to Serve.* New York: Artisan, 2003.

Rosen, Diana. *The Ice Cream Lover's Companion: The Ultimate Connoisseur's Guide to Buying, Making, and Enjoying Ice Cream and Frozen Yogurt.* New York: Citadel Press, 2000.

Weinstein, Bruce. *The Ultimate Ice Cream Book: Over 500 Ice Creams, Sorbets, Granitas, Drinks, and More.* New York: William Morrow and Company, Inc., 1999.

Websites

Chowhound: For Those Who Live to Eat. Ed. Jim Leff. Fall 2003. www.chowhound.com/main.html

Citysearch.com. *2002 Best of Citysearch: Best Ice Cream in the United States.* best.citysearch.com/cities/2002/7778/?cslink=cs_boc_left_nav

Buchanan, Nathan. *Committee for the Analysis and Debate of Various Aspects of Ice Cream.* Fall 2003. www.cc.utah.edu/~nb7939/newcadic/

CustardList.com. Summer 2003. www.custardlist.com

Ehler, James T. *The Food Reference Website.* Fall 2003. James T. Ehler. www.foodreference.com

Ellison, Jim. *Ice Cream Ohio.* Summer 2003. home.netcom.com/~ellisonj/icomain.html

Mann, Steve. Home page. Summer 2003. www.cgl.uwaterloo.ca/~smann/IceCream/

Moore, Holly. Home page. Fall 2003. www.hollyeats.com

Seltzer, Debra Jane. Home page. Fall 2003. www.agilitynut.com/roadside.html

Soda Fountains Near You. Ed. The Prairie Moon Co. Fall 2003. www.prairiemoon.biz/sodfounneary.html

Stern, Jane and Michael. Home page. 2003. www.roadfood.com

Stradley, Linda. *What's Cooking America.* Summer 2003. www.whatscookingamerica.net

University of Guelph Dairy and Science Technology Department. *Ice Cream.* www.foodsci.uoguelph.ca/dairyedu/icecream.html

Wilson, Steve. Home page. Summer/Fall 2003. www.users.nwark.com/~piperw/icpage.htm

PICTURE CREDITS

Note: Any pictures not listed below are by the author or from the author's collection.

From the collection of America's Ice Cream & Dairy Museum at Historic Elm Farm, courtesy of Carl and Sherry Abell and Steven Stolph: Chapter 1: Rabbit pewter mold, page 21. Chapter 2: Sweetheart chair, page 36; Good Humor face mask, page 44. Chapter 6: Hand-crank freezer, page 98. Chapter 7: Dippers, page 119.

From the collection of the American Sign Museum, courtesy of Tod Swormstedt: Chapter 7: Nesbitt's Frosted Orange sign, page 123.

Michael Arnold: Chapter 4: Chocolate Shoppe freezer, page 70; Chocolate Shoppe hardening room (below left), page 71. Chapter 5: Kitt's Frozen Custard, page 85; Leon's Frozen Custard, page 94. Author photo, page 176.

Courtesy of Bruce and Mark Becker: Chapter 3: bottom photo, page 59.

Chris Chapman: Appendix 1, Big Dipper Ice Cream, page 128.

Courtesy of Dairy Queen: Cone photo, page 94.

Courtesy of Dippin' Dots: Chapter 5: Close-up photo, page 91.

Courtesy of Dreyer's: Chapter 4: John Harrison photo, page 69.

Courtesy of Good-Humor-Breyers Company: Chapter 2: Kids eating Good Humor bars, page 30; Harry Burt photo, page 44; Good Humor men, page 45; Good Humor man with dog, page 47. Chapter 3: Sponge Bob Square Pants half gallon, page 61. Chapter 4: Breyers Ice Cream truck, page 66.

Courtesy of Häagen-Dazs: Chapter 3: *Tres leches* pint, page 61.

Courtesy Handel's Homemade Ice Cream & Yogurt: Chapter 5, Original store photo, page 89.

From *Ice Cream Collectibles* by Ed Marks (Schiffer Publishing Ltd., 2003). Reprinted with permission.: Chapter 1: Eskimo pie ad, page 18. Chapter 2: Saturday Evening Post covers, pages 32, 38 and 111.

From *Klondikes, Chipped Ham, & Skyscraper Cones: The Story of Isaly's* by Brian Butko (Stackpole Books, 2001). Reprinted with permission: Chapter 1: Interior of Isaly's, page 13; Klondike ad and Skyscraper cone, page 23.

Tonya Malench: Chapter 5, Ted Drewes, page 80.

From the collection of Allan "Mr. Ice Cream" Mellis: Chapter 1: Boys on Johnston's ice cream tin, page 10; Boy in M.C. & S. Co. tub, page 11; Ice Cream for You and Me sign, page 12; White Mountain freezer ad, page 15; Soda jerk dispensing syrup, page 16; American Druggist cover, page 19; Artic Cream Co. tray, page 22. Chapter 2: Old soda fountain interior, page 33; Shaking valentine, page 35; Movie promo shot, page 37; Soda Fountain Magazine cover, page 38; Soda Fountain Service magazine cover, page 38. Chapter 3: Well "Soda" I valentine, page 56; Gene's Ice Cream sign, page 63. Chapter 4: Hood's ice cream sign, page 76; Gridley ice cream sign, page 79. Chapter 5: Peerless ice cream sign, page 88. Chapter 6: White Mountain freezer ad, page 100; Neuman's tray, page 102; Ice cream tray, page 107. Chapter 7: Cremo truck, page 118.

From the collection of Angela and Tom Sarro: Chapter 1: Drugstore interior, page 16; Ice cream vendor, page 17; Soda jerk at fountain, page 20; Dixie Cup lids ad, page 24. Chapter 4: Bridgman's ice cream sign, page 74; Hood's ice cream ad, page 77. Chapter 6: Boys with dasher, page 96; Junket Freezing Mix, page 98; Junket ad with girl, page 99; Auto Vacuum Freezer booklet cover, page 101. Chapter 7: Snaider Syrups, page 113.

From the collection of John and Carol Skurulsky: Chapter 2: Coca-Cola tray, page 39. Chapter 3: Pineapple ice cream sign, page 58. Chapter 7: Hot Fudge sign, page 112; Banana Split ad, page 114.

Jane Swanson: Chapter 7, Fiberglass cone, page 114. Ice Cream Capital of the World Visitors Center.

Courtesy of Wells Dairy/Blue Bunny: Chapter 4:, page 77.

Courtesy of Dr. Steven C. Wilson: Chapter 2: Wilson with his collection and world's smallest steam-operated ice cream freezer, page 43.

From the collection of Ye Olde Mill/Velvet Ice Cream: Chapter 2: Sundae sign, page 33. Chapter 7: Shift workers with sundae sign, page 117; Vintage milk shake machine, page 125. Off-Duty Pick-Up Sign, page 173.

About the Author

Writer and editor Shannon Jackson Arnold has always loved ice cream. During college, she spent a summer scooping ice cream at Steve's in New York City and never tired of sampling new flavors each day. The former editor of *OHIO Magazine*, she offers workshps and retreats for writers through her company, The Inspired Writer, and writes about food and travel for a variety of publications. She currently resides in Delafield, Wisconsin, with her dairy-loving husband and milk-sensitive daughter. When not out sampling ice cream at stands and parlors, she can be found at home making her own.

Got a Great Ice Cream Tip?

The best part of working on this book has been discovering new things about ice cream — a great parlor, a talented ice cream maker, a fascinating bit of history or trivia. If you have a favorite brand, a treasured parlor or a fascinating fact to share, please let me know. You can submit tips via my website at www.everybodylovesicecream.com